Search & Rescue
in Colorado's
Sengre de Cristos

Kevin G. Wright

JOHNSON BOOKS
AN IMPRINT OF BOWER HOUSE
DENVER

Printed in Canada
Cover and text design by D.K. Luraas

Library of Congress Control Number: 2015949708
ISBN: 978-1-55566-464-0

10 9 8 7 6 5 4 3

To The Memory Of

David Boyd

Kevin Hayne

Jesse Peterson

Lygon Stevens

Mark Stice

Kristen Weiss

Contents

Foreword

By Wayne K. Sheldrake, author of *Instant Karma*

The locale of this book, the Sangre de Cristos, is distinctive, indeed. One of "the longest mountain chains on earth," when viewed through the thin, cold, prismatically clear air of the desolate high desert to the west, the serrated dorsal granite of the Sangre de Cristos frays the spectral-blue edge of sky—especially dramatic where sharp 13,000- and 14,000-foot peaks are enameled with snow. At sunset, the shining upturned blade of the northern sectors appear to slice a blue vein above as they are drenched with pink light.

Panoramically and incisively stealing horizon, satellite photos show an elongated fossilized profile, captured in the deer-like prance and signature nod of a kokopelli, completely apropos, since Native Americans tradition teaches of the corpulent (though craggy) Blanca Massif as a mythical womb, origin of The People. Sneak closer from the desert flats—toward Kit Carson, Crestone, and Crestone Needle (or Challenger and its neighbors)—and the iconic picture inspires comparison to the Tetons, Tibetan Himalaya's, the Andes: threateningly beautiful, perilously seductive.

Closer still, the problems of Sangres become explicit. Face-to-face the summits are nothing like a neat knife-edge silhouette. Thanks to a geological basement of faults, granite-rendering folds, and flatiron flipping lift, they are a gargantuan, cragged trash-heap. Think the dizzyingly illogical but obviously deadly angulate of a column of sharks teeth, or a bucket dump of razor-glass debitage. Mountains maddening, lusterless, latticed with oceanic upthrust and efflorescent with acute and obtuse majesty.

Awing. Daunting. Alluring. A place with the obvious power to kill the drone and doleful plaints of civilization, the Sangres' temple-like aura is potent, but it's a solid half-day drive for most of its closest urban visitors. Once there, even by guidebook it's hard to penetrate very far without rigor and a goal. Its 14ers and (quietly) world-renown technical faces require altitude-gaining, scree-smearing tramps. Consequently, headlong adventurers are soon in zones where serious rescue will take hours or days, if possible at all. Distinctive, indeed. Even the spidery reach of cell phones, GPS signals, etc. falter or fail here, lending to solitude that is its own Siren.

As president of Alamosa Volunteer Search and Rescue, this was Kevin Wright's demesne. Alpine, intimate, desolate—it's been his Shangri-La since boyhood. He'd be the first to tell you that in fiction one need only *arrive* in

Shangri-La. Ah, victory! In real life, the adventure too often turns dire *on the way out.* Then SAR—"your best friends on your worst day"—manifests as mythological hero/guides in the flesh. If you're lucky, you're saveable. If not … you will be conveyed with the care, compassion, and honor befitting a beloved fallen warrior.

A better option (for you and SAR) would be to keep reading. Read like you were SAR. Enjoy the harrowing action and learn. As you do, say a prayer of thanks to a brotherhood/sisterhood that has your back if your own Shangri-La ever becomes your personal living hell.

Acknowledgments

In January of 2014, I mailed out a letter requesting support from the regional county sheriffs, search and rescue (SAR) leaders, national park superintendent, and other key personnel involved with SAR operations in the Sangre de Cristo Mountains of Colorado. I intended to write a book to educate the public about the Sangre de Cristos, small rural SAR operations, and mountain survival skills, and I requested their expertise and insights.

I am deeply grateful to the following individuals who contacted me and agreed to be interviewed for this book: Captain Cindy Howard of the Custer County SAR Team and Ranger John White of Great Sand Dunes National Park. Thank you Sheriff Fred Jobe (retired) who offered me full support, and thank you to Sheriff Dave Stong (retired) for his support while I led the Alamosa Volunteer Search And Rescue team.

Thank you to these current and former SAR personnel who endured my interviews, including Jess Caton, Mick Daniel, Eric Lutringer, Donna Mabry, Andrew McClure, and George Rapoza. Other SAR personnel that I consulted during the writing of this book include John Gilmore, Mike Henderson, Christopher Lavery, and Suzi Rasmussen Hopper. There are many others in the greater SAR community who I spoke with less formally, and for everyone who contributed to this book, those listed as well as those unlisted, I am grateful.

Thank you to the families of the subjects whose stories I share in this book. It is my intention to lessen suffering and save lives in the future, and sharing the stories and lessons in this book will contribute toward that goal.

Thank you to the photographers who graciously have allowed me to use their pictures in this book including Ryan Adams, John Gilmore, Chris Stark, and Don Thompson.

Much gratitude to my mountaineering mentors: my father, Charles Wright, and my junior high teacher, Lindon Wood. I have used the skills they taught me to save lives; I and many others are grateful.

Thank you to my mother, Judith Wright, for teaching me compassion; it is my guiding light regarding the first noble truth: life is suffering.

Thank you to my wife, Autumn Wright, who supported me in numerous ways throughout this project.

Thank you to the author of *Instant Karma,* my friend Wayne Sheldrake, for his moral support throughout this project's process.

Thank you to my friends Dani Coleman and Cammie Newmeyer for their support reading early drafts of chapters and taking the time to suggest edits and modifications.

Thank you to graphic artist Shannon Bruns for illustrating the book's maps.

Thank you to Mira Perrizo at Big Earth Publishing for making this book possible.

My deepest gratitude to search and rescue personnel and their families, especially those heroes I worked with on the AVSAR team from 2006–2011, "… so that others may live."

Introduction

SAR in Colorado's Sangre. Unabbreviated and translated, this means *search and rescue in Colorado's blood.* This book is a collection of true search and rescue stories from the Sangre de Cristo Mountains of Colorado. From 2006 to 2011, I served on the Alamosa Volunteer Search and Rescue (AVSAR) team, an all-volunteer, non-profit organization that responds to all emergency incidents in the Blanca Mountain Group. For three years, from 2008 to 2011, I served as president of AVSAR. In that time, I witnessed much suffering; I also witnessed incredible heroism.

The number one reason I wrote this book is to honor the heroic men and women who volunteer their own time, resources, skills, and potentially their lives to serve on small, rural mountain search and rescue teams. Their bravery in the service of others is the embodiment of heroism.

The second reason I share these stories is to honor all the subjects and their families who have suffered immensely or perished in the Sangre de Cristos. In sharing these narratives, my intent is to show compassion and aid others wanting to avoid similar tragedies.

Third, I wrote this book to educate mountaineers and the public about the reality of mountain SAR operations, specifically the challenges faced by small, rural all-volunteer teams that cover some of the most demanding mountainous territory in the contiguous United States.

The fourth reason for writing this book is to educate the public about basic wilderness survival in mountainous terrain. I taught a course at Adams State University called "Introduction to Search And Rescue, A Class for Heroes," and much of that survival and SAR information I've included in this book.

Historically, annual AVSAR mission fatality rates range between 50 and 80 percent, so this book gives the reader an accurate sense of the proportions of mission endings.

I hope you find these stories engaging, but I also hope they could serve to save your or another's life in a wilderness survival situation.

The Sangre de Cristo Mountain Range

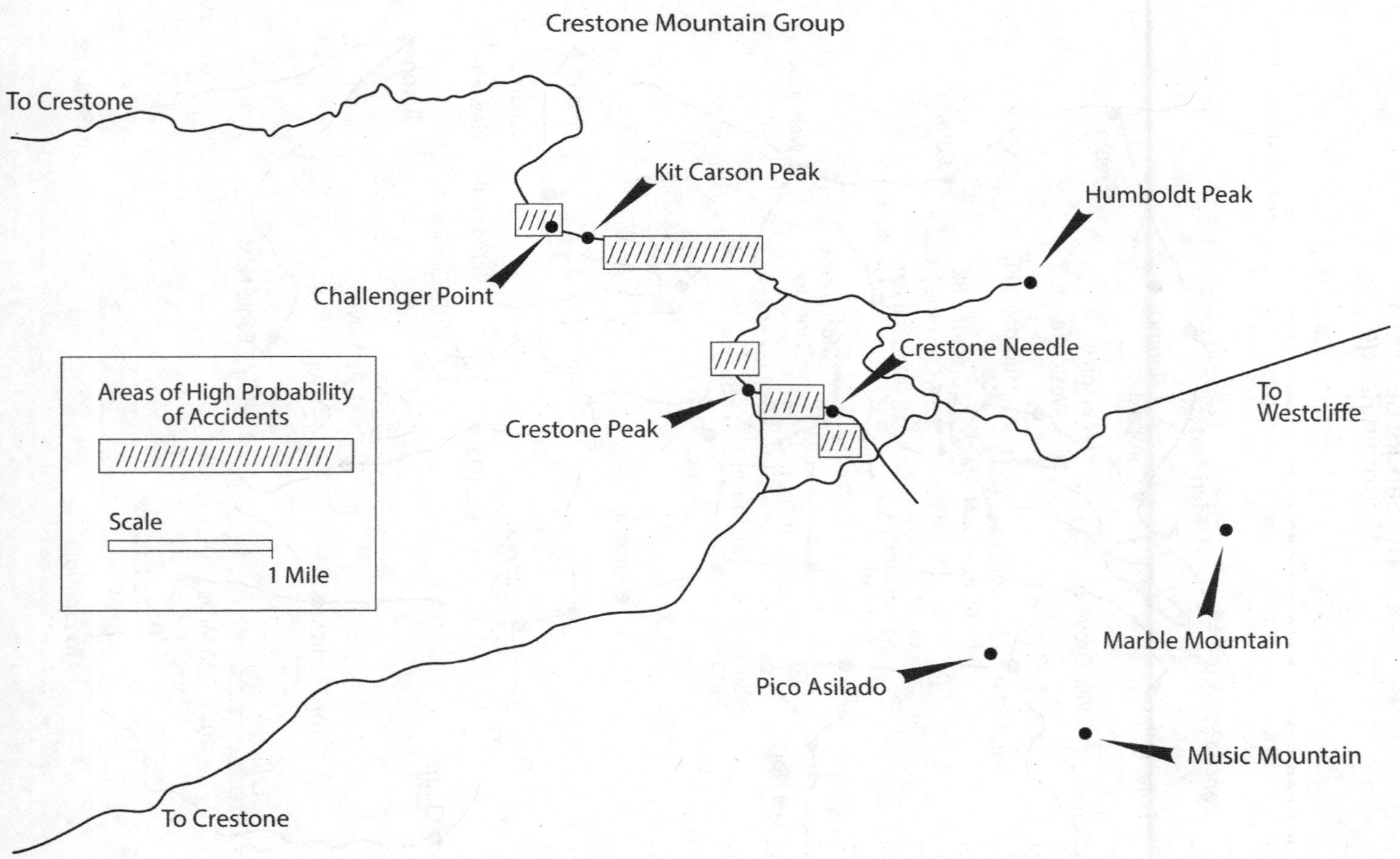

Crestone Mountain Group

To Crestone

To Crestone

To Westcliffe

Humboldt Peak

Crestone Needle

Kit Carson Peak

Challenger Point

Crestone Peak

Marble Mountain

Music Mountain

Pico Asilado

Areas of High Probability
of Accidents

Scale

1 Mile

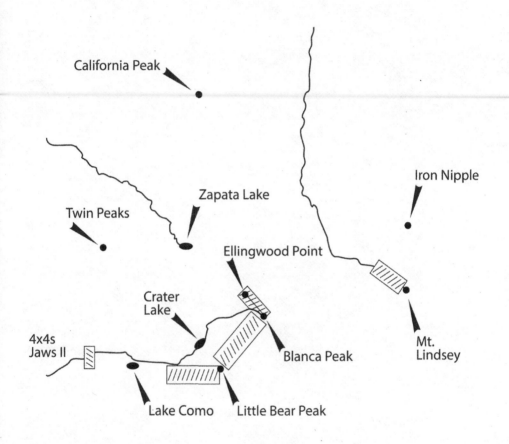

Blanca Mountain Group

California Peak

Iron Nipple

Twin Peaks

Zapata Lake

Ellingwood Point

Crater
Lake

4x4s
Jaws II

Blanca Peak

Mt.
Lindsey

Lake Como   Little Bear Peak

Areas of High Probability
of Accidents

////////////////////////////

Scale

3 Miles

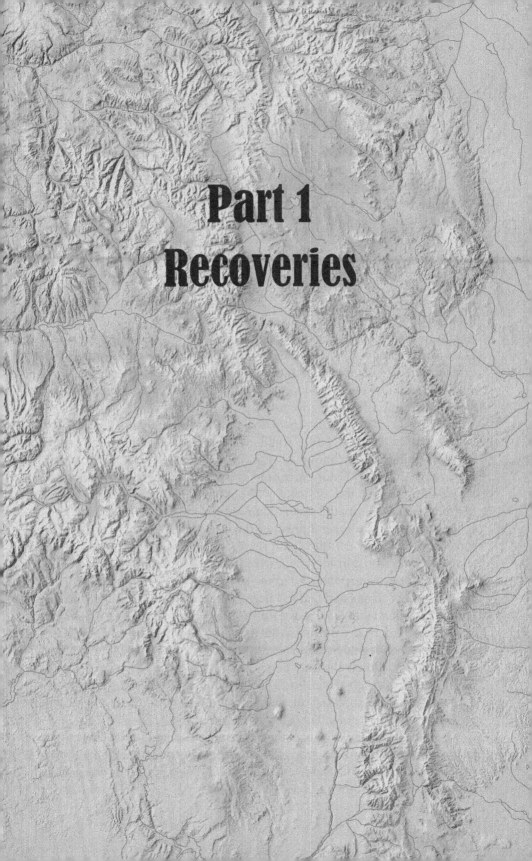

Part 1
Recoveries

Lygon Stevens
Little Bear Peak, January 10, 2008

"Along the golden spine of a mountain, I've felt that the closest I might get to some pure existence could be those instants when I might say, *I am wind, light, rock, awe, and nothing more.*"
—Katie Ives, *Alpinist* magazine

Between 2006 and 2013, I taught middle school language arts. Part of my eighth-grade curriculum was reading the short story *To Build a Fire* by Jack London. My reasoning was that the protagonist's hypothermic death was an excellent literary excuse to teach my students a lesson about extreme cold; the San Luis Valley of Colorado, where we live, is one of the coldest environments in the lower forty-eight states.

January 11, 2008, the day that the mountaineering legend Sir Edmund Hillary passed away, it was a frigid negative 10-degree morning in the San Luis Valley, locally known as "the SLV." As I drove past my neighbor, the steamy Colorado Gator Farm, and south on the flat, straight Highway 17 from Mosca to Alamosa, I noticed the sun rising over a cloudless Blanca Mountain Group. From the distant highway, the mountains indicated atmospheric calmness; for several previous days, fierce winds had been blowing snowy "rooster tails" off the alpine ridges. These rooster tails, when I had taken the scale into consideration, were hundreds of feet long. That Friday, the ridges appeared arctic but windless.

I arrived at school and had just begun the first class of the day when my cell phone began vibrating. I looked at the incoming caller ID, and "State Patrol Dispatch" motivated me to step out into the hallway, making sure the classroom full of eighth graders could see me through the classroom door window.

My students knew the only personal calls I took were emergency calls from the 911 dispatch center, and I had previously made it explicit that my attention could be necessary to coach people through difficult emergency medical procedures, potentially life-saving procedures.

A call such as this was one of the rare things that could completely focus an entire middle school classroom. The class was perfectly silent, pretending to be busily working, but their pencils weren't moving. This class was getting a lesson on eavesdropping and active listening.

As a leader on the county's search and rescue (SAR) team, it was proto-col for an injured subject or his/her hiking partner to be patched through directly to me. This time it was not a patch, just the dispatcher. I took down the initial information—a rescue was in progress for a twenty-two-year-old male and a twenty-year-old female—siblings. The previous day they were caught in an avalanche while trying to ascend Little Bear Peak. On the slope near the base of the Hourglass Couloir, a wind-deposited slab cut loose as the two climbers traversed it. The brother had finally gotten out of the canyon and called for help the next morning, after an injured, restless night at their highest camp.

I responded that I would see if I could get away from work, and I told dispatch that I'd get in contact with the team's executive secretary, Geri Mor-rison. I knew Geri would be helping coordinate communication and oper-ations. Upon being told by my principal that he couldn't find a substitute teacher and that I would need to stay and teach my classes, I called Geri and was given more details.

The male's name was Nicklis Stevens, a young but accomplished moun-taineer for his age. He and his sister, Lygon Stevens, had recently summited Denali, over 20,000 feet high and in the Arctic Circle in Alaska. They also had experienced mountaineering trips to Ecuador and around the U.S. They were used to bitter-cold mountainous environments—they were mountaineers.

During their ascent, close to the summit of Little Bear Peak near the base of the infamous Hourglass Couloir, the last thing Nicklis remembered was the slope breaking into pieces around him, losing his sense of direction as he found himself cartwheeling in an increasingly fluid powder, and then he sensed becoming weightless, as if he had just been hurled into a large void. He was correct—he and his sister had just avalanched off the top of a large cliff band encompassing the cirque above Little Bear Lake.

Miraculously, Nicklis regained consciousness an undetermined amount of time later. The avalanche buried him in concrete-hard snow up to his waist. With a pounding headache, symptoms of respiratory distress, and the panic of realizing his sister was nowhere to be seen, Nicklis dug himself out of the avalanche debris field about a thousand vertical feet below where they had triggered the slide. The debris field was enormous.

Nicklis took his ice axe, its titanium adze bent from the tumbling and forces of the avalanche, and spent a great deal of the remaining day's sunlight probing, calling out, looking for any sign of his younger sister, Lygon. This "coarse search" for his sister was heartbreakingly unsuccessful, and as the sun began to get low in the sky and the temperatures began to drop, Nicklis' new priority became his own survival. Because of his headache, facial laceration, respiratory distress, location, and the time of the day relative to a very cold upcoming night, Nicklis' survival was still precarious. High above treeline, surrounded by nothing but rock, snow, and ice, with a setting sun, painful injuries, and having just survived a horrifically traumatic event, Nicklis rallied himself and slowly, deliberately, carefully, ascended the avalanche path. Over and over again he turned and scanned the avalanche debris field below.

As Nicklis crested over the ridge, there was still no sign of Lygon. He quickly descended the north-facing access couloir that linked Little Bear Peak's west ridge with the valley containing Lake Como and Blue Lakes. By the time he returned to their last camp, it was dark and the temperature was below zero. Nicklis was beyond fatigued. He crawled into his sleeping bag in the tent that was set up in a primitive cabin on the shore of frozen Lake Como, and tried to sleep.

After a nightmarish attempt at sleeping, Nicklis began moving down the mountain before the first light of dawn. He descended what had taken his sister and him two days to ascend in three hours. Just after sunrise, Nicklis Stevens breached the mouth of Chokecherry Canyon beneath Lake Como to emerge at a location overlooking the San Luis Valley. He finally had line of sight to at least one cell phone tower. He dialed 911 and made contact with the region's emergency dispatch.

The 911 center patched him through to an on-duty Alamosa County sheriff's deputy who then requested SAR support. Dispatch then contacted Alamosa Volunteer Search And Rescue (AVSAR) team leadership. I apologized to Geri that my principal couldn't let me go, but I'd be on my way first thing after the last bell of the day. Geri understood, and I wished her and the team good luck and a reminder to be safe. Then I went back to teaching, my students eagerly asking as they passed me in the hallways, "What's up Mr. Wright? How's the rescue mission going on Mount Blanca?"

"I don't know. There's a team of dedicated folks doing their best to save a young man and a young woman involved in an avalanche. Beyond that, I don't know—I'm here with you guys."

A couple hours later my phone vibrated again. It was Geri.

"Can you get here Kevin?"

"Not until after school. What's going on?"

Flight For Life had flown up two SAR techs, hard-core dudes named Don Thompson and Barry Bertin, as close to the Lake Como cabin and Little Bear's west ridge access couloir as they could. Don was an ultra long-distance athlete, and Barry was an experienced technical climbing paramedic, both having gone on several demanding SAR missions together in the past.

The helicopter had flown in and hovered over the landing zone (LZ). The techs put on their backpacks and jumped into the powder. From the pilot's perspective, the techs briefly vanished. From the techs' perspective, it was like jumping into a dense cloud, blind and difficult to breathe. After a few seconds, both techs swam for the surface and waved off the helicopter.

As the helicopter rose away from the hovering insertion and started its descent back down the valley of rock, ice, and snow, the techs knew that this was a one-way trip. There was nowhere a helicopter could safely land in the deep powder; they'd have to walk out the five miles, which in these condi-tions would be the energy output of a summertime twenty miles. The "drop off" zone was very close to Little Bear's standard route, so it only took min-utes for them to find Nicklis' footprints leading to and from the Lake Como cabin and the west ridge of Little Bear Peak.

They began following the footprints up the steep talus field. The near 40-degree talus was now under at least ten feet of snow. Nicklis' and Lygon's trail was just a barely perceivable line in the crystalline blanket of soft powder. As the slope increased and the techs had to kick in the teeth of their snow-shoes harder, they both felt and heard the sound that all mountaineers dread when negotiating avalanche country slopes. The ground gave away just an inch or two, a weak layer in the snowpack collapsed, and it produced a rever-berating "Whumpf!" sound. Sometimes, this is the last sound mountaineers hear before they find themselves in the midst of a gigantic slab avalanche. The trigger of an avalanche is the weight of the traveler(s) on the snow caus-ing a fracture line across the slope (known as the crown of the avalanche). Then huge blocks of snow, sometimes several feet thick, break away and slide on a weak layer such as decayed hoarfrost and air or an icy layer formed after repeated frost/thaw cycles before additional layers are added.

This process is what occurred to Nicklis and his sister. Their weight had triggered an enormous avalanche on a 40-degree slope that traveled ap-proximately 1,000+ vertical feet, including a path that took them off a large, 100-foot-high cliff.

When Don and Barry felt the telltale sign of settling and heard the whumpf sound move out away from their epicenter, they looked at each other and knew that their priority, rather than getting to the avalanche field, was to get themselves back to the command post without dying from an avalanche or exposure. Smart, experienced, lead techs keep their priorities straight even under duress.

Geri said that Flight For Life had tried to insert Mick Daniel, another AVSAR tech (and close personal friend), into Little Bear Lake Gorge, where the avalanche debris field was located, but the cloud deck had descended and winds had increased, so Mick's insertion had been aborted midflight by

Photo taken by author during a mission to observe the slope that avalanched and killed Lygon Stevens. This photo was taken from high up on Little Bear's southwest ridge looking northeast toward Little Bear Peak's summit. The avalanche's path is the upside down "triangle." The total area of the slide was approximately 1,000 feet across at the crown and more than 1,000 vertical feet. Lygon's body is in the snowpack near the bottom point of the triangle.

the pilot. Geri said her biggest worry right now was Don and Barry getting back to the command post safely, which was located at the trailhead for Lake Como. This was the beginning of the infamously rugged Lake Como 4x4 road. If they couldn't get out by sunset, it would be a very, very cold night. Command post temperatures were predicted to drop to twenty-five below zero Fahrenheit. Geri prepared me for one of my biggest concerns—responding to the rescue or recovery of a fellow SAR team member. I understood her worry, and I said that I'd be on my way as soon as possible.

At the last bell of the day, I was out the door of my classroom before the first student. I carefully pulled out of the middle school parking lot, waving at moms and being very mindful of all the kids, my students starting to file en masse out the doors. Once beyond school grounds, however, I turned onto the highway and drove as fast as was safe for the conditions to my home. I floated over some longer patches of black ice as if I weren't attached to the earth at all, and I left a huge snow plume behind my car.

I stopped off at home just long enough to grab my 72-hour SAR pack;

this time of year it was my largest expedition backpack filled to the brim with enough equipment and supplies to be able to survive unsupported for three days in the frigid, arctic-like wintertime wilderness. I said a quick hello and goodbye to my wife and dog, my dog being very sad as he had learned from a history of SAR responses what the equipment meant; my wife was no more thrilled. I walked out the door just as the sun set behind the San Juan foothills to the west.

En route to the command post, I called Geri and asked for an update regarding the status of Don and Barry. Had they made contact with anyone since their drop off? Geri relayed to me their experience with some snow layer settling and whumpfing as they had started ascending the west ridge. Upon realizing what the avalanche conditions were indicating (extreme risk for more slides), they had switched their objective from getting to the debris field to getting out alive.

They had immediately begun following Nicklis' lonely return track down to the Lake Como cabin and beyond. Before my call, both had gotten back to the command post, but Geri expressed that she was still worried about one of them. Barry was stable and on his way home via his own vehicle, but during the descent Don had gotten much colder. Upon reaching the command post, Don was behaving in a manner indicating mild hypothermia, so on-duty hospital medics began treatment in the back of an ambulance and hooked Don up to an EKG; they found erratic cardio-electrical patterns (common, if not expected, in cases of hypothermia), so Don was transported to the local hospital in Alamosa, the San Luis Valley Regional Medical Center.

Geri sounded simultaneously concerned and relieved; I felt the same way. I was relieved that Don and Barry had egressed from the field before dark. Temperatures were beginning their dive below zero.

I arrived at the command post (CP) as the last of the ultraviolet light illuminated anything fluorescent orange as if it were under a black light. The CP was located at the Blanca Peak–Little Bear trailhead out in the sandy, treeless, desert flats at the base of the peaks' piñon pine flanks. From the CP, one could see the whole mountain group as it loomed over us. We could see where the piñons changed to lodgepoles, ponderosas, and aspen, then on up to treeline and the alpine slope and ridge where the incident had crowned (been triggered and begun sliding). From the CP perspective, Little Bear's southwest ridgetop just blocked everyone's view of the debris field. In the low UV light, the mountain seemed especially intimidating, like a predator high up on a cliff watching over its newly acquired prey.

I parked my car alongside the other twenty vehicles along the edge of a large sandy, flat dirt parking lot, and I was met by Mick, my friend from

Adams State University, who had earlier tried to fly to the avalanche field via Flight For Life. Mick was the director of the university's outdoor leadership program as well as an outstanding local mountaineer, skier, and mountain guide.

As he walked up to my car I unrolled my window, "Hey Mick! It's good to see you. How's it going?"

"Take a look around. This thing's a circus. Media's everywhere, people are showing up from the Front Range wanting to help. We've still got a couple AVSAR techs up there trying to get to the avalanche via snowmobile and on foot."

"Who's in charge?"

"Undersheriff John Bianca. He'll be glad you're here. You know the sheriff got word that Buckley Air National Guard out of Aurora's going to provide some support tomorrow? We should have a Blackhawk coming in first thing in the morning to provide personnel lifts up to the debris field. Good thing you can speak that military lingo because pretty quickly we're going to need someone who can coordinate the SAR personnel, the law enforcement personnel, a bunch of civilian volunteers, and the military."

Mick looked at me and paused for a long period. "Kevin, it's not their fault, but the deputies don't have a damned clue what it's like up there on those ridges and cliffs. These good ol' boys don't go more than a hundred feet from the comfort of their warm cruisers when they're on duty. And you know the military and outsiders don't know the intricacies of our mountains. We need a mountaineer, who knows what the hell's going on up there, to stay here and coordinate."

"I hear you. Let's go find the undersheriff."

Right before I turned off the car and pulled the key from the ignition, I checked the outside temperature—minus 15 degrees. I knew it would drop another ten degrees during the night.

Mick and I saw Undersheriff Bianca's cruiser parked over where the large media vans were parked. Walking toward the undersheriff's vehicle, we passed a small red sedan, located about center of the large crescent shape made by the response vehicles. I motioned toward it and asked Mick, "Subjects' car?"

"Affirmative. That's Lygon's. Nicklis is with his parents now. I think they're with a victim's advocate at a hotel." SAR techs on snowmobiles had intercepted Nicklis while he descended the Lake Como road, so he was off the mountain and off site. The sight of the empty, dark little car was lonely and sad.

"How's Nicklis? What'd they find out at the hospital?"

"Earlier I had some time to go interview him myself. He's a tough young man. In addition to being hurled off a cliff and losing consciousness during a massive avalanche, he had a laceration to his head requiring sutures, three broken ribs, and a punctured lung. He said that in the morning as they were ascending the west ridge, they got whumpfing, the same conditions reported by Don and Barry. Don and Barry both confirm that there's two sets of tracks going in, just one coming out. Lygon's still buried."

"I know. She's gone. Our real mission, now that Nicklis is safe, is going to see if we can't recover her without getting anyone else killed or injured. Who's up on the mountain still, and what are their objectives?"

"Jess Caton and Steve Morrison. They went in a couple hours ago to see how close they could get in via snowmobile and hiking."

"What kind of gear do they have? What's their overnight survivability?"

"They have their 72-hour packs, they're geared up and prepared. Remember Jess' famous solo rappel on Little Bear's northwest face with the body a couple years ago? You could drop those two into hell, and they'd survive. But the last I heard is that they've aborted their attempt to get up in the gorge and are making their way back."

"I hope so, because right now they're in hell, and it's not a cozy, warm hell. It's that black cold void, a lack of any energy, a vacuum of temperature like outer space."

We walked up to Undersheriff Bianca's old Chevy Caprice police cruiser. The temperatures were dropping quickly, and all day Undersheriff Bianca had been acting as the incident commander and public information officer, disseminating information to a number of media agencies as well as to the distressed family. He looked rightfully exhausted. I introduced myself as one of the SAR team leaders, and I explained that I wanted to help as a mountaineer and an air force security forces veteran, a guy who could speak the many different "languages" of the situation.

I could tell Bianca was happy to be relieved. He gave me a brief summary of the situation and introduced me to the media reporters.

About that time, we received a phone call from the local retail outfitters, Kristi Mountain Sports, our local version of R.E.I. The owner of the shop, Eric, was calling to give us a heads up that several men had come into the store and just purchased avalanche beacons. The men had mentioned they were family members of the avalanche victim. Eric said that he wanted to pass along anything that could help us keep people alive. I was grateful for the heads up, and my sentiment was the same.

Bianca serendipitously added, "I just got radioed by the deputy at the highway cattle guard. The subject's father and boyfriend are in-bound.

They'll be here in a minute. Literally. Can you help me talk them out of hiking in?"

"Affirmative."

For a moment, I flashed back to my job in college. After I had left the military, I worked as a security guard in a busy, large trauma-one emergency room. One of my primary duties was to secure people's valuables as the trauma teams cut off their wedding rings, found their wallets in pockets, etc. When the results of everyone's efforts failed, the attending doctor, sometimes a young ER resident, or more often an OR surgeon, would ask me to accompany him/her to communicate to the family that their loved one had passed, and I would then hand over the valuables. I summoned my previous experience delivering the news to a parent that his child had died. In this case it wasn't a head-on collision, it was tons of snow and lack of oxygen.

We watched the car's headlights slowly creep up to the parking area from the highway. The lot was partially illuminated with the lights of media vans. In the increasingly cold temperature, the vehicles' exhaust was visible longer and rose around the vehicles. The temperature was already nearing twenty below. As I stood next to Bianca's vehicle, I began flexing my muscles against myself, over and over, as if working out doing small pushups and jumping jacks, a method of building heat internally, a synthetic pre-shivering technique I had used in the air force when I was stationed in the Upper Peninsula of Michigan as a Strategic Air Command security specialist. I thought about the time I was operational (in the field) for two weeks during a cold snap that included ambient temperatures as low as minus 48 degrees Fahrenheit. It had been drilled into me a long time ago—anything below minus 20 degrees is dangerous, and all non-elite, non-essential personnel should stay protected indoors.

Mick, Bianca, and I watched the car slowly pull into the parking lot, unobtrusively. It parked off to the side of the lot with all the SAR responder vehicles, not with the media or visitors. We assumed it was Lygon's father and boyfriend. There were full packs and gear in the vehicle with them. We meandered up to the car as they began to sort their gear.

As we walked up, Mr. Stevens rolled down his window.

"Good evening, sir. I'm Kevin Wright with Alamosa Volunteer Search and Rescue."

John Bianca then added, "Kevin, this is Nick Stevens, Senior, Nicklis Junior's and Lygon's father."

I took my hand out of its mitten and shook Mr. Stevens' hand. "I'm sorry to meet you under these circumstances, Mr. Stevens."

Mr. Stevens never broke eye contact after shaking my hand. Looking into his eyes, I saw the same desperation I had witnessed in the ER—that of a father wanting to have some hope that his daughter could still be alive. He began by asking the most obvious question, and he had asked it with his eyes long before his lips moved, "Kevin, what are the odds? What are the odds that my daughter survived and could still be alive?"

I wished very deeply the truth was that there was a chance that Lygon could have survived, somehow managed to dig herself out of a debris field after her brother had vacated, and that she was alive in their camp, but being honest was far, far more important than giving any hint of false hope.

"Zero, sir. You'll only be putting yourselves at risk of another avalanche if you go up to the site on the ground. If that happens, we'll have to prioritize all resources to your incident. We're expecting to have a Blackhawk helicopter available to ferry personnel to the site tomorrow morning. Imagine yourself only halfway to the site when you see those flights go over. Please don't go in right now."

Like the ER, I watched as Lygon's father processed the understanding that one of his children had died in a tragic accident. I stepped away from the car window and looked up at the clear, frigid sky, the frosty moon surrounded by a halo in the arctic-like atmosphere blurred in a tear. I felt the moisture on my cheeks begin to freeze.

After seeing Mr. Stevens and Lygon's boyfriend, Tim Hall, off site on their way back to a hotel, with one of the law enforcement officer's night optics devices (NODS) I watched Jess and Steve work their way through the piñon pines en route back to the command post. The NODS were an updated generation from those I had used in the air force, and it was easy to see Jess and Steve as they maneuvered their snowmobiles through the little ruts and gullies between the command post and entrance to the Little Bear Lake gorge. At these temperatures, even in my coldest weather boots, just standing around was causing my toes to slowly go numb.

Just sitting on their ATVs, Jess and Steve would likely be in the early stages of hypothermia upon getting back to base. I watched as Steve came in, his full face mask iced-up, like some Hans Solo character on the planet Hoth. I wanted to yell out, "Good to see you're back before we closed the blast shields!" but there were too many media flocked around, and it was far too serious and somber a situation. I watched Steve beeline for his vehicle on his snowmobile. He slid the snow machine up on its trailer behind his truck, jumped in his truck's cab and fired it up obviously eager for its heater to bring him back from Hoth's brink.

I turned toward Jess and was surprised to see 9News and other media interviewing him like a deer in the headlights—a very cold deer with icicles hanging from his nostril hairs. I watched Jess give an quick excellent statement regarding his and Steve's unsuccessful attempt to get up to the debris field, especially considering how obviously cold he was. Basically, the snow and terrain proved impossible for snowmobiles or ATVs. Hiking in was a considerable distance, and it would take several days.

After the lights had gone down from the interview, Jess stowed his snowmobile on its trailer and started warming himself for the drive home. I sighed some relief knowing there was no one in the field any longer at risk of freezing.

I walked over to the media crews packing up their lights and interview equipment, and I addressed them directly, authoritatively, "Hey fellas, you remember me saying not to interview my guys coming out because I wanted to debrief them first? I'd appreciate it if you'd allow the responders some time to warm up and gather their thoughts before you get statements." Their response was that it had been the subject's family and friends who had called news broadcasts and requested that they report the incident and request any available volunteer support.

"We're just reporting the news."

"I know, and I respect that. It's just that I've got to keep everyone who's still alive, safe." I realized that this media attention would likely mean hoards of well meaning, but totally unvetted, unknown outsiders showing up to help in the morning. With the frigid temperature and extreme avalanche conditions, all these volunteers would be liabilities and a complication/distraction for the officially trained county and regional SAR responders. The next day suddenly had the potential to turn into a chaotic disaster.

I checked with Undersheriff Bianca about who would be acting as the sheriff's office incident commander the next day. Learning it would be a deputy named Brian Cooper, my hopes raised. Brian was a big-hearted cop, and he was probably one of the tallest men in the valley. A giant, his voice was deep and calming, a reassurance amidst chaos. Brian was also a master at acquiring the assistance of outside organizations—personnel and equipment that occasionally became necessary to perform more complex missions. In this case, I wasn't surprised to learn from Bianca that Brian was the one who secured the support of the Air National Guard out of Aurora's Buckley A.N.G. base.

A Blackhawk crew was expected to take off from Buckley early the next day to help ferry in a team of avalanche-certified personnel to assess the debris field and what steps we could take to bring Lygon home. After checking with Bianca, I also sat and warmed up in a car with Mick, who had earlier been on the flight to the debris field, when wind and a low cloud deck had turned him around. Mick helped me contact Jack Hunt, the president of the

Rio Grande County SAR team. Jack was a world-class ice climber who wrote the ice climbing guidebook for the San Luis Valley, *Life by the Drop*. Jack confirmed that he would be able to respond the next day along with a couple of his top-notch SAR techs.

By the time Mick and I had finished our conversation, only Mick, I, and a deputy were on scene. Mick and I knew sleeping in the cars would require leaving them on all night, and we would only get fitful car seat naps, so like everyone else we elected to drive home. As Mick's taillights slowly crept back to the highway, I stood beneath the moon, stars, and the easily visible arm of the Milky Way, gazing up at the west face of Little Bear Peak illuminated by their light.

With my night optics, I could see the faint snowfields and slope that had avalanched. I couldn't see the cirque that held the debris field; from this low vantage point, Little Bear Peak's southwest ridge hid it. It was a surreal scene, almost too vivid to be reality. As the painful, minus 20-degree air started creeping down my neck, I shivered, and I thought about Lygon. With all the evidence that had been presented to me, I estimated that she most likely was buried under at least twenty feet of hard-packed, concrete-like debris. I took solace knowing that she likely didn't suffer at all. I imagined that the same tumbling, disorientation and fall over the cliff that had knocked Nicklis out had done the same to Lygon. After being knocked out, buried in the snow, she would have quickly suffocated having never regained consciousness.

In the dark, brutally cold silence, I prayed to Lygon's spirit. I wished her love, and in that spirit of love, I asked her to help me protect her family. I asked her to help me bring her body home to all those who loved her so much, without anyone else being killed or seriously injured. Even in the extreme, biting cold, I felt a subtle, deep warmth and presence as if a wave of love had flowed down the mountain through me. In the midst of chaos, pain, shock, and horror, I was reassured by a deep sense of peace and love.

I drove home for a short nap between midnight and four a.m. Neither my wife nor dog acknowledged me coming home or getting up. Like an air lock, I made sure to close the bedroom door before opening the main door out into the frigid darkness. After idling for about fifteen minutes, my car's engine temperature rose enough to begin thawing my windshield. Its outdoor thermometer reading was minus 25 degrees. As I drove under the twinkling stars back to the trailhead, I wondered what animals might be out scurrying. This is an eternal threat to the safety of those on rural highways. A few years prior, a friend had hit a black cow standing in the middle of the highway in the middle of the night. Hitting a cow, at highway speeds, at night (when no one might notice the wreck) in those temperatures, possibly in one of the many zones without cell service could easily result in a fatality. I took my time, kept my speed at 55 or below, but I saw no sign of life.

Overnight the command post security deputy had been replaced by an older, reserve deputy, and this smart old gent had moved his security checkpoint to the cattle guard gate at the highway, a perfect chokepoint for any vehicles coming in and out of the area. I rolled down my window to check in with him, and I was met by a rush of extremely cold air I felt whirl around my ankles as I watched the warm, moist air of the car's cabin rise into the sky. Before the sun rose, it would drop another degree or two.

I could tell from the deputy's expression that he didn't want his window open for any longer than I wanted mine open. As we talked, we looked like smokers exhaling, our breath mixing with the curtain of steam rising from the tops of our windows. I explained that I'd been assigned as operations manager for the day, and I inquired whether anyone had passed through, in either direction. "No sir. We're the only folks for miles from what I can tell."

"Thank you. What was the directive you were given?" I asked.

"That this trailhead is now closed to the public. Only responders, family, and the media are allowed in. The sheriff's considering this very likely a recovery instead of a rescue, so although the public lands remain open, he's closing the road until the investigation's over."

"Good call. As the media show up, would you mind explaining that there will be an area they are assigned to, and they need to check in with me before anything else?"

"Yup, no problem."

"Could you also give me or the incident commander a heads up if any of the subject's family members or friends come through?"

"Planned to anyway."

"Incident commander's still going to be Deputy Cooper?"

"Yes. That's who I'm expecting."

"Excellent. Thank you. It's going to get busy today. Good luck, and thanks for securing this arctic post overnight."

"You're welcome. Good luck yourself."

I sat and planned as the day's first light silhouetted the mountain's profile. The dark, flat ridgeline was its highest at the summit of Little Bear Peak. I knew that below that dark mass, Lygon's body was peacefully at rest. The headlights of a small caravan of cars turned off the highway and passed the deputy at his makeshift entry control point. He didn't radio a heads up.

As the cars pulled into the sandy parking area, I was happy to see that the first folks arriving at the trailhead were my personal friends and long-time members of the AVSAR team. As the day's operations manager, one of my primary duties would be to coordinate the day's activities including keeping track of all responding personnel, especially those who I would deploy into the field. I started a sign-in roster with several columns: name, organization, medical qualifications, winter mountaineering experience, and avalanche certifications.

In addition to AVSAR personnel, I expected personnel from the Alamosa sheriff's office, Rio Grande County's SAR team, personnel from the Colorado Avalanche Information Center, Air National Guard helicopter personnel, media, ambulance personnel, American Red Cross personnel, Lygon's family and friends, and because of the previous night's media coverage, well-meaning citizen volunteers from all over the state and region.

Because of their trauma, desperation, and feeling like they needed to do whatever they could to support bringing Lygon back as soon as possible, I didn't blame the Stevens family and friends for contacting the media and requesting support from everyone. They were doing what they believed would be the best support for the incident's objective; however, the well-meaning request would have the opposite effect as to what was intended. Untrained, well-meaning volunteers often fail to see that they are actually a liability, and at a minimum will distract the trained, cohesive responders, thus slowing down the operation; in a worst-case scenario, these well-meaning volunteers become subjects themselves and thus reprioritize the mission from the original objective to rescuing the responders.

As the sky transitioned from its star-filled dark blues to its starless lighter hues, vehicles arrived in droves. The first personnel were the AVSAR techs. They, like me, represented a second wave of responders, the fresh contingent group who had been out of the area or unable to get off work the previous day. Yesterday's initial responders also showed up, some as advisers, some as witnesses, but everyone who had been active the previous day made it clear they were too exhausted for redeployment already.

Jack Hunt and some other members from Rio Grande County responded early. It was my first physical introduction to Jack, and upon meeting him, he fulfilled every one of my expectations based on what I knew of him. He was indeed the "hick-hippy" he described himself as. He had young eyes but weathered powerful hands; he had an easy smile and inviting laugh, even under the circumstances that we were meeting. Shaking his hand, I could feel the solid grip of a lifetime climber. Jack's crew, like him, looked like a weathered collection of modern-day Jeremiah Johnsons.

In addition to the core of regional SAR responders, the other group I was especially happy to see was our local American Red Cross volunteers. They were often the scene's impromptu victims' and responders' advocates, providing food, drinks, listening outlets, hugs, and morale boosts when they were most needed.

Also arriving before the sun rose was Deputy Cooper, several media trucks, and a few volunteers who had driven overnight from locations as far away as Wyoming. One of these volunteers said he had pulled off the highway only long enough to take a short nap. He wanted to be at the command post at first light. I deeply hoped no well-meaning volunteers would get injured traveling. When I inquired what equipment he had brought with him (wondering if he had crampons or ice tools I could commandeer for one of my team's techs who did not possess his own), he surprised me by producing a small daypack, like the one I carried books to school in as a kid. I inquired what layering he had brought to manage the extreme cold (I said this through his half-rolled down window, frost obviously built up on my mustache and eyelashes). He replied, "I brought a winter field jacket." It was then I noticed he was wearing military green BDUs, the jungle type with the green, olive, and black-splotched pattern.

"Do you have anything to layer on top of those fatigues?"

"I brought the matching gortex shells. Windproof and waterproof."

I tried to be as respectful and succinct as I could, watching the line of cars coming in from the highway. "Those fatigues are cotton. In these temperatures, what'll happen is you'll put on your shell, start moving hard and fast and build up heat, you'll unknowingly sweat into the cotton, and then you'll stop moving, either because you've reached your goal, you're injured, or you need to rest, and these temperatures will plummet you into a hypothermic state in hours, if not minutes."

"I had no idea it was this cold here."

"Few people do. Sorry you drove all this way for me to tell you you're not being deployed beyond this trailhead. Everyone's safety is my first priority. Getting to the subject is the second."

"I understand. Who would have known it would be twenty below zero?"

"I think it's closer to minus twenty-five."

Over the course of the morning, I had the same conversation with nearly two-dozen well-meaning good Samaritans from around the region.

Unlike the night before, the media didn't seem nearly as eager to speak with folks; the need for sensational stories was not as great in the mornings as the evenings, and the tone of the command post was changing. The military couldn't officially help us (officially as a training mission) unless we were attempting a rescue, not a body recovery. Even though there still was no official call of death, the media and everyone else at the command post knew the reality. The mission's objective was a recovery, not a rescue.

After checking in with the incident commander, Deputy Cooper, I briefed the media as the operations manager and public information officer. Whenever I could, I briefed them about the current situation and plan. At that time the plan was to await the arrival of the Blackhawk. After it landed, we'd shuttle in avalanche-certified technicians to survey the scene.

About that time Deputy Cooper received a radio transmission that the Stevens family had just turned off the highway. They were only a minute or two from arriving at the command post. I looked up at the peak, the west face's details easily discernible, but still softened by the early morning light. I said a brief prayer to Lygon, and I asked her to help guide me in protecting her family.

Although I had met Lygon's father, Nick Senior, and boyfriend, Tim, the night before, this was the first time I met Lygon's younger sister Lexy, her brother Nicklis Junior, and her mother Sarah. Justifiably, they all had a look of traumatized disbelief, the first stage of grief, and they often just gazed, fixated on the looming mountain. I assured everyone that I would do everything I could to bring Lygon back to them as soon as possible. Unfortunately, at the moment, that meant patiently waiting for the arrival of the army Blackhawk helicopter, inbound from Aurora, east of Denver. I passed along to Lygon's family as well as the media and everyone standing by that the army expected to take off from Denver around 0800 hours and be at the command post about two hours later.

As the sun finally rose above the ridgeline of the Sangres and illuminated the command post, the air temperature was still well below zero, about minus 15 degrees. Wearing all my thermal sock layers, my feet would still quickly go numb after thirty minutes exposure to the temperature. Had I been moving it would have taken far longer for the cold to creep in, but when outside the protection of my vehicle or Deputy Cooper's sheriff's vehicle, I was doing nothing physically demanding; I was just standing, literally just chilling.

I continued to add legitimate SAR personnel to the mission roster well into the morning, and as the time for the Blackhawk arrival got closer, I ranked everyone on the list according to their avalanche certification levels, winter survivability, ice/snow climbing skills (based on demonstrations during trainings), and medical qualifications. From this list I prioritized those SAR responders most qualified to be put in harm's way and survive as the first "hasty teams." They would be flown to the debris field via helicopter, assess the scene, do whatever they could to safely recover Lygon, and return unharmed.

Unfortunately, this method of prioritization did not sit well with a couple volunteers who had responded from distant locations, as well as a couple inactive AVSAR techs. All of these disappointed volunteers were surprised when I explained that because they hadn't participated in recent AVSAR trainings, none of the active AVSAR techs knew them, knew their skill levels, and frankly putting them on a helicopter to be flown into isolated wilderness in extreme winter survival conditions would be outrageously stupid and an act of dangerous liability.

The estimated time of the Blackhawk's arrival came and went. Upon checking in with Deputy Cooper, I learned that the helicopter had been late leaving Buckley, the preflight requirements and fuel-up taking longer than the pilot and copilot had anticipated. The Blackhawk was expected to arrive by 1100 hours, just enough time for the Colorado Avalanche Information Center experts to arrive. They were driving in from along the northern Front Range. As we began finalizing the individuals who would be on the first sortie in, as well as what field team members' responsibilities would be, I was notified that the subject's father, Nick Stevens Senior, as well as the subject's friend and minister, Jim Doenges, were requesting to be part of the field response.

My initial reaction was simply, "No way. The subject's father and minister will be far too much of a distraction and liability. They're not objective rescuers, they're too invested. If fate killed them, in addition to what's already occurred, how would that affect the surviving Stevens family?" I understood their desire to take part, but initially my reaction was a plain and simple negative.

I continued planning, explaining people's roles, and the objective—to reach the debris field, and if possible, conduct a rough scuff search. Then if necessary (and possible) conduct a finer probe search, locate Lygon's body, recover her, and bring her back to her family and the coroner. Of the dozen people who were properly qualified and up to the task, I began assigning field roles including asking Jack Hunt, Rio Grande's president and local ice guru, to take pictures of the scene with several different cameras. I assigned another person as a lookout, who while the others were working, would post himself in a good vantage point, and upon any additional avalanches triggering and descending into the same cirque, would sound a loud whistle notifying all the others to employ defensive tactics, if possible. The techs on skis with the most downhill skills, I asked to position themselves in the most dangerous spots, so that if the alarm were raised, they'd have the greatest chance of getting out of the slide's way. Sometime in the midst of this planning and assigning, I was approached by Lygon's friend and mountaineering mentor, Jim Doenges, a minister for the Climbing for Christ organization.

Jim again requested that he and Lygon's father be allowed to fly into the field with the team. Again I explained the dangers and the liability; however, Jim had been watching the planning and had seen the sign-in roster as I had passed it around during the morning. He pointed out that he was a highly qualified mountaineer with both avalanche and medical skills; Nick Senior was also an experienced wintertime mountaineer. Jim said that if allowed to fly in, he'd take Nick away from the immediate danger of additional avy run-outs, and they would remain simply as relatively distant observers. Jim believed that whether Lygon's body was found and recovered, or if she was unable to be recovered at that time, either scenario would be easier for Lygon's family to accept, especially her father, if he were present to see all the effort implemented to bring her home. Jim made some good points, so I had him sign in on the SAR roster.

As I finalized the field teams and went down the line of techs inspecting their packs, gear, attitudes, and roles, I was once more approached by Jim. This time both he and Nick Senior assured me that they had the skills to survive overnight if necessary and were both qualified to help others if a contingent accident occurred.

Having already been blunt and brutal getting everyone ready for what might be in store, I quickly assessed what the SAR responders' opinions were in allowing Jim and Nick to be present in the field observing them. I also warned them that if an overnight occurred, they might very well end up in a position "babysitting" the non-vetted within the group.

In my field notes, I wrote that I was surprised that the SAR personnel were all supportive of "giving the father the closure he so desperately and obviously requires." With the feedback and support of the field team, I decided to put Jim and Nick on the third and final Blackhawk flight to the avalanche site. I asked that they both keep a fair distance from the debris field, both for their safety from the continued "hang fire" that remained above them, but also for decreased trauma in the case that Lygon was located. Jim and Nick agreed to adhere to these directives.

As if on cue, the nearly imperceptible sound of a helicopter rotor began pulsing through the frigid air, and Deputy Cooper announced that the Blackhawk was just a couple miles out. He had a direct radio channel with the pilot, and I listened as he gave the pilot directions to the landing zone (LZ) describing our location from the pilot's perspective. "Affirmative. We're about three miles out at your two o'clock." I told Cooper that I'd walk out to the area west of the command post where we had planned to land the helicopter, and I'd give the pilot the final hand signals to aid in landing. I reminded Cooper of the signals I'd give if we needed to abort, and if he saw me give those signals, I asked him to reinforce this by also transmitting the same over the radio. He acknowledged the request with a nod, and I could tell he was focused and eager to get the field deployments underway.

I walked out to the LZ and put my back to the wind, thus allowing the pilot easy visibility of me while also facing the helicopter into a slight headwind giving it a tiny bit of additional lift. It could use all it could muster at the 8,000-foot elevation where we stood.

I watched as the Blackhawk straight-lined toward the command post, and then it made two large circles around the LZ, the first one a little farther out, the last circle close-in. During their last circling, I could see the crew looking out the windows searching for anything that could turn a standard helicopter field landing into a catastrophe, such as a piece of barbed wire, which might be caught in the looping ground effects of the helicopter's air cushion, lifted up off the ground to be spun right back into the helicopter's blades. They were looking but seeing nothing; we had cleared the LZ of any such objects and debris just before their arrival.

Finally, the aircraft leveled out of its reconnaissance, and I responded by lifting my arms in a "Y" over my head—the signal that everything's good, the LZ is safe and ready for use. At this point, the pilots and I, even from a few hundred feet, began a staring contest. Really the pilot was using my eyes as his. If I made any motion for him to abort, he'd rise up and away for another try. Finally I had to close my eyes as the sand particles from the air cushion slammed me with a force nearly hard enough to knock me off my feet, but I stayed standing, and blind I kept my arms up until I heard the whine of the turbine begin slowing down.

Still wiping frozen sand from the corners of my eyes, a car raced into the parking lot skidding to a stop, coughing up a cloud of frozen dust. The ski rack on top of the car had some very expensive, top-of-the-line skis, and I had a pretty good idea who the two bearded mountain-man-looking guys were as they began getting out of the car. With the blades of the Blackhawk still slowly rotating, I walked over to the vehicle and introduced myself, "Hi, I'm Kevin. I'm the operations manager for this incident."

"Kevin, it's good to meet you in person. I'm Ethan Greene, the director of the Colorado Avalanche Information Center. This is Scott Toepfer, one of CAIC's senior forecasters and investigators. Sorry we're so late. We had to drive all the way down from the northern Front Range." I was relieved to know we now had two of the most experienced avalanche experts in the state available on scene.

"No worries. You guys are arriving just in time. As you can tell, the Blackhawk just arrived, and I'm about to start flying responders into the field. How long will it take you to be ready to deploy?"

In the time it took me to ask the question, Scott had already donned his pack. He was getting his skis off the rack, "I'm ready now."

"Awesome. Let me quickly brief you guys about our current situational status, what the plan is, and what to do in case of any contingencies."

Deputy Cooper yelled, "Kevin, the pilots aren't going to shut down completely. They want to make the most use of the time and fuel. We've got to get folks on board asap!"

"Good copy Cooper. Quick briefing and they're outta here. Start the first of the SAR techs loading!"

I quickly summarized for Ethan and Scott what roles I had assigned the techs, and explained the reasoning and decision to involve the subject's father and minister as observers. I asked that they act as field leads as they had the most experience investigating avalanche scenes and keeping personnel safe in risky terrain. They agreed, and I walked with them to the Blackhawk. They'd be on the first of three sorties to transport personnel and equipment to a LZ as close to the debris field as possible.

The pilots communicated that they would require refueling, and they only had so much time they could support us. They would have to begin their flight back to the Denver area by 1500, giving all of us just a few hours to try and meet our objective.

I wished them well, and ended with "Be safe!" and as I walked away, the helicopter's turbines began to accelerate the rotors. As I reached the edge of the command post's LZ, the blades of the rotors bit into the dense air, and the helicopter lifted off on an air cushion of dust and sparkly ice crystals.

In just half a minute we could barely see or hear the Blackhawk enter the gorge it was so small—the helicopter reinforced the mountain's enormous scale. The second group was at the edge of the LZ preparing for their own flight into the bitter icy cold. The third group was also forming up—the group including Lygon's father. I watched him hug and console his wife, Sarah, his daughter, Lexy, and his son, Nicklis Junior. From a hundred feet away, it wasn't Nicklis Junior's head bandages or other indications of physical injury that caught my attention, it was his anguish, his constant gaze toward the mountain, its slopes.

I thought of my own siblings and family, and how broken hearted I would be. I thought of my own near-death experiences, and the effect my passing away would have had on them. I recalled calling my mother after an ascent of Mt. Rainier. When a snow bridge had collapsed under one of two partners, our entire team had nearly been lost into a crevasse. I had intended on calling family members to communicate and celebrate my successful summit, but upon hearing my mom's voice, I could barely speak and quietly began crying—I felt utterly ashamed and selfish at how close I had come to deeply hurting all those around me. I remembered the lesson I had learned working in the emergency room and as a first responder in multiple roles earlier in my life—my role, in addition to recovering Lygon, was to support a trauma-tized family.

In about twenty minutes, the Blackhawk returned to the command post empty except for the pilots and a couple air crew members. The second group of technicians boarded the craft, and just as quickly as the first pick-up, they were en route to the avalanche site.

In the quiet, after the second departure, I walked over to Jim Doenges, the Climbing for Christ minister and Lygon's friend. Jim was experienced in avalanche terrain and had an avalanche level two certification. I knew they would be boarding shortly, and I wanted to ensure one last time that every-one felt prepared for the risks involved. "Jim, I haven't heard yet from the first team, so it seems it's taking awhile just to get to the scene. Are you sure you and Mr. Stevens are prepared for either scenario: one in which his daughter is located and dug out, or the other possibility that she is buried too deep and we won't be able to recover her anytime soon?"

"I think we're as prepared as one can possibly be. In either scenario, it'll be a form of closure, either forever or temporarily for Mr. Stevens."

"If the team locates Lygon, please keep him far enough away that he's safe and not *too* exposed to his daughter's recovery. Seeing her from a distance will be less traumatizing."

"Agreed. I promise to keep him a safe distance."

Again on cue, the Blackhawk's rotors could be heard exiting the canyon. Within seconds, we could all see the miniscule aircraft beelining for the com-mand post again.

Like the previous two drills, the helicopter dropped quickly onto the LZ and a crewman jumped out the side door and motioned for the remaining personnel to approach and jump in. Jim, Nick Senior, and the remaining techs crouched as they moved quickly beneath the moving rotors.

The air temperature was hovering in the teens, near the day's high. The cold air carried the sound extremely well. Everyone at the command post could hear all our radios crackle as Mick, a member of the first group was now on the scene and reporting the conditions, "Command this is SAR 1."

Brian Cooper, acting as the incident commander radioed back, "Go for Command."

"How's the transmission?"

"Loud and clear."

"We've reached the base of the debris field. It's located in the small cirque at the top of the gorge under the west face of Little Bear. It's *massive*. The crown of the slide might be a hundred yards or more across. The depth looks to be a couple feet minimum. It's hard to tell scale without any references but ice, snow, and rock. From crown to debris field, we're looking at a thousand or more vertical feet. There's several more potential avalanche paths that deposit into the same cirque. We're sitting ducks. Keep any nonessential personnel away from the scene. It's too dangerous. Copy?"

Cooper replied, "That's a good copy SAR 1, but it's too late. All personnel are en route to your location already. When Jim and Nick arrive on the scene, keep them as far away from any danger as you can. Look for any tracks indicating someone leaving the site other than Nicklis Junior. Personnel safety is the number one priority. Mick, do what you can in the time you have."

Mick replied, "Good copy. It sounds like the chopper's delivering the third group back at the LZ. I'll radio updates when possible."

"Good copy SAR 1. Be safe."

After the third group had been delivered to the LZ, the Blackhawk flew overhead and passed us on its way to Alamosa airport, where it could refuel. The day was nearly cloudless, a bright blue sky, allowing the radiant sunshine to help the 25 degrees above zero feel relatively warm, even with a light breeze.

Deputy Cooper asked if I'd make a statement to the media; they had been patiently waiting since the morning news. I approached the half dozen reporters and with the mountain as my backdrop described the size and scale of the slide, its location, and a summary of the operation.

Passing 1400, the Blackhawk and crew returned to the LZ and finally shut down to standby. I became increasingly anxious about the closing of the window of time in which we had use of the Blackhawk. Finally, Mick radioed around 1430, "Command, SAR 1."

Cooper responded, "Go for Command."

"We've completed a scuff search and a coarse probe search. The debris is much deeper than our longest three meter probes. It's getting windier up here. How's the wind there?" Indeed the wind was beginning to indicate the first afternoon/evening breezes.

Cooper looked toward the pilots as he answered Mick's question. "They're picking up. How long is it until you can get back to the LZ for pick up?"

Mick answered eagerly, "Maybe ten minutes."

"Good copy. Standby."

Standby? What was Cooper doing? They should get back to the LZ asap. "Deputy Cooper, why did you tell them to standby? They need to get the hell out of there. Tell 'em to head toward the LZ."

"Kevin, what do you mean? They all had large packs and you said earlier that everyone was prepared and equipped to spend the night. I'm thinking that with these winds picking up, and the Blackhawk needing to get back to Aurora, we cut 'em loose and everyone bed down."

"Bed down? Brian, those folks are equipped to spend a night out in an *emergency*. They're in these temperatures, above treeline, in multiple avalanche paths. Please call them and ask them what they'd prefer." I could see this might be the moment in which Mick had predicted having an experienced winter mountaineer at the command post coming in handy.

Brian promptly brought them up on the radio, "SAR 1, Command."

"Go for SAR 1."

"Would you guys be okay spending the night? The Blackhawk crew said they can come back tomorrow and do the pick-up then. Do you think you could locate her by then?"

Without any hesitation Mick replied, "That's a negative Command. We're almost back to the LZ already. Please get us out of here as soon as possible. Temperatures are dropping fast. Winds should be okay for a bit longer. We'll be ready in minutes. Start the flight now if you can."

Cooper looked at me with a smile and nod, "Good copy."

At nearly 1500 on the dot, the Blackhawk returned from its flight in. The pilots had to be far more conservative in adding mass when creeping up into the higher, less dense air on the way up. If the craft needs only to descend, it can add as much mass as it can take off with. All the personnel and equipment that had taken three separate flights to lift up to the scene took only one single flight to fly out. A dozen personnel total had been on the scene, and I was personally relieved to see each face exit the helicopter. Mr. Stevens was obviously still distraught. I approached him and explained that all the SAR leadership would convene for a briefing and planning as soon as the Blackhawk crew had departed, and after I had debriefed the avalanche experts. He returned to his family, and I took solace watching them form a small prayer circle.

I walked with Ethan and Scott, the CAIC avalanche specialists, back to their car as they returned their alpine skis to the top of their car rack. I asked Jack Hunt, the president of Rio Grande County SAR, to join us. I asked them all their frank perspectives regarding the scene.

Jack was the first to answer my most pressing question. He said, "There were two sets of tracks into the top of the avalanche, and only one set leaving the debris. Lygon's still there, and she's buried deep."

Ethan followed up with an answer to my second most important question. He said, "The debris field is in a very precarious position. Any personnel in that environment are at risk of further avalanche activity."

I collected the cameras I had given Jack to take digital pictures and film pictures of the scene, and even through the digital's small LCD screen I could see the enormous scales involved. With some rough estimations of the volumes involved, I calculated that Lygon could be under twenty feet or more of snow. It might not be possible to recover her until melt out much later in the spring or even the summer. I looked over at the Stevens family and knew that Lygon would want me to do everything I could to protect them and bring them peace.

After speaking with everyone who had been on scene, I spoke with Deputy Cooper and we decided that it was time to communicate that no further personnel could be risked in an attempt to recover Lygon until later in the season when conditions were safer. We had done everything we possibly could for the moment. Cooper and the other leaders agreed.

As the San Juans' shadows began creeping across the San Luis Valley, and the sun began to set for the third night after the incident, a small group of rescue specialists waited for a moment of grace to approach a family in the midst of prayer.

As we continued to peacefully experience the frozen sky turning from blue to pink, no one noticed the 1970s model Volkswagen Beetle drive up and park. As we were all awaiting a cue from the Stevens family, our focus was not on the small Navajo man who emerged from the VW. I didn't actually notice him until he positioned himself between the circle of family and us first responders. Everyone noticed him when he spoke, "What has happened on Sisnaajini? What has happened on this sacred mountain of Diné?"

Someone in the Stevens' circle humbly responded, "A couple of climbers were involved in an avalanche."

The old Navajo man became angry. "That's a possible consequence for trespassing on Sisnaajini. Those who trespass may die." I immediately walked up to the man, consciously invading his personal space, my face inches within his.

In a whisper only audible to him I said, "Many of the people standing here are the family of a young woman who was killed. You need to leave. These men you've offended, they may be a threat to you."

The man responded loudly, "It is the mountain that's been offended. I say again that trespassers will die. Those who trespass, die."

With that, Deputy Cooper, far closer to being seven feet tall than six, walked up behind the man, bent down a bit, bear hugged him, lifted him clear off the ground, walked over to the VW and proceeded to physically stuff the small man into his car, finishing the process off with Cooper pointing down the two-track toward the highway, "If you don't leave, you're under arrest."

Cussing and visibly upset, the man drove off down the sandy two-track toward the darkening western horizon.

As the sky transitioned to the ultraviolet purple of the first part of the night, mission leadership conferred with the Stevens and their close friends. They explained the heartbreaking decision to prioritize the safety of the living over the currently impossible recovery of the deceased. All present agreed, "It was what Lygon would want."

***

Halfway through the following week, I received a call from the sheriff. He had a peculiar request. He explained that SAR volunteers were only covered by the sheriff's office workmen's comp insurance if we were on missions to rescue or recover people; we weren't covered if we were going after equipment. He explained that even though this were the case, the Stevens family had contacted him asking about any plans to recover Nicklis' and Lygon's equipment, located at their last camp next to Lake Como. The sheriff said that the Stevens family was planning on potentially ascending to the camp to recover equipment, as well as satisfy themselves 100 percent that Lygon hadn't been able to miraculously dig out of the avalanche, ascend up and over Little Bear Peak's west ridge, and return to the camp. In summary, he asked that I put together a small group of highly trained mountaineers capable of recovering the equipment, truly personal volunteers operating on their own, not officially on a county SAR mission thus not covered by any workmen's compensation insurance. I told him I was willing to lead such a small team in the spirit of keeping people safe, and I'd do what I could to recruit some capable souls.

I notified all members on the AVSAR roster of the request and parameters, and two people offered to accompany me: Mick Daniel, who'd been to the scene, and John White, a national park ranger at Sand Dunes National Park. Unfortunately, as the next weekend neared, Mick came down with a cold, and his energy vanished. This left John, but on Thursday night, John called and explained that he, like Mick, was sick. In a very hoarse voice he said, "Maybe if I feel better in the morning, I'll be able to make it."

Friday evening I met Deputy Cooper and obtained a sheriff's office radio. Although not an official mission, the sheriff and Deputy Cooper had asked that as long as I had radio contact with the nearby repeater that I maintain communication and regular check-ins. I explained that I'd have radio capability until I entered the canyon containing Lake Como, but up until that point and immediately upon returning to that location, I'd be able to do communication status checks. Deputy Cooper provided a list of equipment I should expect to find and have the team recover including a tent, Lygon's backpack, skis, ski poles, clothes, food, some other minor essentials, and Gerry Roach's *Colorado 14er Guidebook*. According to Nicklis, he had left their last camp with everything set up in the Lake Como cabin, a small, drafty shack next to the frozen lake, just in case Lygon had somehow miraculously dug herself out of the avalanche and returned to their last high camp.

Saturday morning I left my home at approximately 3:45 in the morning, so I'd be at the trailhead at 4:30 to prep and get an early start. As I stepped out into the darkness, the temperature was painful. The thermometer read minus 25 degrees—temperature so cold that it burned to breathe in too quickly. Driving out to the trailhead, for curiosity's sake, I stuck my hand out into the windchill's effect. With a temperature of minus 25 degrees and a wind speed of 60 mph (how fast I was cruising), my fingers felt the equivalent of negative 69 degrees. At this frigid temperature, my fingers' nerves transitioned from an uncomfortable burning-like sensation to a relatively comfortable numb in less than a minute. It took several times longer for sensation to return, and it did so after a period of stinging, like an intense version of one's arm going to sleep.

As I pulled into the parking area, where just a week before there had been dozens of vehicles, people, and the occasional helicopter, in the current cold and darkness there was no car, not a person, nothing but the dark ominous profile of Little Bear Peak and the Blanca Massif, silhouetted by the twinkling of the stars in the eastern sky. The car's thermometer read minus 24 degrees. I pulled out my cell phone to see if there was a text or call from John. Maybe his flu, just coming on, had miraculously gotten better and not worse? On my cell phone, there was nothing. I thought about Mick and John, two AVSAR friends who were constantly going above and beyond to help others. It made me proud that they wanted to help, and I was sad that they'd be battling low energy, sniffles, and the regret of not getting to go up the mountain with me. I'd promised myself I'd take good field notes so I could pass along to Mick, John, and the rest of the team what my experience had been. Plus if anything ever happened mid-mission, notes and photos on my body would record the period leading up to my demise.

I took a few warm field notes, cracked the car's window and watched as the moist warm air rolled out into the atmosphere. I looked up at the mountain's profile, and I knew exactly where the dark mass hid Lygon's body. The previous week's memories were fresh. I thought of Lygon's family, their pain, their grief, their anguish. I knew it was the sort of suffering that would drive Lygon's father and brother, as well as a number of mountaineering friends to ascend back up to their last high camp. If they went to that effort, it wouldn't be unfathomable from there, they may try to climb the west ridge to look down upon or even go back to the debris field and continue to look for their beloved.

If it were my family member, I would likely try and do it myself, just to feel like I was doing something, anything to combat the feelings of loss, chaos, lack of control. I thought of the previous weekend and listening to Lygon's family members and friends describe her—a brilliant, spiritual, charismatic, athletic, inspiring young woman, who felt more at home in nature than she did anywhere else. I recalled someone quietly and compassionately sharing, "If Lygon could have chosen the place she would be called home, it would have been in the wilderness, as close to God as she could find herself. Lygon's spirit is at peace." Indeed, that was suddenly the sense I was feeling, but simultaneously, I also knew Lygon wouldn't want to endanger anyone, especially her beloved.

I looked at my watch, and it was now nearly 5:00 a.m. In the middle of winter, it was still pitch black, not even a hint of light in the sky. In these temperatures, I knew it would not be safe to travel alone. I thought of the main character in Jack London's *To Build a Fire*, how he had been warned by the old timers of Sulphur Creek not to travel alone below a certain temperature. In the past, I had operated as a military specialist in ambient temperatures as low as minus 47 degrees, but anytime I was isolated, exposed to temperatures lower than minus 20, I was very anxious. Below minus 20, there is very little room for error. Little room for error and attention to detail are the lessons of London's short story as well as my training in the air force. As I finished organizing and packing up the last of my gear, I thought of the main character at the end of London's story, dead and frozen. I thought of Lygon.

I've rarely prayed in my life, but around 5:30 a.m., as I stepped out into the wicked black void and donned my pack, I faced east, the mountain, Lygon, and I bowed my head. In the quiet I meditated, "Lygon, I sense that although physically I'm alone, spiritually you are here with me. I sense your love, and in the spirit of that love I ask for your guidance and protection. I ask that in the spirit of love, you protect me getting to your camp, the camp you shared with your brother. Help me get there, help me bring back the equipment that your brother left in camp for you. Please protect me and your family with your love."

As my breath pushed through the balaclava, its moisture froze, and instantly a thin layer of frost began forming on its exterior. Some of my breath rose up along my face, and as it passed my eyes, ice began forming on my eyelashes.

As I had learned from experience and in survival training working in the "northern tier" with the air force, difficult terrain such as mountainous deep powder snow can slow a person up to five times the amount of time it would take to cover the same distance on easy terrain (and that's with snowshoes).

If I thought about my goal, exactly five miles away, I became overwhelmed by the scale. Five miles in the summer is a few hours of steep hiking, but in the winter, I'd be putting out an equivalent amount of energy as a marathon. Like any big physical goal, I knew to chunk it into smaller more manageable pieces. I decided to focus on just a hundred yards at a time. Alone, I had to be very careful and take as little risk as possible; at any time if I calculated or sensed too much danger, I would simply turn around—I could always try again in the future. I also remembered that although I was choosing the more risky option of traveling solo, Deputy Cooper knew my exact travel path, I'd be in radio contact with him the majority of the mission, and there was minimal objective danger from avalanches—I would only be crossing a half dozen or so run-outs. In my mind, the real danger was someone choosing to ascend the west ridge from Lake Como, as Lygon and Nicklis had done the week prior. I ultimately justified my choice to go solo as I knew, unlike most other folks, I had a great deal of arctic environment training (which lowered my subjective risk), and I knew I could move very fast solo and avoid running the risk of a larger team not making the objective at all. As long as their equipment remained at the camp, Lygon's family members and friends would continue having a reason to ascend to the camp and be tempted to go up the west ridge. I decided what calculated risk I would be taking was worth the potential reward, and the motto of search and rescue came to mind, "We take these risks, so that others may live."

As I began taking small steps away from the car, I listened to the unusual squeak of the snow under my boots, the sound of the ultra cold. I adjusted my face mask so that, with the help of the nearly imperceptible northerly wind, my lashes would remain thawed.

"Let your love keep me safe Lygon." As I said this, I sensed a warm, loving presence, and I quickened my pace a bit. As my car receded to the southwest, I floated over the last sandy flat section of the trail. There was a dusting of snow, and little snowdrifts behind taller rocks and bushes, but otherwise in the forbidding darkness, it felt like I was afloat between billions of stars twinkling above and the soft, smooth sand.

There was still no light as I started up the "baby heads" section, so named for the size of the rocks that covered the trail in a cobblestone effect. In the darkness under the beam of my headlamp looking out ahead, I could not see them, but the rolling of my ankles verified their shapes. I knew the piñon pines surrounded me, the dark forests to either side of the road. If I were to get off the road, I would find myself surrounded by miles of unending piñon pine trees, crisscrossed by the occasional ATV trail.

As I began traversing the alluvial formation under the proper peaks and passed the first large aspen grove, the first hint of ultraviolet light began illuminating the sky. I checked my thermometer, minus 20 degrees. The temperature was slightly warmer, and yet it was the coldest part of a calm morning. The San Luis Valley was experiencing a common occurrence for the high alpine desert in the winter, a condition called a temperature inversion. An inversion is a thin layer of the atmosphere where the normal decrease in temperature with height switches to an increase in temperature with height. In these conditions, one can climb up out of the cold into much warmer air. I looked forward to getting out of the sub-zero temperatures. I stopped and ate a granola bar. Briefly exposing my hand to peel the food, and even with my glove liners remaining on, my fingers quickly felt the chill set in, and my body began cooling without the added heat of near aerobic exercise. It was difficult to put my mittens back on.

I continued hiking and enjoyed watching the San Luis Valley slowly turn from a dark blue sea dotted by islands of city lights to its usual cornflower blue sky over a snowy desert parceled into grids by highways and roads. I gained elevation quickly as I traversed the piñon pine section. The snow more consistently covered the ground deep enough that I could clearly walk along and read the tracks of the snowmobiles and rescuers from the previous week. The week had eroded the tracks, but they were still clear.

Near where the tracks of the snowmobiles had encountered Nicklis, I imagined what the scene would have been a week prior, and I imagined what the rescuers and Nicklis must have been thinking and feeling at those moments. I sensed the relief myself.

I stopped to have another granola bar at the last turnout before entering Chokecherry Canyon, the mouth of the gorge that leads 4x4 enthusiasts, hikers, and climbers up to the three fourteeners of the group—Little Bear Peak, Ellingwood Point, and Blanca Peak. The thermometer still read in the negative teens.

The sun's direct rays were about to hit me as I entered Chokecherry Canyon. Here the road stops ascending, and it descends briefly into the mouth of the canyon. From this point I'd have the last line of sight to the local law enforcement radio repeater, so I pulled out the sheriff's radio and I made a call directly to Deputy Cooper on an alternate channel. I let him know I was the only one who wasn't sick and was headed up, I gave him a brief status report, I said the temperature was manageable, but if I got injured and stopped moving, I would likely only have hours to be rescued before succumbing to the cold. I told Cooper to call in the regional SAR cavalry if he didn't hear back from me by dark. He replied, "Copy that."

I switched off the radio to conserve the batteries, and I turned and began the short descent into the canyon. The snow was starting to drift over the road becoming a true obstacle in places, but as long as I stayed on the drifted over snowmobile tracks, I remained afloat in the deepening powder.

Near "Jaws 1," the first of the major vehicle rock obstacles along the Lake Como 4x4 road, the first rays of sunshine finally hit me directly. I briefly stopped and checked the thermometer. It had risen to nearly zero degrees. I was at the transition of the temperature inversion, and my elevation had allowed me to escape the significantly colder temperatures just below.

Near the deadly "Jaws 2" obstacle, I knew I was nearing the location where the initial snowmobile team had intercepted the two SAR personnel, Don and Barry, who had been dropped off by Flight For Life a week before. The snowmobile team had also previously intercepted Nicklis, so I was glad the snowmobiles had packed down the trail, especially since entering the canyon. The snow was deep powder on either side of the packed down snowmobile tracks. At the top of Jaws 2, the second major rock obstacle in the 4x4 road, the snowmobile tracks ended. I stepped off the tracks to test the snow that lay beyond, and I sank to my waist. Without snowshoes, I couldn't continue. I put the snowshoes on quickly, but my sweat-soaked inner mittens still froze in the time it took.

As I started into the deep power, I realized even with snowshoes I was sinking into the froth, and it was going to take considerable movement and energy to make the camp, more than another mile up the canyon. I stopped to catch my breath, and I asked Lygon to continue keeping me and her family safe. As if on cue, a little flock of chirping birds flew up to me and landed on a close-by spruce. I felt comforted and secured by the birds.

I slowly lifted one snowshoe out of the fluffy powder, then another, then another. I set myself to a steady pace that kept my heart rate around 130, and let the quiet, peaceful setting flow around me. I headed easterly, upward into the sparkles of light on the surface of the snow, reflecting magically through the pines. Unperceivable via any depressions in the surface snow, I could sense the snowshoe tracks left by the Nicklis and Lygon as well as the two rescuers from the prior week.

As I came up into the "flats" of the lake, I knew I was nearing the cabin. One last time I stopped and took in the isolated wintery mountainous setting. One last time I asked Lygon's spirit to keep me safe, and in a gesture that seemed beyond any possible coincidence, the small flock of birds reappeared. This time they flew ahead, guiding me the last hundred yards to the cabin.

I approached the cabin from the south. I could see the snowed-in tracks from the east; the slight depression of my SAR brethren's trail from their drop-in LZ that had been higher up, easterly in the canyon. They had followed the tracks originally set down by Nicklis and Lygon on their way up, as well as Nicklis' solo descent.

I slowly approached the cabin, taking pictures documenting what I found before disturbing anything. As I snowshoed up close to the cabin, I saw Lygon's skis propped up in the snow, just as she had left them a week ago. In a traumatized state Nicklis had left them, along with the tent and equipment, just in case Lygon miraculously survived. The skis there, with their owner nearby but no longer alive, made me feel isolated, alone in the wilderness. I found some peace remembering that this was the setting for Lygon's last morning. It was a place of indescribable beauty.

I began documenting the scene, noting the time and the temperature. It was 11:30 a.m. It had taken me just about six hours to ascend from the lowest parking area to the cabin. It was 10 degrees above zero. The wind had increased, and consistent breezes with small gusts were regularly dusting the sparse forest around the frozen, snow-covered lake.

I opened the door of the cabin and found a fully set up tent. The Lake Como cabin was more of a shack, and in the winter it provided little protection from the wind and snow. In the week since Nicklis had left the camp (and the two rescuers had passed it and briefly checked it for Lygon), the tent had remained untouched. I took a picture and stepped into the cabin, out of the majority of the breeze. I dropped my pack and immediately lit my stove. In the high temperatures of the day, I figured a little external finger warming and some hot chocolate for lunch would be especially motivating.

After ingesting some gorp and liquid chocolate, I shook off the tent and slowly unzipped the front door. I photographed everything as I found it: a sleeping bag, clothes, food, water, the guidebook, odds and ends of equipment. I packed up all the equipment and loaded it into my expeditionary pack, which up to that point carried only my essential winter survival equipment.

Nicklis' and Lygon's tent, set up in the Lake Como cabin, January 19, 2008 (author photo).

I emerged from the cabin with an enormous and heavy pack. I took some solace in knowing that at least it was downhill from the cabin. Before I lifted the pack, I added Lygon's skis and poles to its sides. She had left them and switched to her snowshoes for good reason. The snow conditions were not advantageous for skis. Now the skis and poles served to add several more pounds to an already outrageously heavy rig. I was thankful knowing I could follow my own tracks out, not needing to pack down a virgin path. Downhill, no trail packing, my only burden would be the girth of the pack.

My Mountainsmith pack bore the weight well and distributed it in a manageable way, but it was still 80+ pounds. I was glad I wouldn't be using any energy to descend. I took pictures of the empty cabin documenting that nothing had been left behind, at least nothing in this canyon.

Lygon was in the parallel canyon immediately south of the camp; Little Bear's west ridge separated the two canyons. In the midday light, I looked up the access chute that Nicklis and Lygon had ascended gaining the west ridge's standard route. From below, I couldn't see their tracks. I thought of Lygon's body at rest deep under the snow, and I promised her I'd be back for her as soon as I could safely.

I left the cabin at 1:00 p.m., and I covered ground descending much faster than on the way up. I was back to Jaws 2 in an hour, and I was very happy to unstrap the snowshoes.

The pack was heavy, but knowing I was racing an early midwinter sunset around 4:30, I wanted to make sure I had plenty of time to radio in before the cavalry got called up. It took me half the time to descend as it had to ascend. At about 3:00, I was back to the mouth of Chokecherry Canyon and called out to dispatch and Deputy Cooper. I was glad when it didn't take but a second for Cooper to return my radio call. We discussed a rendezvous point for that evening. I told him I'd call him on my cell when I got back close to town.

As I continued to descend, I noticed that a second set of tracks had been made after the ones I had left that morning. They looked as if someone had either followed me or come out of the woods and descended my tracks. In the deep snow, I figured it was likely a mountain lion or bobcat, as the bears were all hibernating, skipping the existential challenge of these extreme, sub-zero nights.

Just a short time before sunset I ran across a patch of perfect Styrofoam snow that acted as a "track trap." These "traps" are spots at which travel is choked down to a concentrated location and the tracks are well preserved. An experienced tracker can use tracks to distinguish a vast amount of information. In SAR that may sometimes be the track of a ten-year-old child's shoe. In my case, I found I was tracking a large cat, a lion that had traveled in the same direction I had traveled on the ascent. The tracks didn't tell me how much longer after I had made my tracks that the cat had made its tracks. The thought of a lion stalking me seemed a little over-reactive, as there wasn't a record of a predatory animal attacking a human in the Sangres. Even statewide, lion attacks are extremely rare. Less than ten have ever occurred historically. I knew far more likely that the lion came along the tracks some time after I had passed and had followed my tracks for the same reason I had used them—they were located on a snowmobile trail and the snow was packed down.

I almost needed a headlamp to cover the nearly treeless lower section of the trail, the last mile in which I had a line of sight to my car. It was near dark as I walked over the baby heads again. In the summer, I usually returned to the trailhead, overheated, parched, ready for a long drink at the local brew pub. That night, the temperature was already in the negative teens, and my fingers had a difficult time differentiating the proper car key, and then turning it to open the door lock was nearly impossible. Upon entering the car, I threw all the equipment into the backseat and dove into the front seat. I turned the ignition and slumped over into the passenger seat, fetal position, eagerly awaiting the warmth of the engine. After ten or fifteen minutes of near sleep-like meditation imagining somewhere warm, I sat up, turned on the headlights, and started down the sandy two-track toward Alamosa.

Right around 6:00 p.m. in extremely frosty air, I met with Deputy Cooper and transferred all of the Stevens' property to him. He thanked me on behalf of the family, and I said I was glad to help. Deep down I was afraid the Stevens or random good samaritans would be back soon.

About a week later, the Alamosa Volunteer Search and Rescue team held its monthly meeting. It also acted as the Stevens Mission After Action Review (AAR). This meeting and review served as our opportunity to reflect on what we did well and would repeat on future missions to increase success, and then for the sake of our own safety and the safety of our future subjects, we also critiqued what we did poorly and would avoid repeating in the future.

From the pictures taken of the slope and debris field, I estimated that the volume of snow was enough to have buried Lygon twenty feet deep. As regional SAR teams called to offer their support, it wasn't easy to explain that everyone may have to wait for the melt out as late as summer.

My most immediate concern was that the standard summer mountaineering route took one up and across the west ridge of Little Bear. This was the route that slid on Nicklis and Lygon, and this is exactly what others should avoid in getting to a spot to observe the debris field.

***

I began to obsessively, daily track the snowstorms and windy periods. I had a hand chart I filled in using Weather Underground and NOAA data. I made a mental model of the snowpack in different spots on the mountain, based on the data and my weekly drives past it on Highway 150. I photographed the snowfields as they changed after large snowstorms and windstorms, with rooster tails blowing off the ridges hundreds of feet high at times. Sometimes entire faces would be there one day, the next, bare rock. Massive slab avalanches often occurred that spring—more and more snow that I knew was depositing on top of Lygon.

I passed along my reports and observations to the sheriff as well as other interested and appropriate parties. Everyone knew that until later in the year, we were all on standby. We had to wait for Mother Nature. She was the one in charge of timing Lygon's homecoming. My priority was keeping everyone as safe as possible until then.

It does not make any sense to risk the living over a body, not in civilian mountain SAR. I reinforced to everyone I spoke with about my concerns regarding continued avalanche risk. I suggested to everyone that ideally we would begin observing the original debris field area from the southwest ridge, accessed from a network of roads on an unincorporated private subdivision. I thought the best access might be to park along the Lake Como access road, still down on the rocky baby heads section, and then traverse through the piñons over to the mouth of Tobin Creek. This was also the base of the southwest ridge of Little Bear Peak. If one followed the ridge directly, it provided an excellent observation point and stayed clear of avalanche danger.

As had been my concern, it was the Stevens family who was the most motivated to get into the field initially and begin looking for Lygon. Her father Nick and Climbing for Christ minister Jim, the two men who had flown into the gorge in January, led the effort to secure a safe route to Lygon's location.

The Stevens contacted landowners in the subdivision and acquired written permission to use their properties as base camps, and they immediately began scouting a route up the southwest ridge. They found that they could drive up to the highest corner of the subdivision's private roads. It was far more advantageous to drive up from the west than the south. Still very steep, the west's approach is a little more gradual than the south's that goes through an aspen grove and rises quite sharply.

At the northeast corner of the private roads nearest to Tobin Creek, one has an amazing view of the valley floor, approximately a thousand feet below, immediately surrounded by twenty-foot piñon pines. If one launches off into the trees without a compass, GPS, breadcrumbs, etc., then disorientation becomes a potential hazard. Ultimately, as a well-supplied lost mountaineer, one could descend straight away from the mountains out onto the flats of the treeless valley and walk to a highway, but within the vast piñon pine forest that skirts the entire Sangre de Cristo mountain range, it is easy to get lost trying to hit an exact point within the forest. Orienteering must be done with precision.

In addition to acquiring permission to access the mountain from these private properties, the Stevens also found a "trail" of pink ribbons. I assumed a hunter left behind a trail of fluorescent surveyor's tape during an excursion, tying bows in the outer branches of piñon pines. This "pink ribbon" route brought a hiker from the parking area, across Tobin Creek to the base of the southwest ridge of Little Bear Peak.

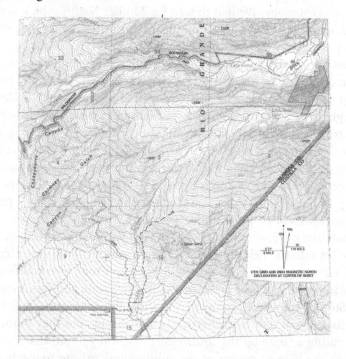

Map of "pink ribbon" route up Little Bear Peak's southwest ridge (image provided by Stevens family, spring 2008).

After the dry creek, the route traversed an old burn area, presumably from a lightning strike. After that, it climbed a steep section a couple hundred yards long and gained the rocky ridge just east of the mouth of Tobin Creek. By the time I got ready to scout the route myself, the Stevens family had added their own pink ribbons all the way up to treeline on the southwest ridge. Anyone who attempted the route got a huge cardio and pulmonary test. Anyone not in superb physical shape was quickly stopped.

At the beginning of May, I asked everyone on the rescue team who might be interested to join me. I planned the trip to see the debris field for myself. I didn't think we'd come across any evidencing surfacing for a long time, but I could get a sense of the scene. A team member named George Rapoza offered to go with me, and I was happy to have him be a hiking partner. George was a former surfer, who many years ago broke his neck while surfing by diving off his board in shallow water. His surfing partner initially did not recognize that George was paralyzed and couldn't swim, but luckily after realizing the gravity of the situation and that George couldn't move or breathe, he rescued George from drowning. George came back from that experience by a combination of luck, spirit, resilience, and mental strength. I knew George was a tough fellow, and I also appreciated that he was safe in risky environments.

We began at sunrise and quickly gained the ridge, possibly too quickly as I began feeling a bit light-headed. I somewhat enjoyed the altitude euphoria, the sound of my heart pulsing at 150+ beats per minute. Having switched over the ridge from its highest southern points to its north slope, George and I went from an environment of cool, wet, occasional patches of snow, to a slope covered in about six to ten inches of wet snow draped over everything, making the scree and talus look like a smooth surface, punctuated by little holes, spots where the snow had fallen away between larger rocks. I could not imagine a better way of breaking one's leg and in the worst possible location. Even in dry perfect conditions, we were attempting to cover virgin scree and talus rock slopes, with rocks the size of soccer balls to mini fridge—everything under foot was extremely prone to rolling and moving so that the surfaces we were treading on were more often moving than not, especially after putting weight onto them. In the snowy conditions, it was this same challenge but adding to it the rock being covered with ice and snow that hides all its detailed features. We very carefully, very slowly descended all the way to the gorge's base. From there we planned to follow the creek up to Little Bear Lake, then the pond above that, and then the cirque with Lygon's body.

It was here when I stopped. "I say we call it, George. This is a recon mission. I can see the higher parts of the gorge, and everything's covered in a blanket of snow. Let's turn around and see if we can't get back up on the ridge without snapping any legs."

George was nodding, "That's an affirmative."

As we got to the bottom of the ridge, back to the burned out forest, I heard voices coming up through the piñons below us.

"George, do you hear voices?"

"Yes."

"That must be the Stevens. They said they might be up here this weekend."

In a few minutes, the voices became clearer and clearer until the Stevens family and some friends emerged from the piñons. I said hello and very much enjoyed making the acquaintance of their dog, a young yellow lab. They were on their way up for another observation of the gorge. I passed along what the conditions of the route were like, especially beyond treeline, and we all expressed gratitude toward each other and everyone involved in the recovery of Lygon. They said they weren't going beyond the high point where they could look down onto the location of the debris field. After a few minutes, we continued on our separate paths.

With a couple hours to spare before sunset, George and I returned to my second vehicle, a 4x4 Toyota Tacoma. The Corolla was a great highway vehicle for getting me to trailheads, but for a rocky 4x4 approach like this, I drove my truck. We took our time driving back to Alamosa.

As the sun set later that afternoon, I thought of the Stevens camped up near treeline. We had said nothing explicitly, but the Stevens had asked when I thought the regional bears would be coming out of hibernation. I explained that this was happening as we spoke but that I had seen no sign to indicate any such activity in the Little Bear Lake gorge. We were all in a race to recover Lygon before a hungry momma bear might scavenge her. Bears are known for being able to eat everything a human body offers, including even the large bones such as the pelvis and cranium. I wondered if we'd truly be able to reach Lygon before scavengers did. I was sure her family wondered the same. If it came to be that indeed scavengers reached her first, I thought of this pleasing Lygon, knowing her body had given back directly to the environment.

Later into May, the Stevens family and the sheriff became increasingly concerned about Lygon's recovery. I had hung signs at the trailhead asking any early season mountaineers in the area to be on the lookout for signs of scavenging such as ravens, crows, vultures circling, or tracks of coyotes indicating approaches from below. My plan was that as soon as possible after Lygon was located, I would recover whatever remained of the scene as quickly as possible.

I contacted the sheriff and asked what lengths we could take to recover Lygon's body regarding the use of cadaver dogs and helicopters (necessary to transport the specialized dogs and their handlers). He pointed out that although standard operating procedure was that no aircraft are to be used for recoveries, nor any lives put at considerable risk, the Stevens family had communicated a willingness to help support the process in whatever ways they could. After negotiating on all parties' behalf, the sheriff okayed and coordinated an operation in which a few specialized SAR technicians would fly in with a cadaver dog, locate Lygon, extract her from the snowfield, and fly the dog, handler, and body back out. This would spare a large number of ground personnel having to hike into such an isolated, dangerous location. In one discussion, I predicted that at least one SAR member would sustain a significant injury if we brought in 24+ personnel.

This prediction came true even before a large-scale SAR attempt at a ground operation could occur. On one of his reconnaissance ascents of the southwest ridge, Lygon's dad fell and fractured his collarbone, a very painful injury, especially if one is isolated in a mountainous wilderness environment. Since I had warned him that any use of our limited local SAR resources would detract us from the ultimate quickest recovery of his daughter, Nick Senior didn't contact authorities when the injury occurred; instead, he performed a self-rescue with his partners on the trip. A self-rescue off the southwest ridge of Little Bear Peak while managing a broken clavicle is a feat of painful endurance I'd just as soon not imagine.

***

Early in the morning of June 11, I awoke before sunrise and drove two and half hours from my home outside Mosca to Saint Mary Corwin's Hospital in Pueblo, Colorado. It was after sunrise by the time I pulled into the hospital's parking lot, and the day shift crew was in the process of replacing the midnight crew. I must have looked awkward walking up to the entrance of the hospital in mountaineering garb with a large pack, strapped with an ice axe, crampons, and a construction pickaxe. I wondered if some of the looks I was receiving were, "Why is that guy wearing a red Petzl climbing helmet?"

After checking in with the main desk, I found my way to the Flight For Life desk and administrative office. None of the day shift folks had arrived yet, so I sat in a waiting chair and took the chance for a small doze. What felt like an instant later, I was awakened by a Flight For Life pilot.

During a past training I had acted as a landing assistant for this helicopter pilot, Ed Lockwood. Flight For Life was exactly its namesake, an air ambulance service, one of the few that was capable of flying mountain missions at Colorado's high altitudes. Colorado locals know FFL because of their helicopters' bright orange color. The service uses A Star helicopters, a model that was made famous by landing at the top of Mount Everest in a promotional stunt. In this case, the sheriff and the Stevens family convinced FFL that its service, meant to be utilized as an air ambulance service, might be put to use in this recovery to prevent injury to the two dozen-plus ground rescuers that would be required for a proper ground recovery operation. I consider courage that's applied for the benefit of others as heroism, so Flight For Life is an organization of very brave heroes.

"Good morning Kevin. Good to see you again."

"It's good to see you too, Ed."

"I'm going to head in and grab a weather report, do a few things in the office, and I'll be right out. Then we'll head up to the roof, do a flight inspection, and we'll be off."

"Awesome. Thanks. See you in a few."

As I waited, several more FFL personnel showed up, including the flight nurse and the flight paramedic who I'd be accompanying on our flight that day. My job was to guide the FFL team into the right gorge as close to the debris field as possible. After we had landed, I was going to get out, stay and set up the LZ, and help land the team every time they came in with a new SAR tech. When all the techs had rallied, we were going to ascend to the debris field, locate Lygon, and bring her home.

After we took the elevator to the roof, I watched carefully as Ed nimbly and mindfully finished his preflight check of the aircraft. I marveled at the capabilities of my fellow man. The thought that as a community we had the capability of launching an advanced medical air ambulance straight off the roof of a hospital and fly virtually anywhere within its fuel range to render aid to a person in a struggle to live … the overall scene put me in a state of awe.

We boarded the aircraft. Ed, the pilot, sat in the front right seat, I sat directly behind him so I could help him sight things below us, next to me in the middle rear sat the flight nurse, and on the left hand side of the craft sat the flight paramedic. In that small helicopter, the three of us side by side were a tight squeeze. As the turbine fired up and warmed, I could feel the breeze buffet the aircraft, and I was reminded that for all their power, size, and capability, these types of aircraft were very, very lightweight.

As the engine became engaged with the rotors, the aircraft's power shuttered and surged through its lightweight frame. I watched Ed engage the rotor blades' angles so they bit into the air, and I felt the helicopter lift into the wind and rise away from the hospital. After a brief climb with our nose faced into the wind, the pilot turned and put the wind to our tail. It remained at our tail until we were about half across the Wet Mountain Valley, the eastern equivalent of the San Luis Valley on the Sangres' west side. The Wet Mountain Valley, receiving the moisture from upslope weather patterns, was much greener and lush than the west side, in a rain shadow from all directions but the south. We were headed directly for Mosca Pass, a low notch in the Sangre de Cristos, a common spot for such aircraft to use while flying between the San Luis Valley and Pueblo. At the higher altitudes, the winds were blowing in from the west, and they were gusting pretty forcefully. On occasion, the helicopter would get slammed by a gust and it reminded me of getting slammed by a wind gust while riding a bicycle along the highway as a semi blazed pass.

As we flew over Mosca Pass, I recalled a story told to me by a fellow AVSAR volunteer, John Gilmore, about flying in a FFL chopper over Mosca Pass. John was a red-headed charismatic Robert Redford'esque lead paramedic for Flight For Life out of Pueblo. Often we traded off acting as incident commanders or operational managers for incidents. On one of the occasions of us having to hurry up and wait, we passed the time storytelling.

John and the rest of the crew had flown out of Pueblo in the late summer afternoon in "the best part of your worst day," in this case for an off-duty cop. Vacationing with his family, four-wheeling in remote backcountry, the off-duty officer ended up in a situation where his several hundred pound four-wheeler rolled and knocked him unconscious. He was lucky, as many ATV accidents result in death.

In the time it took the FFL crew to respond, approximately an hour, the patient had regained consciousness, began to interact normally with family, and other than a headache and a little bit of nausea (normal symptoms of a concussion), he didn't show any indications of a more troubling issue such as intracranial pressure (ICP) build-up. After the initial medical assessment, John felt the patient needed to lie down on the gurney on the flight to the hospital, however, he opted out of restraints. The patient was not presenting any signs or symptoms warranting restraints.

As they were flying back to Pueblo, in the darkness of sunset, the talkative friendliness of the cop tapered off. John attributed it to the mesmerizing sound and vibration of the helicopter's turbine and rotors, but another part of him sensed it was odd. John checked the patient's vitals. Heart rate and respiration were present and normal, blood oxygen normal, everything seemed normal. John asked the patient a question, but in response instead of intelligible language, all John could decipher from the background noise was a murmur.

Well, at least we're only about twenty minutes out, thought John. We should be landing very soon. We're probably over Mosca Pass.

In the darkness, John sensed the patient start waving an arm. He thought he heard a question, "Where am I?" Then maybe another question, "What's going on? Who are you? Why is it dark?" John realized what was happening—the head trauma (possibly exacerbated by the quick rise in altitude) had likely induced a swelling of the brain. John was witnessing initial signs of ICP. "I need to get out of here," the patient murmured. In some sort of blind, dark, nightmare, the patient began wrestling John, and John could feel the patient reaching for the helicopter's door handle, a handle not unlike a car's handle—it's just that instead of stepping out of a dark car, the patient was going to step out of a helicopter flying at approximately 14,000 feet, about a mile above Mosca Pass.

Trying to force the off-duty cop to stay lying down on the small gurney, John found himself being arm-barred into submission; however, John had the advantage of home court. In the darkness with his free hand John reached and grabbed a hypodermic needle filled with a paralytic and sedative, a combination of drugs that would paralyze and simultaneously knock out the delirious, defensive patient.

Like a scene in a dramatic comedy, as John readied the syringe, the patient defensively knocked John's arm and the needle went flying into the darkness.

Without allowing the situation to get any worse, John's intimate knowledge of the environment came in as a handy survival skill as he knew exactly where the syringe would be waiting from "muscle memory," and having dropped hundreds of syringes over the years and knowing where they ended up, he reached down to a spot he knew well.

In the dark A Star, John's free fingers found the syringe exactly where he expected it, and without wasting any time, the injection hit its mark, and the patient was safely restrained.

The strengthening wind gusts brought me back to the moment, and I focused on the objective—recovering Lygon. As we cleared over the rise of the pass, we could see the dust rolling along the valley floor in waves of dust bowl-like images. It was obvious that the wind had scratched our plan. The pilot explicitly said that any sort of landing or close-to-ground maneuvers were out of the question. I inquired about an attempt to fly over the snowfields where I suspected Lygon's location to be for the purpose of observation. Ed pointed out that it was "on the way back." Plus, Ed could do a reconnaissance on the gorge from which we'd eventually recover Lygon soon, even if it didn't happen that day.

As we neared the GPS coordinates for the entrance to the canyon, Ed began ascending. He turned and we did flybys of the canyon's entrance, power checks, and he said we'd be able to fly in but he didn't want to get in a situation in which he didn't have enough lift or space to turn around. I watched as he powered up the turbine and pointed us into the mouth of the canyon. I could clearly see the top of the gorge, surrounded by cliffs and steep snowfields, and I could already see the snowfield I believed to be the debris field of Lygon's location. I heard Ed ask the medic to watch for canyon proximity on his side. There was nothing to give us clear scale, such as trees. It was just rock and ice, and it was passing us below and to our immediate sides at what appeared to be very fast speed.

As we approached the top of the gorge Ed came over the headset and explained that he planned on flying up the west face of the peak, virtually stalling the aircraft while it spun around facing down, giving us time to scan the snowfields directly below us, and then dive and fly out of the gorge having never gotten too close to the terrain. Although helicopters can hover, they operate fundamentally just like planes, and they prefer to be flying into a headwind or with the lift of sustained forward flight.

In the time that we approached the snowfield, zoomed up the face of Little Bear, stalled and rotated, and then fell nose down toward the snowfields, I never saw a trace of evidence on the surface of the snowfields. I did notice the flight nurse grabbing her pant legs and tucking her head forward with her chin against her chest—in crash position. The whole maneuver made me physically ill with an exaggerated motion sickness reaction. I asked Ed to crack his window for some fresh air. The breeze suppressed my desire to hurl. I was airsick the entire flight back to Pueblo, a trip lasting just over twenty minutes.

As we departed the aircraft, I thanked the crew very much and joked that we should do it again sometime.

Thirteen days later, on Tuesday June 24, the winds were calm and all seemed well for the next attempt to fly a cadaver dog team into Little Bear Lake gorge. This time, I asked if the air crew wouldn't mind picking me up at the base of the mountain, where they could fly me and another person into the gorge, after dropping off the flight nurse and medic at the trailhead and staging area. This would spare me the drive to and from Pueblo, around two and a half hours one-way from my home. This time, I planned to send in Mick and the dog handler first. I'd follow with another SAR tech, and a third sortie would fly in another tech and the mining-style pickaxes we planned to use to exhume Lygon from the snow and ice. Even in the coolness of early morning, it felt summer-like and warm. The snowfields were melting out very quickly, and little remained of seasonal snow. Unlike our attempt on the 11th, I expected this day to be successful.

I watched a deputy tie a long strip of fluorescent surveyor's tape to the tall antennae on one of the law enforcement SUVs, an impromptu windsock. Word came that the helicopter, Life Guard Four, was en route, about twenty minutes away. This mission allowed for a full cold stop so that everyone could confer and we could brief each other on aspects of the plan. I led the mission briefing, going over the usual basics including expected hazards and protocol. That day's pilot, Dale Geanetta, like Ed, was another legendary mountain pilot. He and I had trained together in the past.

The author, pointing up, briefing Lygon Stevens' recovery team June 24, 2008. Counter-clockwise from bottom left is AVSAR's Geri Morrison, SARDOC handler Anne-Marie Cooper, Alamosa County Sheriff Dave Stong, Flight For Life nurse Jayson Perry, AVSAR tech Mick Daniel, Flight For Life pilot Dale Geanetta, and Flight For Life nurse Teresa Stockebrand (photo by Chris Stark, reprinted courtesy of the *Daily Camera*).

The plan was to locate Lygon first. After location was determined by the dog, we'd get the tools on scene necessary for exhumation. Thus after going over expected weather, communication, contingency plans, etc., the cadaver dog Mally along with the dog's handler, Anne-Marie Cooper, were the first to board Life Guard Four and fly into the gorge. Next went Mick, who'd be acting basically as the handler's guide. I'd fly in with a second AVSAR tech, Geri, the team's executive secretary and a nurse with the local hospital. Last, Geri's husband, Steve, a long time rescue team "renaissance man," would fly in with additional extraction tools. I watched as Anne Marie and Mick took off and vanished into the canyon's expanse.

I was surprised at how quickly the helicopter returned for Geri and I. We quickly buckled in and put on helmets with headsets for communication with Dale. He, like all the FFL pilots, was the best of the best. The communication was pretty much unneeded as Dale had just flown in Mick and Marie, and he knew exactly where he was headed without any communication from

Geri or I. As we flew in, he pointed and said, "That's the landing zone, that little bench above the lake. I'll be in-bound with Steve very soon, and then I'll pick you up later."

Geri and I quickly got our backpacks out of the craft and walked about a hundred feet away before crouching on our knees and watching as Dale lifted off to fetch Steve. I asked Geri if she would like to wait for Steve, and the two of them could ascend together. Geri liked that idea, so I ascended the talus leading up the gorge to the debris field alone.

As I rounded a corner above a marshy pond where the talus angle steepened, my radio began to crackle. Unfortunately, it was so garbled it was unintelligible. I knew that there was radio traffic, however, and I knew this indicated Mick or someone else was communicating something of importance. At about the same time as the radio crackled, I also heard Mally, a black lab, barking incessantly somewhere in the gorge above.

I guessed that the dog had found Lygon, and the radio crackling was the report. Later I would find out that the radio transmission was coming from a mountaineering/spotting team the Stevens family had positioned high on the southwest ridge. They had spotted Lygon's body in the middle of what they described as a snowfield that looked like the hand of God.

The handler and dog had initially passed Lygon, continuing up the lowest part of the cirque's confluence. Looking up the snowfield while catching his breath, Mick noticed Lygon first. He noticed her at the same time the radio reported her location to be the snowfield above them. Mick had a similar reaction as I had upon initially seeing Lygon.

As I came around the corner, I saw Mick above me on the snowfield. Above his location was Lygon's body surreally floating above the snow. As I approached closer, the effect grew even more surreal. Lygon's body looked as if she were facing the sky, arms open wide, floating a foot above the snowfield. Maybe I was hallucinating from the altitude a bit?

I reached the location where Mick, and now Anne Marie and Mally had stopped, where they felt comfortable not disturbing evidence or the scene. I knelt down a bit to get a better look at how Lygon was levitating. In fact, she wasn't hovering just above the snow, rather her body had become a shield for the snow directly beneath her, so the snow had melted out all around her, but the snow directly beneath her had remained, allowing her at that moment in time to be suspended about a foot above the snowfield around her. The white snow beneath her was hidden by her shadow adding to the optical effect of levitation.

After the entire recovery group was assembled near Lygon, I initially approached her body photo-documenting my movements and the scene. I

Mick Daniel standing next to Lygon Steven's body on June 24, 2008 (author photo).

started by photographing Lygon's body from about thirty to forty feet away, showing her in relation to the scene around her from a distant perspective. Then I walked in and did a close-up circling of her body overlapping the scene and background. I then took close-ups of her body and evidence around the scene.

The positioning of her body looked like she was forming a cross, her face and upper body facing the heavens, upward. Her lower torso was facing the slope, downward, so in the space of her lower torso, mid back to pelvis, her body was twisted 180 degrees. This position told me that, like her brother, she had been knocked unconscious during the slide. Had she been conscious as she fell and the motion stopped, her position would not have been so twisted and "relaxed." Unlike Nicklis, however, Lygon had ended up deep under the snow. It appeared to me she had peacefully suffocated while unconscious. The scene's evidence gave me a great sense of peace and closure.

Lygon had been melted out for what I estimated to be a several days. The ice and snow had preserved her well, her exposed skin mostly mummified from the cold, dry conditions. We all gathered around her and meditated or prayed. I thanked Mother Nature and Lygon for keeping us safe up to that moment.

After completing documentation of the scene including some field notes and last pictures, a couple of us positioned a cadaver bag beneath the snow pedestal on which Lygon balanced, and we carefully rolled her into the bag, as if we were rolling a live patient into a sleeping bag. We placed Lygon's remains in a SKED litter, not ideal compared to a Stokes litter, but lightweight for such a small team. As we finished processing and documenting the scene,

I was grateful that Lygon's family members and friends, who were observing us from high up on the southwest ridge about a mile away, were too far away to make out any details of the process. I was also pleased to see them begin their descent of the ridge—likely eager to get back to the command post to support the Stevens family.

Now the plan was to get back to the LZ and prioritize flying Lygon, Anne-Marie, and Mally back to the command post. If possible, maybe the rest of us could get a helicopter lift out too. We radioed the trailhead and asked for a status and how long it would take to get the helicopter back to the landing zone. They said it wouldn't take long, maybe fifteen minutes, but that we'd best be making haste as the winds were beginning to pick up, and they didn't know how long they'd be able to get us safely. Soon they'd have to return to Pueblo.

We looked at each other and I could tell that no one wanted to spend the night out waiting for FFL until the next day. I radioed that we'd be back to the LZ shortly, and they should standby ready for take-off soon. I told the team we'd have to move quickly to ensure our pick-up.

Descending the snowfield the SKED litter was ideal as a sled. Luckily we kept our glissade under control. Once the five of us switched over to the talus at the base of the snowfield, a half mile to the LZ suddenly seemed a gargantuan task, if not impossible.

Like many missions before, we broke the task down into miniscule manageable parts. Unlike in many movies, the act of only five people moving a body over terrain composed of boulders and talus requires exorbitant amounts of energy. I recall looking over at my partners and being unbelievably proud at the sweat dripping from their brows and noses, working as strenuously as I'd ever seen people pushing, yet pausing to give the cadaver dog Mally praise, taking her reward toy and tossing it far ahead of us so she'd egg us on with her desire for continued praise. Even though she wasn't the one who truly found Lygon, she was made to feel she had, and we rewarded her the same. When I estimated we were twenty minutes from the LZ, I radioed the command post, "We're at the LZ and ready for a ride back!"

"We're en route. See you in twenty."

The additional pressure of knowing we had to be at the LZ in twenty minutes helped the five of us, six including Lygon, cover what normally would have taken twice as long. We had just gotten to the LZ when the rotors of Lifeguard Four were audible. A minute later, Dale was landing the helicopter exactly the way he had already several times earlier that day. Lygon's body, Mally the dog, and us SAR techs stayed hunkered down in the subalpine brush as Dale shut down the rotors to a full stop.

He and the flight paramedic got out, and Dale explained he was worried that this might be the last flight out for the day because of increasing winds, so we needed to act quickly and decisively. The flight medic tucked a family heirloom blanket around Lygon, a request that had been made by the family that it be used as a shroud for Lygon on her last journey out of the wilderness. We loaded Lygon on board, and without wasting a second, the turbines sparked, were quickly roaring, and the helicopter lifted off.

In the quiet, I felt the pressure lift of months of commitment to recovering Lygon, just as the helicopter had just risen. Lygon's family could finally be at peace. I was deeply relieved and even happy with the prospect of having to walk out. If we were lucky, Dale would be able to get back and lift Mally and Anne-Marie out. The SARDOC dogs were too special to hike until collapse or until their pads bled; if she had to walk out from this isolated spot, she'd most likely become injured.

I imagined the scene at the command post with the sheriff and the family receiving Lygon's body after all these many months. I enjoyed some time lying down in the soft alpine grasses, warming myself in the sunshine, listening to the wind whirl around the canyon. A few minutes later, the radio crackled and the sheriff said that winds were picking up too much for another flight.

I responded quickly requesting that if at all possible, the dog and handler get lifted out. It would be a difficult hardship on the dog to hike her out.

After a long pause, the sheriff responded and said Dale would give it a try.

Twenty minutes later, the helicopter returned, struggling against the small wind gusts more than I had seen it do all morning. I was happy that one last flight was being made for the sake of the dog and her handler, but I was also happy I didn't have to get on board with them; although it would take me hours to hike out the distance they would fly in minutes, the idea of repeating my experience with helicopter-induced motion sickness was more than plenty to help me feel gratitude for a "long afternoon hike."

Dale touched down, and Anne-Marie and Mally jumped on board L.G. Four. The chopper breached into the westerly wind one last time, and the four of us stood up, buckled our backpack straps, and began descending Little Bear Lake gorge via Tobin Creek.

It took us a little over an hour to descend to the same location where George and I had turned around about a month prior. This time there was no snow hampering our descent, but because of the morning's activities, we were all spent. We took our time descending, stopping often to enjoy the views of the San Luis Valley, filter water for our bottles, eat high-carb treats, and reflect on the usual wonders of the mountains and life. Although we had all just been honored to act as Lygon's first pallbearers, a solemn and serious honor, as we reached lower elevations we became more and more the group we were when we trained—simply a highly cohesive small team of mountaineers who love mountains and feel absolutely at home and joyous in nature.

That close to the summer solstice, the light lasted until late in the evening, and in the last crepuscular rays of the dusk, the four of us AVSAR techs, following a trail of pink ribbons along Tobin Creek, wandered out of the piñon pines onto the private road where Sheriff Stong himself waited to pick us up. On the drive out, he briefed us about Lygon's reception at the command post, and he personally thanked us.

The Stevens family buried Lygon Stevens on June 28, 2008, at Estes Valley Memorial Gardens in Estes Park, Colorado.

David Boyd
Little Bear Peak, September 4, 2008

"We climbed onward, searching, always searching. Searching for handholds and footholds, for piton cracks and the right piton. And searching ourselves for the necessary human qualities to make this climb possible. Searching for adventure, searching for ourselves, searching for situations that would call forth our total resources. For some it is a search for courage. Perhaps if we can learn to face the dangers of the mountains with equanimity, we can also learn to face with a calm spirit the chilling specter of inevitable death."
—Royal Robbins, American Alpine Club publication

From the autumn 2008 semester until the spring 2011 semester, I taught a three-credit elective course at Adams State University titled Introduction to Search and Rescue. After the death of Lygon Stevens, who had been a twenty-year-old student at the University of Northern Colorado, many students became interested in the incident as well as SAR. As the president of the county rescue team, several friends and leaders from Adams State University approached me and asked if I would be interested in teaching a night course on the topic. In addition to it being an opportunity to give an age group that was high risk for wilderness accidents a taste of what the reality of a SAR response entails, I knew I would also be able to hand pick and recruit some outstanding future SAR technicians.

There were already several university stars on the local county AVSAR team, so when I announced to them that I'd be teaching an elective course on the subject, several were very eager to sign up to get credits for what they already volunteered to do. Starting a new university course, it was comforting to know that several of the course's students would already know me, be able to vouch for the course's value and safety, as well as be able to act as belay assistants when we went out into the field for the course's "labs."

During one of these classes at 8:50 p.m., on the evening of September 4, just ten minutes before the class got out, all at once my phone and several students' phones began vibrating simultaneously. I would have thought it an amazing coincidence if I didn't immediately recognize that all the phones belonged to us folks on the county SAR team. We were getting

50

paged for a SAR call-out, so I condensed the last ten minutes of the class into just a few brief minutes, and I turned the students loose with my usual send-off, "Be safe!"

I watched as the students who were on the team all read their text messages and listen to the voicemails that were now trickling in. I quickly packed up the class resources for the evening, which had been my 72-hour SAR pack, including my Wilderness First Responder (WFR) kit. I had demonstrated what my real-world pack consisted of by packing and unpacking everything in it for the class. I had been explaining what minimal gear a SAR tech was expected to take on any field deployments during the summer and early autumn seasons. I kept this pack in my trunk, but this evening I realized I had taken my summer mountaineering boots out of the trunk meaning to exchange them with my heavier autumn/early winter boots, and in that process, I had forgotten to finish—I was without boots.

Cameron Roberts, a particularly intelligent and strapping up-and-coming EMT closed his cell phone and grabbed one of my bags of equipment to help me get out to my car in one quick trip. As other students in the class (who were also on the SAR team), and I walked out to our vehicles, Cameron briefed me about the call-out. "Kevin, there's a missing person up on Little Bear. His domestic partner in Texas called the sheriff to report that he has a SPOT device, and his location waypoints haven't changed since early afternoon. She told the sheriff that this wasn't like him at all. He's an ultra endurance athlete, a driven type-A medical doctor, and she's reporting the only reason he'd be stopped like that is something catastrophic. The sheriff provided GPS coordinates for the waypoint, here they are," and Cameron handed me a small piece of paper with the latitude and longitude of the subject's beacon's location.

"Thanks, Cameron. What time did the subject's partner say the waypoints started showing up in the same location?"

"Sometime in the afternoon. But the signal must be weak or nearly blocked because they're not coming in consistently. Some have come in just a few minutes apart, others more than an hour."

"Was the emergency signal activated?"

"No."

I thought that this wasn't a good sign. By the brief description of the subject, if he had dropped the SPOT device, he would have already come out of the area and contacted his partner. If he were injured and conscious, he would have initiated the emergency signal. I sensed that with the little evidence already presented, we were likely responding to an unconscious or deceased subject. Not knowing what his condition may be, we would need to get to his location as quickly as possible. The temperatures at and above treeline were near freezing. An injured, semi-conscious or unconscious subject would succumb to hypothermia relatively quickly.

"Thanks for the briefing, Cameron. We'll all need to get out to the command post as safely and quickly as possible." By now we had walked out to our vehicles, and as I threw my pack and extra equipment into the trunk, I noticed the empty spot in the car trunk that normally held my boots. *Damn it*, I thought to myself. I lived twenty minutes from town in a perpendicular direction to the trailhead and I wouldn't have the time to fetch the appropriate footwear. On this night, on this mission, I'd be in my favorite Orvis dress shoes; ironic, as I had just finished the class in which I made it very clear that SAR techs would not be deployed who showed up at the command post unprepared, without proper equipment to endure 72 unsupported hours in a wilderness environment. I figured I'd be acting as incident commander (IC) at the command post anyway. If worse came to worse, the Orvis model I was wearing was one of their more beefy, utilitarian, rugged-soled, full leather shoes. I could have probably walked to California in them if I had to; they'd make Utah at a minimum.

"I'll be heading directly out to the trailhead so I can act as IC and coordinate. I'll see those of you who can make it out there shortly. Pack enough insulation and illumination. This is going to be a long night. Drive safely, and be extra vigilant for wildlife on the highway. There's a lot of elk and deer out where we'll be setting up the command post."

Cameron answered for the small group of students, "Will do," and with that, we all jumped in our cars and went our separate directions.

I knew that some of the other SAR folks were already headed out of town, probably five to ten minutes ahead of me. I hoped there would be enough of us responding to send out a hasty team as soon as possible.

Out on the alpine desert highway, that late at night, the line of vehicles headed north on Highway 150 to the trailhead was obvious. It looked like the final scene in the movie *Field of Dreams,* in which all the headlights of the cars line up for miles, although our line of vehicles wasn't as dense nor as long, and it led to the command post for a somber objective.

In a matter of ten minutes, a dozen SAR personnel vehicles filled the trailhead's parking area. I was happy to see our 4x4 specialists, the cavalry as I called them, arrive. It was their modified Frankenbeast 4x4s that would shuttle us in and out of "battle." Although the vehicles' overall speed was not that much greater than someone in a jog, they saved considerable amounts of energy, especially in the case of transporting a litter with a victim or a body down the mountain. In this mission's case, I still did not know what to expect—a live or deceased subject. Was David Boyd still breathing, awaiting our arrival in an epic battle to survive?

As the team converged and prepared to launch into the mountainous wilderness, Corporal Spangler, Deputy Terrell, and I briefed the team on a couple different possible scenarios. One was that the subject's stationary GPS coordinates were inconsistent and non-emergency because he was on a north-facing slope, limiting line of sight and performance of GPS devices relying heavily on equator/southerly based satellites, and that he was stationary because he was injured, awaiting our response, especially as nightfall set in and temperatures dropped. The worst-case scenario was that David had fallen a considerable distance, possibly descending the wrong couloir, and he now lay at the base of a steep, rocky cliff, deceased.

Until I knew for sure, we had to keep striving to be the rescue of someone who was still alive. We formed a hasty team including Jess Caton, Tish Caton, Steve Morrison, Geri Morrison, Roy Hood, and I, all high-angle or medical technicians. Initially I offered to stay as the IC, but the field team members asked that I go with them. Our job would be to respond as quickly as possible, locate the subject, stabilize him, and await additional team members to do a patient transport to a helicopter LZ—that was, if the patient were still living. If David were deceased, he would ride back to the command post in one of the 4x4s.

Staying behind at the command post willing to act as the contingent team and standing by until further notice were Chris Lavery, Cameron Roberts, George Rapoza, Jose Salcedo, and Rob Mabry. Jess grabbed a radio from one of the sheriff's personnel, did a radio communication check, and we headed into the cool darkness around 2200 hours.

I rode with Roy in his modified lifted Jeep, while Steve and Geri rode in Steve's modified Frankenbeast Blazer, and Jess and Tish rode in their modified Jeep. Just like the boys in *Stand By Me*, when one is heading off into the dark wilderness with the objective being to locate a highly traumatized or deceased subject, it makes sense to go in groups of personnel with high levels of trust and confidence. In our SAR team's case, except for Roy and I, the vehicles were husband-wife teams. The husbands had highly modified 4x4 vehicles and were men with extraordinary stamina and strength, especially at altitude; their wives were medically qualified and experienced in high-angle environments.

In the conditions and environment into which we were heading, I wanted to know I had teammates who were tough enough to manage whatever obstacles and trauma we were to encounter; but simultaneously I wanted teammates experienced and sensitive enough to admit our limitations and voice safety concerns when those issues arose.

Roy had taken his Jeep's side doors off for ease of getting in and out of the vehicle, and the cool air rushing through the open door made me glad I already had on several layers of clothing. I was also happy to have more layers in my pack because the temperature would only continue getting colder as the night progressed.

Just before midnight, we passed Lake Como, and cruising alongside its northern shore, the water's surface became a mirror of the stars above. The lake smelled rich and earthy, delicious in the late summer. It smelled like autumn at treeline. The smell of pine campfires still lingered from the previous evening.

At midnight, all three vehicles reached the point above Lake Como where hikers seeking to ascend Little Bear Peak leave the road and begin their climb of Little Bear's west ridge. We parked the vehicles and used a combination of attraction tactics to get anyone's attention who was conscious and in that gorge. We positioned the vehicles so their headlights faced up and illuminated the north-facing slopes of the west ridge. We flashed the headlights and honked the horns. The echoes bounced back and forth and up and down the valley. We shut off the vehicles' engines, and we peered toward the slopes, looking for any indication of life, any movement at all. We listened carefully to any sounds that indicated David's possible location. All we heard was the babbling water under the talus boulders. Ice and snowmelt dripping and gurgling, creeping its way toward the brook that connected Blue Lake with Lake Como. Blue Lake was the major lake in a small set that sits on a treeless bench above Lake Como. Above Blue Lake vehicle traffic ceases, and the trail becomes a single track that zigzags up a steep section of cliffs referred to as "the waterfall" by locals.

Several times the six of us cycled through turning on and off the headlights, using spot lamps, honking horns, whistling with dual-chambered extra loud survival whistles, and listening as intently as we could. Nothing.

The canyon was steep enough to blot out the majority of the southern hemisphere, crucial in proper GPS-unit functioning. Every single one of our GPSs, although different models and using different antennae systems, weren't working. We knew from mapping the coordinates on maps and in our minds, David's last GPS coordinates indicated he was on the north-facing slopes somewhere between Little Bear Peak's northwest face and the access couloir. After receiving no indication of signaling back to us from the western boundary of where we knew David's beacon was, we jumped back in the vehicles and slowly ascended the 4x4 road on its way to Blue Lake, above Lake Como. On several occasions, we stopped the vehicles and repeated the attraction tactics cycle.

The author (with his rat terrier) next to Lake Como. Litte Bear Peak's summit is above the author's head, and the standard west ridge route ascends a couloir just out of this picture to the right. Many have died in the couloirs in the upper right of this picture (fish-eye lense photo at sunset, July 17, 2009, by Adam Wright).

When we got to the base of the northwest face of Little Bear Peak, and the road swung significantly toward the north, we turned the vehicles around. This location marked the farthest east we felt David's beacon could be located. Just as we had on the western boundary, we drove up small inclines so that the vehicles' headlights would illuminate the north-facing slopes of Little Bear Peak's northwest face and west ridge. In the headlights, it was impossible to tell that this is where the prominent west ridge intersects the main peak; in the spot lamps, the face looked contiguous, one massive cliff face, aprons of scree and talus at its base. As the vehicles' headlights swung up the face, both the married couples believed they saw a flash of light. All four thought it looked like a headlamp or a reflection. Neither Roy nor I saw anything. The Catons and Morrisons both described the light located about halfway up the ridge, in the couloir just west of the most deeply notched couloir. We formulated a plan to go investigate the location of the light.

Steve stayed at the vehicles, alternating between idling and being shut off to allow signaling that required sensitivity to sound, and the vehicles' batteries needed to be occasionally charged to ensure they didn't go dead. On the other hand, the illumination of the headlights of the slope was very helpful. Via radio, Steve could also watch our headlamps and coordinate our location in relativity to the location of the light source. He could coordinate our movement and walk us right up to where we hoped David was signaling us.

For Jess, this gorge, its lakes, its peaks, everything was his backyard. He had grown up playing in this gorge. Even in the darkness, on high-angled, high-risk terrain, he felt quite at ease and in his element. Within minutes, he had gotten far ahead of the group. We could easily keep track of each other using our headlamps and Steve's radio coordination. In a very brief time, the vehicles' headlights looked quite small, and we could barely hear the engines cycling on and off. Jess, almost twice the distance above the rest of us, reached the location that Steve said was the source of the illumination potentially signaling us. Jess found nothing.

At the assumed last known position of a clue, Jess began doing a circular grid search, walking ever increasingly large circles around the spot Steve had started him. Tish, Jess' wife, was next to ascend to this high spot, and she helped Jess walk circles on the steep scree slope, just beneath the cliff bands of the west ridge.

As Roy and I ascended, less enthusiastically as we hadn't seen any of the signaling the other four had, we kept checking our GPS devices, hoping that we might get a functional signal. At one point, we both got spotty signals, and both of our GPS units gave us indications of where we were regarding latitude-longitude coordinates. Based on previously known GPS spots, Roy and I guessed that David's last signals had occurred west of our current location, but east of the access couloir's coordinates. We guessed that Jess, Tish, and Geri were searching a bit too far east.

Jess continued to search the slopes, moving easterly, continuing all the way to Little Bear's northwest face at approximately 12,500 feet elevation. Tish searched the slopes just westerly and along the base of cliffs from Jess' position. West from Tish was Geri, then Roy, and finally me, in the most westerly position. At first I had easy line of sight to all members of the search party, but as I ascended the talus, it got steeper and steeper, turned to scree, and as I tried to find the base of the gorge's cliffs, the headlamps of the others vanished. I had climbed into the base of a couloir, and the rock around me blocked my ability to see or communicate with my teammates.

Close to 0300 hours, I traversed as far west as I could on the steep scree. As I came around the corner of a vertical section of the cliff base, the scree dropped off at an especially steep angle, and as I began to descend, I triggered a rockslide. I watched in the headlamp several soccer ball-sized rocks leave the boundary of my headlamp's beam. In the darkness below me, the resulting rockslide sounded enormous. I listened to the slide's sound and motion as it fell away hundreds of feet below me. I could smell the dust rising from the commotion below; it smelled like fireworks, similar to gunpowder, the result of the chemicals in the rocks smashing into each other and vaporizing

The west ridge of Little Bear Peak from Lake Como. The vertical arrow indicates Little Bear's standard route. The horizontal arrow indicates where SAR found David Boyd's body (author photo).

during the slide. I looked down at my beloved Orvis shoes, the full-grained fine leather now completely scratched and rough; the toes especially looked fuzzy, more like a rough suede than the polished leather they had been just hours before. I wished I had my usual mountaineering boots or approach shoes. Even with all the exercise and circulation, my toes were near numb. The designers of dress shoes meant for teaching in a classroom on a college campus did a poor job of insulating them for cold, middle of the night mountain search and rescue work. I knew the shoes only had to remain utilitarian until I was back to my car. I knew the beefy, high quality leather would get me through to morning. I also knew I couldn't afford to replace the expensive shoes any time soon.

I was far beyond the section of the slope illuminated by the vehicles. I was out of sight and communication with my team, and I was standing on the precipice of something large and steep. In the dark, I peered westerly and looked for any sign of David along the cliff base. I couldn't illuminate any landscape very far—anything more than fifty feet away vanished into a dark void. I also had a negative intuition, and I knew that it was time to stop and descend. We had covered nearly all the terrain where we believed David could be located; all the terrain except little ledges and pockets in the cliffs between the lower scree aprons and the high-angle slope just under the ridge.

I flashed my headlamp, I whistled, I listened. I was within a signaling distance of the access couloir. If David were conscious, he would hear my signaling and respond. I listened as intently as I could. I screamed out "DAVE" over and over until I was hoarse and then I sat and I meditated. I sat and allowed the cold air to sneak into my shirt collar and sleeves. I listened to the absence of all sound but the slight breeze. I listened to the rockslides fall away from my teammates' locations. I sensed that David was near, but no longer alive.

I felt a sense of deep gratitude, and my objective switched to keeping a group of sleep-deprived SAR techs safe. I looked at my GPS one last time, and it was blank. No line of sight to the GPS satellites at all. I figured that David's SPOT device was likely on top of the cliff band, or worst-case scenario, he was on an isolated cliff ledge halfway between the top and bottom of the cliffs that separated the ridge from the valley.

From my report to the sheriff based on my field notes:

> At 0300 hours, because of the numerous rockslides, the very dangerous
> nature of the terrain (40-degree talus), the temperature (approximately
> 20 degrees), people's exhaustion and sleep deprivation, and the fact that
> I felt we didn't have a POD [probability of detection] greater than 25% in
> such conditions at night, I communicated to everyone to rally at the top
> of the talus bench. I requested that Jess radio base to prepare the second
> team to transport to our location to begin searching the ridge at first light.
> Soon after 0300 hours, Steve left our location to drive back down to the
> command post and return with the second team. I told the remaining five
> AVSAR personnel to standby and recharge for a first light deployment.

After arriving back at the vehicles, I checked with Steve several times that he felt okay and safe to make the trip back to the command post by himself. Normally, Geri or one of us would accompany him, but he needed every possible spot available for another teammate on his return journey. Steve assured me he'd be safe, and he fired up Frankenbeast and began his slow 4x4 crawl out of the rocky gorge that included the four "Jaws" obstacles, named Jaws for the rock obstacles' abilities to "eat up" machines and men like a shark. I reminded him to take his time and be mindful of every moment, especially as he negotiated Jaws 2.

After the last echoes of Steve's Frankenbeast vanished, I pulled out my sleeping bag from my 72-hour SAR pack that was in the back of Roy's Jeep. Roy put the doors of the Jeep back on, and rather than getting into the bag, I unzipped it, making a large blanket-like layer that I threw over my body and legs. I leaned back into the front passenger seat, a seat not designed for sleep, but it was a lot more comfortable than a mountain ledge bivy or no sleep at all. As I slowly began to fall asleep in a semi-sitting position, the sleeping bag tucked in around my fully clothed body, through the windshield I stared at the dark silhouette of Little Bear's west ridge. I knew that somewhere up in that darkness lay David Boyd. With the current evidence, I now assumed David was unconscious or deceased. Maybe he had snapped his ankle and was merely unconscious in the talus above the cliffs near the top of the ridge. Two GPS coordinates that appeared to be within just a few yards of each other on a map might in reality be hundreds of feet apart, the distance from above being just feet, but the difference in elevation being the top of a cliff and the base of a cliff.

Where was David? I fell asleep hoping that if David were still alive he wasn't suffering, floating in and out of consciousness. I wondered if he had heard our signaling in a traumatized, far away state of mind, not knowing those sounds and lights were meant for him. After gazing into the darkness continuing to look for any sign, my eyes started closing and I nodded off into a light sleep.

Even with the sleeping bag covering me, the Jeep chilled down, and in a relatively short amount of time Roy and I were in temperatures below freezing as the windows frosted a bit from our breath.

If my eyes weren't open and I wasn't scanning the slopes for signs of a faint headlamp signal, I was dreaming that I was scanning the slopes for signals. It was a fitful couple of hours before the first hints of light began giving the slope contrast. Without being able to relax comfortably and truly fall asleep and recharge, I was ready for the light to allow us to begin moving around and continue our search for David. I began to stir, and I gobbled down a couple granola bars. We could all see quite well by the time the last stars were ceasing to twinkle overhead, and we discussed our plan and deployed ourselves on separate missions with the same objective: search for and find David Boyd.

While Steve was driving down to the command post and back to pick up more techs and gear, Jess, Tish, and Geri ascended the access couloir just above Lake Como.

Near the top of the couloir, just above the cliff bands, they traversed the upper part of the west ridge moving easterly, hoping to find David in an easily accessible location, possibly hypothermic and alive, also possibly deceased from injury and exposure.

Roy and I drove up the canyon and turned around. We hoped the perspective and our scopes (Roy had a pair of binoculars, and I had a monocular) would help regarding a thorough visual grid search of almost all the north-facing slopes where David's beacon seemed to be located. Hopefully, by the time Steve returned with the contingent team, either Jess' group or Roy and I would locate David.

From my field notes:

At first light, approximately 0600 hours, Roy Hood and I began scoping the slopes with a monocular and binoculars. Jess notified us that he had received a text message from Steve. Steve had blown out a tire while descending and had needed to return home to retrieve a new tire, so his ETA with the second team was now estimated to be 0800 hours. The five of us remaining decided to break into two groups. Jess, Tish, and Geri would ascend the Little Bear standard route and search the upper north slopes of the west ridge. Roy and I would continue scoping the slopes and coordinate the second team upon their arrival. Two private climbers (a man and a woman) came upon us and notified us that they were planning on climbing Little Bear via the standard route. I briefed them about the potential of finding the subject and what to do if they did. Geri asked them to check the summit log for evidence of the subject being there. The ASO radio was nearly dead, so Jess left it with me. The two private climbers began ascending the access couloir, and soon after so did the three AVSAR techs.

As Roy and I scanned the slope, because his binoculars were better than my monocular, I began asking him to check on colors I recognized as being rare or unnatural.

At approximately 0720 hours, I noticed an unnatural maroon color at the base of a cliff, at the top of the talus in the high couloir just east of the access couloir. When I asked Roy to verify, he stated, "That's him." We watched the location for about a minute and didn't observe any movement. We decided to verify the location and subject's condition 100% before radioing (I knew the radio was nearly dead). We left a note on Roy's Jeep about the two teams' objectives, and Roy and I left for the maroon color's position at 0730 hours.

At approximately 0745 hours, Jess Caton reached a position above the "maroon color," and he yelled at Roy and me to confirm the subject's location. I began taking film pictures as Roy and I ascended the slope around 12,000 feet elevation. At about 0830 hours, approximately 50 feet below the subject, I got a clear line of sight to the subject and was able to verify he was deceased. I radioed ASO several times and was barely able to successfully transmit a "code Frank" before the radio went dead. Roy was approximately 30 feet below me, and I verified the maroon color to be that of the subject's backpack still on the back of the subject. I continued taking pictures as I approached the subject.

The subject was lying face down in basketball-sized scree. He was perpendicular to the fall line, the top of his head facing west, his feet facing east. His legs were crossed, and his arms were crossed, lying perpendicular to his body (down the fall line). He was wearing running shoes, short gaiters, shorts, a long underwear layer under a t-shirt, a glove, a daypack, a helmet, and a Camelbak-like hydrating system. His legs and arms were severely abraded, every inch of which were deeply "cheese-grated." His helmet had three or more high-energy impact points, and his face was flattened. Considering the extent of the apparent injuries, there was very little blood. One of his elbows had soaked his shirt, and there was a little bit of blood leaking from his face. I believed this to indicate that he was deceased by the time his body came to rest in this position. There was approximately an inch of decomposed hail remaining on top of the subject's pants, which were on the slope just feet above him. The glove and pants were nearly totally covered by decomposed hail/snow. This evidence indicated hail/snow had fallen since the subject had come to rest.

Approximately a minute after Roy had gotten to me and the body's location, Jess Caton arrived on the scene. I continued photographing as they began searching the immediate area for evidence. Approximately 20 feet below and to the northwest of the body was an orange emergency GPS device. It was face down but still blinking, indicating power. All this evidence occurred in a straight line following the terrain's fall line directly above and south of the body's position. I believe this indicates the subject was directly above the body's location when he fell. As I photographed the scene and Roy and Jess searched the area, the secondary team began arriving on scene, which included Steve Morrison, Cameron Roberts, Phil Heisey, Rob Mabry, George Rapoza and Jose Salcedo. Tish and Geri returned to the vehicles and awaited our descent. None of our GPS's were working, and only George Rapoza's reported a position at all. I recorded this position estimated to be about 12,400 feet in elevation.

Unfortunately, I do not have the exact coordinate for this report. After handing it to Sergeant Alejo at the mission debriefing, either it was misplaced, blown away by wind, or never given back. Later using Google Earth mapping, I estimated the position to be 37 degrees 33 minutes 54.77 seconds North 105 degrees 30 minutes 28.81 seconds West.

After processing and documenting the scene, Roy, Jess, and I packaged the subject by rolling him into a body bag. When we rolled the body over, I could feel severe deformation to one of the ankles under the gaiter. The subject's face was severely malformed and completely flattened. There was considerable rigor mortis in the body, and it was difficult to keep the arms in line with the torso. Roy, Jess, and I secured the body and scene evidence in the bag, and then secured a SKED litter around the body.

At approximately 0900 hours, Roy and Steve set several pitons in the cliff's base to our west, and they rigged a simple lower system for the body. At approximately 0930 hours, Steve and Rob remained at the anchor station, and the remaining seven of us began descending with the body. After two knot passes, we had descended three 200-foot rope lowers. From this point, the talus' angle eased, so Jess did a body belay of the package. He did this twice, each time using a single 200-foot rope.

At approximately 1130 hours, all eleven AVSAR techs and the body reached the vehicle staging point. Near this time, the two climbers who had left earlier that morning to summit Little Bear returned and passed along the information that Dave Boyd had signed the register around 1430 hours the previous day with the comment, "Three 14'ers in one day!" At 1200 hours, we began descending in the vehicles for the command post.

At 1400 hours, the vehicles, team, and body reached the command post at the Como Trailhead. Possession of the body was transferred to Sergeant Alejo, chief ASO investigator and Alamosa County deputy coroner. Sergeant Alejo debriefed me, and then Deputy Richard Terrell and I debriefed the team. The debriefing ended at approximately 1500 hours, and AVSAR personnel were released.

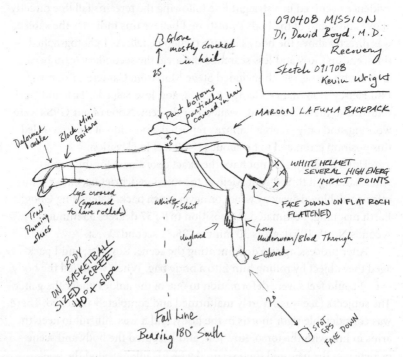

Diagram of Dr. David Boyd's final resting position. Sketch done using several pages from the author's field notes just days following the recovery.

By the time all of the personnel and vehicles had returned to the command post, temperatures in the valley were quite warm, and David's remains were not holding together well. Us technical pallbearers had brought David's body in a body bag secured in a litter back to Steve's 4x4 Frankenbeast. While slowly descending the technical road in this makeshift hearse, David's body had begun leaking fluids from the bag into the vehicle. After we had transferred David's body to the coroner, I apologized to Steve as he indicated that he'd have to replace some carpeting. "No worries Kevin, I meant to do it anyway." This was Steve's reply no matter what. Steve, Roy, and Jess made up AVSAR's "cavalry" in those days, and it was this legendary cavalry that deserves much gratitude. That trinity of fellows, between their generous donations of materials, skills, and time, have saved many lives and recovered numerous bodies (bringing needed closure and peace to families). I love those three heroes.

I loved my teammates so much (and still do), that as their lead, I'd occasionally make executive decisions to help them avoid unnecessary drama and stress. For example, in the case of David Boyd's incident, even though the sheriff asked me to share with the team that David had ridden a very expensive mountain bike up the mountain as part of his ascent, I did not share with the team that David's GPS unit and bicycle were still on the mountain. My reasoning was that I was concerned well-meaning volunteers would risk injuries, or SAR techs would use up energy searching for material possessions and then a mission to find a child would come up, and several techs wouldn't be on their A-game. I led a team of heroes that saved lives; they didn't fetch bicycles.

From my field notes:

On Monday, September 8, 2008, I was contacted by Sheriff Stong that the subject's regular GPS unit and bicycle were still in the area. I notified him that I would pass this information along to the team in case we might recover it in the future. I also asked for permission to contact the family, as they had left a voicemail on Saturday at 1000 hours requesting that I brief them about the scene's evidence. The sheriff said I could, but I was to remember the guidelines of professional discretion.

Upon speaking with the subject's stepbrother, I was asked about the subject's location and condition. I reported where we had found him and that evidence indicated he had fallen a long distance and was deceased before coming to rest. The subject's stepbrother then communicated that he had tried to contact the local media about false statements that had been reported. He said that David had never "sent" distress signals, rather the device simply sent waypoints to an online program. That the times of the signals had been mixed up, and that the actual times indicated that David had already summited Blanca, Ellingwood Point, and Little Bear on Wednesday, September 3, 2008, and sometime around 1530 hours had gone off route. He said the waypoints then became inconsistently sent, but all from the same location over a period of several hours. Thus, he said he believes David simply got off route and fell to his death, not suffering a long battle with an injury or such. At 0700 hours, Tuesday September 9, 2008, I emailed Sergeant Alejo this information.

Several days afterward, I read a report on 14ers.com that area hikers reported a large thunderstorm had passed through the area around 1500 hours September 3, 2008. This report is congruent with the evidence of hail/snow at the scene. A report of a rockslide in the area around 1500 hours was also made on the 14ers.com forum, but this could not be verified, and evidence at the scene neither confirmed nor denied this possibility. Lastly, I learned from the forum that the subject was experienced in hiking Colorado fourteeners, and that Dr. David Boyd, M.D., was a very respected and loved member of his community.

I thought that after the busy summer and fall SAR season ended, I might run up on a weekend later in October or November and grab the bike. The GPS unit, I figured, was lost forever. Although the sheriff pointed out that the GPS unit likely possessed the coordinates where David had cached his bike, the GPS unit was likely deep in the scree where we had recovered his body. By the time we left the scene where we had recovered David, the hail and snow had melted out, and after scouring the slope several times, we found no further evidence. David's GPS was probably high up on a ledge he had impacted, or it had rolled and tumbled into a crack, snuggled deeply under scree and talus that will hide it until the mountain grinds it to powder over eons.

When I first started exploring the Sangres, I had used bicycles, just like David, and just like David, I had ditched my mountain bike in the aspens and pines at the mouth of Chokecherry Canyon near Jaws 1. The concept of a bike is great, but the reality is that beyond Jaws 1, the two-track is too steep, rocky, and loose to be of any real help (especially if you have a pack and intend to mountaineer higher up). With a bigger overnight pack, the energy it takes to balance and fight the loose gravel surpasses simply hiking the trail. Descending from this point on the bike uses different musculature than walking, but it barely conserves energy, even going down.

Since I didn't share with anyone else that David's bicycle was cached somewhere up on the mountain, I was surprised when the sheriff contacted me and asked me if I might know who had stolen David Boyd's bicycle. The sheriff explained that David Boyd's bike had been a several thousand dollar model, and it had recently shown up for sale on eBay. He was in the process of investigation. I was glad to tell him I hadn't originally obeyed his directive to notify everyone on the team. "Sir, I'm the only one who knew the bike was up there. I hadn't passed along the information to the team. I was withholding it so no one would waste energy recovering equipment until later in the season."

The sheriff was a little surprised, but immediately his curiosity turned to the others who knew about the bicycle. A few days later the investigation would find that one of the sheriff's deputies had spoken to local firefighters about it, and it was a local volunteer firefighter who was guilty of going up the mountain, finding the bicycle, stealing it, and selling it on eBay. I was glad the sheriff criminally charged the suspect. The GPS is still in the process of becoming dust.

Several weeks later, I learned of the results of David's autopsy from the Alamosa coroner. As I had suspected, David had expired by the time his body came to rest. Thus, even though he was highly abraded and deformed, there was very little blood on scene. The autopsy revealed that during his fall down the cliff, David sustained a blow that fractured a rib that pierced his heart, instantly causing death.

If I could go back to that moment after David had summited his third peak in the "Triple Slam," I would have urged him to be very cautious. Most accidents happen on the way down, after the athlete feels the objective has been gained, so it's just time to put it on cruise control for the descent. In David's case, he could have been under duress, likely trying to descend to treeline before a large thunderstorm moved in and covered the mountain in a blanket of hail. If I could just go back in time and be at that location right then, I'd stop David and point out to him he was about to go off route. I'd remind David and anyone else who is up on that ridge in similar circumstances that the non-technical, non-deadly route has earth, soil, dirt at the top. It is NOT a set of boilerplates, large domes of rock, big talus boulders, or the tops of solid or crumbly slabs. It is earth, not rock, that leads the way back to Lake Como.

It is a very important lesson of seasoned mountaineers to take enough time on the way up to stop, turn around, and memorize the visual route down. If one does not do this consistently on the way up, the way down is visually and for most purposes a new route. In technical terrain such as the west ridge of Little Bear Peak, similar to the standard route up Crestone Needle, one must memorize the route down on the way up. Mistaking similar couloirs on these peaks results in death.

In late summer of 2010, Jess and I guided David's stepbrother, John, to the location where we found David. After seeing the location of his brother's incident, Jess and I led John to a nearby waterfall. There, John said goodbye to his brother and spread some of David's ashes where his spirit had been so fully alive.

As we carefully drove down the canyon, we all spoke of the pain of loss, and how deeply it affects families, friends, and in David's case, so many patients' lives.

Kristen Weiss
Great Sand Dunes National Park, December 2, 2009

"Oh cold, cold, rigid, dreadful Death, set up thine altar here, and dress it with such terrors as thou hast at thy command: for this is thy dominion! But of the loved, revered, and honoured head, thou canst not turn one hair to thy dread purposes, or make one feature odious. It is not that the hand is heavy and will fall down when released; it is not that the heart and pulse are still; but that the hand was open, generous, and true; the heart brave, warm, and tender; and the pulse a man's. Strike, Shadow, strike! And see his good deeds springing from the wound, to sow the world with life immortal."

—Charles Dickens, *A Christmas Carol*

Every year in early December, near the end of the autumn semester, Adams State University puts on a winter holiday party for its faculty and staff. The university holds the party in the Luther Bean Museum, a section of Richardson Hall, the university's administrative building. The museum's enormous grand room, its two-story ceilings, its decorations and lights, live music, free food and wine—everything culminated in a mystical holiday setting.

On the evening of Wednesday, December 2, 2009, I was at the annual party, listening to the classical Christmas caroling and chatting with friends. At 7:41 p.m., my phone began vibrating, and I was disappointed that caller ID showed, "Colorado State Patrol Dispatch." Dispatch often called to connect me to a subject who needed guidance in the field. Since it was after dark and well below freezing, I could not imagine who would be needing guidance, but three glasses of wine into the evening, I found a quiet corner in a hallway where I could speak without distraction.

One of the basic expectations of our rescue team was that we were honest with teammates when we were too intoxicated to respond legally and safely. The standard operating procedure was that if we were in no shape to respond, we would not answer the call-out request coming from the team's executive secretary, so as not to waste her time as she was calling everyone out. In this case, as one of the team's lead officers, taking a call directly from CSP, I decided to answer the phone and if it came up, explain that I could not drive and respond to anything for three or four more hours, but after that I would be good to go.

I flipped open the phone and hit accept, "Hello, this is Kevin."

"Kevin? Director of Alamosa Volunteer Search and Rescue?" The steady, assured voices of dispatchers calmed me. I didn't know exactly which dispatcher I was speaking with, but I knew that whenever any of them called, I immediately loved the tone of direct, efficient communication. In this case, a woman's higher-pitched voice was that much easier to hear in difficult conditions; also there's something reassuringly motherly about feminine voices.

"This is Kevin."

"This is CSP dispatch, and the sheriff asked that I call you so you can put the team on standby for deployment in the morning."

I was secretly happy that I didn't have to report to anyone in my inebriated merriment. Now I could enjoy the rest of the party drinking water, and when I got home in a few hours, I could pack for the morning's business, sleep a bit, and get an early start.

"What time and location does the sheriff want us?"

"The sheriff requested that any available AVSAR personnel rally at first light at the visitor center out at Great Sand Dunes National Park."

"Good copy. Did the sheriff mention what the mission objective will be?"

"No. He said you'll be working with the law enforcement rangers who'll call and brief you by phone later this evening."

"Okay, thanks for the call and info. I hope it's a slow night for you guys."

As I flipped closed the phone another call came in. Caller ID showed it was Chief Ranger Jim Bowman from Great Sand Dunes National Park.

I flipped open the phone again. "Hello, this is Kevin."

"Kevin, this is Jim Bowman, national park ranger out at Great Sand Dunes."

"Hi Jim. I just got off the phone with CSP dispatch, and I was told to put the team on standby for a rally at the visitor center in the morning. First-light deployment. What's going on?"

Jim explained that earlier that day a dune field visitor had brought a purse into the visitor center. It had been filled with drifting sand, and as the rangers inspected the purse, they became suspicious when the contents included a wallet with a driver's license, car registration, car keys, a pair of shoes, and some unpaid bills. The driver's license, registration, bills, and letter were all the property of a young woman named Kristen Weiss.

About this same time, law enforcement rangers investigated the license plate of a lone, unoccupied vehicle parked in the main dunes parking lot. They found that the tan, 2000 model Honda sedan was registered to a Kristen

Weiss of Colorado Springs, Colorado. All the car's doors were locked, but the sunroof was wide open.

Connecting the purse and car, rangers used the keys to enter the car and search it. They found a partially completed résumé and two four-packs of wine coolers with the bottles missing. Upon researching Kristen's credit card purchases, it was found that she had made a purchase at a Walsenburg liquor store approximately 12:30 p.m. on November 30.

Since Kristen was now a missing person, rangers contacted the Colorado Springs Police Department (CSPD) to do a welfare check on Kristen's residence. Soon afterward, CSPD replied that no one was at the residence, and they reported that Kristen had had previous contact with them regarding her despondent state.

The rangers did a search of the immediate area surrounding the car and parking lot, and they employed attraction tactics such as sirens and overhead light bar lights to help the subject, Kristen, orient herself if she were in line of sight or within an audible proximity to the parking lot or the road that connects the park's entrance to the visitor center. The rangers also patrolled the parking lots, campgrounds, and nearby trails on foot. This resulted in nothing, and at this point the park's personnel recognized that they might be searching for a despondent subject, so they called AVSAR for support and additional personnel. Because video cameras at the park's entrance had documented the time when Kristen had entered the park two days prior, and because of having spent two sub-zero, windy arctic-like nights out exposed, I knew the probability of her being alive was near zero, and risking other's safety was not warranted until first light, Chief Ranger Bowman and I agreed to rally "the troops" at the visitor center at 6:30 a.m. This time of first light would be the safest time to begin searching in brush for Kristen. In the dark, the vegetations' sticks at eye level could easily result in injuries, and I had a strong intuition about Kristen's profile from the facts shared with me over the phone.

The next morning, it was just below zero as I drove past my closest neighbor, the Colorado Gator Farm. In the dark predawn light of my headlights, the thick steam rising off the geothermally heated pools momentarily would block out my vision, and for moments I felt like I was in an aircraft in clouds. This was not unusual for such cold conditions.

In the few seconds it had taken me to walk from my front door to my detached garage, my face had felt the high humidity breeze, and I was reminded of the difference between ambient temperature and windchill temperatures. In the temperature of negative 5 degrees, the 10 mile-per-hour wind made the temperature feel like negative 22 degrees. In such conditions, exposed flesh becomes frostbitten in approximately 30 minutes.

I arrived at the Great Sand Dunes National Park Visitor Center (VC) as the sky began transitioning from pitch black to dark blue, a few minutes before 6:30 a.m. Lead Ranger John White greeted me, and soon after I introduced myself to several other rangers including Tillman Cavert, Melanie Rawling, and Patrick Meyers. Around that time, a caravan of vehicles filled with AVSAR personnel arrived, and I was happy to see George Rapoza, Andrew McClure, Mark Martinez, Josh Copelan, Christopher Lavery, Mike Henderson, John Gilmore, Suzi Hopper, and Jade Wright (no relation to the author).

After introductions, everyone made their way to the conference room in a non-public area of the VC. Like a war planning room, the walls of the conference room were covered with maps of the park. It was a perfect setting for the planning and discussion of the day's mission.

The meeting began with an announcement by park personnel that CSPD had done another welfare check, and no one was at Kristen's residence. As I began to ponder all the evidence that had been presented, I started the search at one of Kristen's last known points (LKPs). Kristen's LKP was her purse, located out in the dune field just a few thousand feet from her car. All evidence pointed toward Kristen being in the park. Everyone was shown an enlarged picture of Kristen's driver's license photo and given her description to aid in the search. She was a twenty-seven-year-old female, five-feet five-inches tall, one hundred forty-five pounds, with red hair and blue eyes.

In SAR missions, regardless of the agency, it is custom to follow FEMA protocol and assign leadership specific rank and roles. The purpose of this is to aid in the most effective response to an emergency incident that often requires the quick adaptation of a large group of responders to a rapidly changing incident. Using the universally followed protocol, commanders direct the responding personnel from multiple agencies to where they are most needed as quickly as possible.

In this emergency command and control system, the highest-ranking role is the incident commander. The person in this role has the primary responsibility of acting as the mission's overseer.

The next in the chain of command is the operations manager; this person acts primarily as the mission's planner and coordinator. In this mission's case, the national park leaders requested that I act as operations manager. I accepted this role and began brainstorming possible scenarios that would explain the evidence we were facing.

Several scenarios were discussed, including Kristen getting lost in the dunes, being despondent and having taken her life in the park, or the un-likely scenario of a criminal abduction. John conveyed that rangers would go through park entrance station video again, carefully looking at all vehicles exiting the park for any evidence that might indicate if and when Kristen may have possibly exited the park.

After discussing each scenario and their probabilities, I explained that with the given evidence and feedback, I believed we were looking for a sub-ject who was despondent and who had likely taken her own life. I described the "close-in phenomenon," a statistical occurrence in which the highest probability of the location of a despondent subject is within a quarter mile of the subject's last known point (LKP). In this incident's case, Kristen's LKP was the location of her purse, in the west part of the Medano Creek flats in the sands where the dunes begin to rise. I thought Kristen would be located within a quarter mile of where her purse was found, or a quarter mile of her car.

Operating under the suspicion that Kristen had taken her life, I explained my theory was that Kristen would likely be within proximity to the parking lot, or just beyond line of sight of the ridge in the dune field. If she wasn't in either of these locations, I believed our next search area would be to move down the dry Medano Creek flats.

I requested two searchers to ascend to High Dune and visually scan all the pockets and dune valleys not visible from the parking lot or Medano Creek flats. Upon completing this objective, these two searchers would then descend back to Medano Creek and walk up the dry creek bed approximately one mile in a northerly direction. I requested the remaining searchers do a "line search" of the Medano Creek flats and brush around the parking lot and the location of where the purse was found out in the sand flats. Follow-ing the line search, personnel would then continue down Medano Creek for approximately two miles. Upon reaching that point, personnel would turn around and do a second sweep of the area.

George Rapoza and Andrew McClure volunteered to be the team that would ascend to High Dune and cover the dune field and the dry creek bed north of the parking lot.

Ranger John White requested to act as a solo hasty team and scout ahead of the large group along the two-mile dry Medano Creek bed south of the parking area. John's reasoning was that responders had historically found many subjects in this area. Even though AVSAR hasty teams were always a minimum of two people, John being solo was not an issue as he was follow-ing NPS protocol, and he would have clear radio contact and line of sight to the rest of us conducting the slower line search.

At 7:30 a.m., an hour after we rallied at the VC, all searchers but Suzi left the visitor's center. She remained to meet Red Cross personnel who, because of the brutal environmental conditions, were responding in support of the searchers. She would also be available to act as an impromptu victim's advocate in case any of Kristen's family or friends arrived, and she could coordinate anyone else who required it, such as additional SAR responders. The weather report as we all walked out to our vehicles to drive from the VC to the dune field main parking lot indicated dangerous conditions.

When I arrived at the main parking lot at 7:45 a.m., the temperature had risen to two degrees Fahrenheit, and there was a sustained westerly wind of approximately 10 miles per hour, the resulting windchill equaling negative 13 degrees Fahrenheit. As we embarked on our separate objectives, I watched George and Andrew quickly cover the flat ground of the seasonally dry Medano Creek bed and begin ascending the 700-foot tall High Dune.

John White departed walking south, his objective to hastily cover two miles of the dry creek bed looking for any evidence that indicated a direction of travel (footprints, discarded clothes, empty wine cooler bottles, etc.). The rest of us, totaling ten people, walked single file into the brush north of the parking lot about two hundred yards. Once there, we lined up east to west, with about a hundred feet of distance between us. We were now within visual and speaking range of the people immediately to our right and left, and the line we formed now stretched approximately a thousand feet through the brush. I positioned myself in the middle of this line so I could help coordinate everyone staying in formation and more quickly respond to either side of the line if searchers found evidence. I reminded everyone on the line that as we moved south, I would stop the line every twenty to thirty feet so that searchers could move laterally east-west and carefully observe any locations that evidence could be hidden (such as in thick brush, high grass, little pockets and washouts in the sandy soil, etc.). I had a vision that Kristen had wandered from the dunes back to the brush and laid down in the brush. I wanted to make sure every little depression and pocket in the willows and cottonwoods around the parking lot was checked and cleared.

As I watched George and Andrew's silhouettes traversing the dune's ridgeline, I hoped the windchill wasn't too much worse than it was where we were. The wind made facing west difficult as I hadn't brought any ski goggles and my eyes watered up coping with the frigid breeze. I gave the command for the line to make its first steps twenty feet into the brush and grasses. Perfectly as instructed, everyone moved south and then walked briefly back and forth on the east-west line making a thorough visual search of the ground in their separate sectors. I was very pleased as I watched everyone overlap just a bit in their sectors, ensuring that no "holes" occurred during the search.

The rangers ended up mostly to my right (west), and the AVSAR personnel mostly to my left (east). The rangers farthest west spread out several hundred feet from each other because the sandy flats were far easier to cover. The cycle of stepping forward and stopping, searching our section of the line, and then stepping forward again took several long, cold minutes, but in each cycle everyone remained as mindful as the first. We all knew that if we allowed even a small gap in our search, we could miss vital evidence. We all knew that our objective, which we could come upon at any moment, was a deceased young woman.

At 8:25 a.m., as the line reached a position just south of the parking lot, the farthest west searcher on the line, Ranger Tillman Cavert, called out to the searcher next to him that he observed what he believed to be the subject. After verifying what he saw with binoculars, he was certain that approximately two hundred yards ahead of us (south of our present location) he observed Kristen, and he keyed the mic of his radio and announced to all of us that the subject had been located.

I stopped the line and walked west toward Tillman's position. By the time I emerged from the thick brush and trees, I observed Tillman, Patrick, and Melanie (all three rangers who had been farthest west on the search line) standing next to a small mound of sand in the middle of the dry creek bed about a hundred and fifty yards south of my location. As I walked south to their location, I was quite amazed that Tillman had successfully observed the subject, as far away as he had been; it was nearly impossible to tell if the mound of wind-blown sand had formed because of a body or because of one of the driftwood logs that occurred throughout the sandy flats. All three rangers posted themselves about twenty to thirty feet from the Kristen's body, and I was happy to see that no one had approached Kristen too closely; everyone was sensitive not to disturb evidence. I thanked Tillman for the acute observation and successful find, as this would help bring her family closure more quickly, as well as it would help keep searchers safe by limiting their exposure to the extremely cold environment.

With the rangers as witnesses, I circled Kristen over-viewing the immediate scene 360 degrees. Kristen's body was laying face down, body east-west, her head easterly. As I circled over to her south side, the windward side, I had a much clearer view of Kristen. Quoted from the report I provided the sheriff:

I observed that the female body was face down in the sand, long red hair blowing in the wind. Her top was covered by a small pink and white spaghetti-strapped shirt. Her blue jean pants were pulled down just below her buttocks; thus, her entire lower back and buttocks were exposed to the elements. Sand had drifted around her, covering half or more of her body in sand drifts. She was lying facing east in a symmetrical prone position (legs straight), her arms underneath her torso, partially buried under sand. It was impossible to see her face, her hands or under her. I could see on the lowest parts of her body, where the "sand line" met with the atmosphere, some evidence of blood pooling, but her exposed flesh was still very life-colored.

I asked Patrick to direct the AVSAR techs to form a north-south line in the brush, farther apart than they had been during the search, about two hundred feet east of the body's location. This line would serve as a scene perimeter, and their new objective would be to ensure that no park visitors would emerge from the web of game and single-track foot trails that criss-crossed the brush between the day camping area and the Medano Creek bed where we were all located. Although this early and frigid, the likelihood of a park visitor in the area was near zero, but I did not want any visitors accidentally exposing themselves to the scene.

Patrick nodded and walked northeastward where AVSAR techs were emerging from the brush. I could see him giving hand signals indicating the new scene perimeter. I asked Tillman to remain near me as a witness, and I asked Melanie if she would position herself north of our location, approximately two hundred feet or more and act as a backup to Patrick and the SAR personnel. The likelihood of someone approaching from either the south or west in those conditions during that time of the day was zero.

Although I had been granted permission to process scenes involving fatalities by the sheriff without having to have a deputy or coroner present except at the trailhead for transfer, in this case I decided that the scene required the investigatory skills of personnel more qualified than myself. From my report to the sheriff, "As the evidence presented a young female who was partially undressed, I immediately called the Alamosa sheriff's office and requested investigators be sent to the scene because of the potential for sexual assault or other foul play. I also called the coroner's office and requested personnel be sent to the scene."

At approximately 8:45 a.m., the park's superintendent, Ranger Art Hutchinson, and Ranger John White were on scene, and soon afterward, Alamosa County Sheriff's Office Investigator, Corporal Spangler, arrived on scene.

Just after 9:00 a.m., Sheriff Dave Stong and the Assistant County Coroner Harry Alejo arrived on the scene. With all necessary personnel present, we began processing the scene by carefully documenting everything as we found it. All of this occurred in ambient temperatures in the single digits, windchill below zero. After Kristen's body was carefully secured in a cadaver bag and put in a litter, Sheriff Stong, Corporal Spangler, Coroner Alejo, and myself carefully sifted by hand the sand that had been around and under Kristen's body.

From my original report:

> The body's exposed skin that had contact with the sand was darker from blood pooling and generally the skin had a layer of attached sand. The woman appeared to be in the process of trying to take off a blue short-sleeve, lightweight sweat suit top that was still wrapped around her neck. Her left arm seemed caught in both her shirts, thus her arm lifted both shirts toward her shoulders exposing her left breast. The body's face, although dark and sand covered, appeared to be the subject. Several of us on scene went and got the wheeled litter for moving the subject. We returned with the litter and placed the subject in a cadaver bag for transport. The sheriff, myself, the assistant coroner, and Corporal Spangler, using our fingers, combed the sand that had been underneath the subject for any additional potential evidence. There was none. We loaded the subject into the coroner's vehicle at approximately 0930 hours, and the AVSAR, national park service, coroner's office and Alamosa sheriff's office personnel conducted a line search of the Medano Creek flats, west of the body's location, from the parking lot to the lowest flanks of the dunes. No additional evidence was located.

After completing the final line search to locate any possible evidence between Kristen's body and where her purse had been found, I debriefed AVSAR personnel and released them about 11:30 a.m. I thanked all personnel who had been involved, especially the volunteer SAR personnel and the rangers who had come in during their off-duty time to assist in the search. I was also especially grateful for Adeline Lee, the lead Red Cross volunteer, who had been in the parking lot since 9:00 a.m. providing warm food and drinks to all the responders. She saved a couple personnel's fingers from frostbite that morning (the rangers and SAR personnel had shown up ready for a day-long search and were well prepared, but some of the other responders had shown up forgetting their beanies and gloves).

A few minutes after the coroner, sheriff, and investigator left the scene, the Red Cross and AVSAR personnel, myself included, drove in a caravan out of the park. Most of us were headed back to Alamosa.

The next day, I called Ranger Bowman and asked if any additional findings related to Kristen had come up. He verified that at approximately 2:00 p.m. on Monday, November 30, Kristen had entered the park alone, wearing the same shirts she was found wearing post mortem. There was no evidence that Kristen had left or reentered the park after her initial entry.

On Christmas Eve, the autopsy results returned from the coroner. From the Christmas Eve *Alamosa Valley Courier*:

> Alamosa County Coroner Mike Rogers Wednesday said autopsy results concerning the death of 27-year old Kristin Weiss at the Great Sand Dunes National Park on Dec. 2, 2009, do not indicate any kind of foul play. Rogers said the autopsy indicated Weiss, of Colorado Springs, died of asphyxiation after she apparently fell face down in the sand in an intoxicated state, passed out and inhaled sand into her throat and lungs. He said there were no signs of hypothermia or trauma found on the body.

In early December when the first subzero winds sneak down my neck, I think of Kristen Weiss. I think of her death; I also think of all the helpers, all the responders, all those people who will do whatever they can to show compassion toward those suffering.

Kevin Hayne
Little Bear Peak, Tuesday, June 15, 2010

"For sudden the worst turns the best to the brave."
—Robert Browning, "Prospice"

To visit the agriculturally driven San Luis Valley in mid-June is to visit an American Shangri-La; in the lowlands of the valley, the sprouting fields of barley, canola, and potato stubble take on an especially vibrant color contrasted to the lingering snow and dark cliffs higher up. At treeline and above, the end of avalanche season overlaps melt out, and the thawing cliffs and slopes make this a potentially excellent as well as dangerous season for mountaineering; what benefits a mountaineer gains by more easily ascending steep snow chutes in lieu of loose, rocky slopes, the mountaineer must weigh against the costs of hazards in the form of increased rock fall, loose rock, rapidly changing snow and ice conditions, and weather such as spring thunder snowstorms and near freezing rain, both of which significantly raise the risk of becoming hypothermic.

It was this beautiful time of June in 2010, and driving south on Highway 17 I soaked in the chlorophyll-rich fields. It was after Memorial Day, and I knew the mountaineering SAR season had officially begun. Driving north to south along Highway 17, I paralleled the Sangre de Cristos, and from habit I had taken a long look at the snowfields near Little Bear's summit—the year before I was still in a race with Mother Nature to recover Lygon Stevens.

The snowfields on Little Bear were still covering a significant amount of the west face, and it would still be a dangerous time to have to respond high up on the peaks. I relaxed a bit remembering not to allow the past to stress me out about the present; I also remembered that lightning does strike in the same place twice, in some cases it strikes the same place over and over. Little Bear Peak's standard route has the highest probability of area (POA) of fatalities of any location in the mountain group. Along with the standard route of Crestone Needle, the standard route of Little Bear Peak is one of the most dangerous locations in the entire Sangre de Cristo mountain range. Statistically, I wasn't really having a mystical foreshadowing intuition; I was predicting the inevitable.

This bluebird morning, I was driving into Alamosa to attend a global positioning system/geographical information systems (GPS/GIS) class at Adams State University. It was being offered to all the regional government agency specialists who had use for GPS skills. The city's mosquito control department was learning how to map their nightly fogging patrols. Also present was law enforcement's investigatory folks with interests in precise crime scene uses. I flashed back to a time when I used GPS to help precisely map the locations of body parts, where a scavenger, probably a bear, had spread body parts over a large area of a private property woods—the "back forty" of a large ranch.

As a leader of the SAR community, I sat near the other first responders and explained that my reasoning for being present was making my conversions between the geographical units the FAA uses (pilots) and the units "ground pounders" use (hunters, hikers) more efficient, thus helping quicken a potentially life-saving response. I already knew many of the sarcastic characters I'd be spending the day with.

During our mid-morning break, I enjoyed the company of some fellow mountaineers and first responders in the hallway of the university's science and mathematics building. The hallway was something out of a natural history museum including dioramas with preserved local bird specimens, a large tropical reef aquarium, and a large multi-storied pendulum that demonstrated the rotation of the earth.

Just as class reconvened, my cell vibrated, and the caller ID came up Alamosa Sheriff's Office. I stepped out into the large hallway, took a deep breath, and as the pendulum slowly swung back and forth, keeping time like a three-story grandfather clock, I answered the phone.

"Hello, this is Kevin."

"Kevin. This is Sheriff Stong. I have a very upset, distraught mom on the line. She's been watching her son's location with a SPOT device and thinks he's injured based on information she's watching on her computer. She says his location hasn't moved since around nine a.m. She says he'd never stop that long unless he was injured. She said she has a horrible intuition. What do you think?"

At first I didn't react, I just reflected. I thought about all the previous missions to rescue and recover others, and all the risk those who responded took every time such a mission occurred. It was very likely that the mom was correct, and we'd be deploying soon to help her son, but based on the limited information I had just received, boiling down to the intuition of a mom, in my judgment the risk to the responders was not justified. "Sheriff, I understand and wish I could send twenty-five people out to every incident involving a mother's intuition, but I need more than that to send people into harm's way. Up there is harm's way."

"She's got a sense of urgency that's genuine and convincing. I've got her on the line and am going to have you speak to her directly."

When the sheriff calls one directly, it's always an urgent matter. I knew this had been the case since answering the call. "Okay, sir. Patch her through." With a click, I knew the transfer had been made.

"This is Kevin Wright with Alamosa Volunteer Search and Rescue. How may I help you?"

"This is Beth Hayne, I'm the mother of one of two young men climbing Little Bear Peak, and I believe that one or both of them have been injured and require rescue."

Thus began a conversation that involved many difficult, challenging elements. I explained to Mrs. Hayne I had a very limited number of qualified responders, who I could not deploy and put at risk until I knew with a great deal more certainty that someone was injured and in need of help. I explained that stopped movement too often indicated a transceiver malfunction, or a minor injury requiring far fewer responders, and as hard as it would be to do so, we needed to wait for an emergency signal, continued movement, or for another sign of distress. I told her to continue watching the SPOT device for movement, or an emergency signal, and to be patient. I explained that I had been a young enthusiastic mountaineer like her son Kevin when I was eighteen. I said that based on the location of the SPOT device, the base of the Hourglass Couloir, the two of them were probably just warming up with a warm brew or making the difficult decision to turn back. Just like the sheriff though, I could sense that Mom knew something was desperately wrong.

A couple of GPS classmates were AVSAR teammates, Mick Daniel and Mike Henderson, so when they saw me step out into the hallway and take a call, their attention had already been perked. My look upon returning to the classroom probably conveyed what Kevin Hayne's mom, Beth, had successfully communicated to me. I nonverbally verified to them that there would very likely be a SAR call-out. I sat down in class and pretended to be engaged in the lecture. In reality, my mind was racing through the checklists and flowcharts of what it would entail getting a team of qualified specialists—specialized mountaineering, medically qualified life savers—to a pair of climbers, one of whom was likely severely injured or near dead. I wasn't aware of it, but Mick and Mike were subtly watching my every movement.

As my mind raced, time became distorted and in what felt like just a couple minutes, an hour had passed. The instructor dismissed the class for lunch. While walking to the student union cafeteria and over lunch, I briefed my teammates about the situation.

Walking back from the university's student union, I took my first official mission field note—at 1249 hours, I received another call verifying Beth's intuition and the worst case scenario.

From a scrap piece of paper, my mission field notes begin with, "Deputy Chacon just made contact with 17 y. o. male, Travis Winders. Travis is now with Deputy Chacon at the trailhead. Chacon put Travis on the phone with me. Travis was so upset he couldn't breathe or communicate. I asked Travis to slow down and tell me what happened."

Travis said that he and Kevin had reached the base of the Hourglass Couloir earlier that morning. Because the chute was filled with hard water ice-like snow, the two of them had alternatively chosen to ascend rock faces and ledges along the edge of the steep gully. Several hundred feet up the couloir and just a couple hundred vertical feet shy of the summit with Kevin in the lead, the two of them stopped to discuss the route dead-ending in a wall of ice that funneled to their position. In the midst of this route finding, a handhold unexpectedly pulled free and Kevin fell backward onto the steep, hard snow.

It was difficult for Travis to describe the horror of Kevin's unanticipated, wicked-fast acceleration. Travis said that within seconds Kevin had slid hundreds of feet down the chute, bouncing violently off a wall and out of sight at its base. When I asked Travis to estimate the speed at which Kevin was traveling when he ricocheted off the rock, Travis said it was very fast, maybe 60 mph, "Like a car traveling down the highway."

Travis carefully down-climbed the Hourglass Couloir and very narrowly avoided his partner's fate. Travis exited the couloir and continued down-climbing on the west face of Little Bear Peak. Travis' descent took him across several steep, precarious snowfields, punctuated by bands of rocks. Upon reaching Kevin, who had come to rest in one of the narrow strips of rock between snowfields three to five hundred feet below the base of the couloir, Travis found his climber partner and friend in an extremely traumatized, near-dead state.

Transcribed directly from my field notes from that day:

- subject 100 yds. south of trail at base of Hourglass
- fell in Hourglass
- climbing just left of ice
- hand held broke
- reporting party got to subject's location
- subject breathing hard, extremities twitching
- both arms deformed, broken
- subject unconscious, initially seemingly attempting to crawl
- subject face up

Kevin Hayne . 81

- face very swollen
- subject spitting up blood
- blood coming from ears
- partner stayed with subject for 35-45 minutes
- subject's breathing labored, slow
- Beth Hayne, Highlands Ranch [contact info]

Realizing there was nothing he could do, and there was no way to know if the emergency signal he had pressed on the SPOT device had gone out, Travis decided to self-evacuate as fast as he could back to the trailhead, and as soon as he got a cell signal, call 911. As I neared acquiring all the information I could from Travis, I knew it would likely be the last time I would speak to him. From this point, the deputy would drive him to the sheriff's office to speak with a victim's advocate until his parents could arrive. I didn't write any shorthand accounts of how our conversation ended, but I still remember it.

I remember being in awe of the seventeen-year-old young man faced with a situation and decision most seasoned mountaineers would be hard-pressed to manage: treatment of multiple life-threatening traumas, in a very dangerous environment, on a best friend. Travis repeatedly apologized for having moved Kevin's neck while trying to maintain Kevin's airway. He mentioned that Kevin's neck felt "loose" and he was horrified at the thought that he may have further injured Kevin. I reassured Travis of the truth—that as horrific and traumatizing as the experience was, he had done everything anyone could and had acted appropriately at all times. As we ended our conversation, I told Travis that I was responsible for Kevin, and I promised him that I would bring back his friend.

Deputy Chacon called back a few minutes later at 1303 hours and gave me some more information regarding the incident, including the contact information for the reporting party's father, Sean Winders.

At 1309 hours I called Sheriff Stong and requested that he call the local military bases and ask about any possible "training" support and to put Flight For Life (FFL) on standby.

At 1313 hours I called Sean Winders and spoke to him about his son and Kevin Hayne. In this impromptu interview, I learned that this was seventeen-year-old Travis' ninth fourteen thousand-foot peak and eighteen-year-old Kevin's fortieth fourteener. Both had experience on snow, experience with ropes and crampons, both had SPOT satellite devices, Kevin was marking waypoints, Travis' SPOT was tracking. Kevin was known to be a conservative mountaineer who wouldn't take undue risks.

I walked into the GPS class, now back in the afternoon session, and I motioned for the SAR guys to grab their stuff. I apologized to the instructor, mentioning that it was literally a life or death situation, and as I walked out of what remained of the GPS training, I was wished good luck by several first responders. Out in the hallway, I told my fellow SAR team members that I was about to do an all-member, all-specialist AVSAR team call-out. I was calling in the cavalry ahead of time. I was calling out everyone, and it was going to be a big showing.

"I'll meet you guys out at the usual command post, the Lake Como trailhead flats as quickly as you can get out there. Everyone available will be there. See if you can't get a head start on the rush and help organize 'em as they stagger in."

As I stepped from the "museum's" pendulum hallway into the breeze and mid-day sunlight, I donned my sunglasses and looked through the gaps in the large cottonwoods' shady branches toward Little Bear Peak. I knew exactly where Kevin Hayne was lying. I deeply hoped he was no longer suffering, but I knew he might still be hanging on. I began jogging toward my car.

I jumped in my Corolla and bee-lined for home, about fifteen minutes away; on the way, I called AVSAR's executive secretary, briefed her about the situation, and asked that she call out all the team's members and have us rally at the Lake Como Road trailhead. I called Sheriff Stong, and he informed me that both Flight For Life and the military were gearing up and on their way to assist. The sheriff passed along that the military was sending a Chinook crew coming out of Buckley Air National Guard Base in Aurora, and he thought they'd have a special forces ground crew; excellent news as this would mean that potentially only one AVSAR tech would need to board the aircraft and advise the crew in locating the subject—the military personnel would take care of the rescue.

As I sped north on Highway 17, I looked to my right and focused my vision on the snowfields below Little Bear's Hourglass. I imagined Kevin, near death, struggling to survive and breathe, and then I also pictured him passed, peaceful, no longer suffering, struggling.

The thought of him all by himself, hanging on, waiting for us—as hard as it was, I had to continue to operate as if Kevin were still alive, and his life depended upon our safe, professional response. I called the contact number the sheriff had provided for the military crew, a cell number for one of the pilots. The captain responded that they were refueling and inbound, estimated time of arrival approximately three hours later, 1700 hours. With all the possible communication channels available to the two of us, I thought it ironic that we continued to text as our primary communication.

I slowed down as I passed my neighbor, the famous Colorado Gator

Farm. I frustratingly slowly rolled by all the clueless, happy tourists, giving them plenty of space and safety, but as soon as I rounded the corner to my house, I left a thick cloud of San Luis Valley dust in the air. Sliding to a stop and emerging from the car into my dust cloud rolling up the driveway to the house, I could hear my dog barking with enthusiasm. He had no idea that my stop was just a quick check-in.

Freckles, my mountaineering rat terrier, had plenty of food and water, and I gave him an extra long good bye ritual—a long staring into each other's eyes, a touching of foreheads, and a loving slow pet from nose to tip of his little bobbed tail, a nonverbal, interspecies communication of understanding. Attachment would have to be put aside for a couple days so that another's suffering could be eased. Somewhere deep down, Freckles understood. More likely, he also simply knew the drill—when I showed up like this and gave him the "forehead goodbye," he knew I was leaving, possibly for days.

I already had all my low-angle SAR gear in my trunk, but for what I was headed into, I knew I better grab my high-angle technical gear—my full body harness, some extra personal rock climbing gear, as well as my crampons and an ice axe. I figured I'd be acting as the IC (incident commander), so I'd most likely stay at the command post and keep everything planned and organized, but just in case, I wanted always to be prepared as well as a model of what I expected of my teammates.

I filled my Nalgene water bottles, mixing one up as a diluted electrolyte solution, and I drank my fill of water to ensure that I was starting out as well hydrated as possible. I ate some food and grabbed high energy/high protein exercise treats.

In case I was gone a couple days, I cracked the windows so Freckles would have some fresh air. I bid him a last goodbye, and as I shut the door, he cocked his head to one side to accentuate his focus on me. "See you soon Frecks." I shut the door, and I knew that if anything ever happened to me, the day afterward a friend's wife would swing by. Eventually he'd make his way to my ex-wife.

It would be a horrific irony to kill someone in the process of responding to save another person's life, so I carefully, slowly passed the Gator Farm tourists again, but pulling out onto Highway 17, I floored the accelerator and I recalled my police academy training with the military and what happens if one isn't extremely attentive to details when cruising at highway speeds in excess of 80 mph. I wanted to be one of the first personnel at the command post, readying teammates and the landing zone well ahead of the time they'd be needed.

I turned east on the Six Mile, and as I approached Highway 150, I enjoyed the magnificent, postcard vista of the Great Sand Dunes backdropped by the Kit Carson and Crestone Mountain Groups. The early afternoon was cloudless, and the mid-70s temperature was perfect for a day along Medano Creek. I imagined all the families and young kids building sand castles and playing in the stream surges.

At Highway 150, I turned right and sped south past Zapata Falls. I caught a glimpse of the summit of Ellingwood Point, a fourteener that still had plenty of snow on it. I took note; soon I would be deploying some of my best friends into that environment. As I neared the turn-off for the two-track dirt road that led to the Lake Como trailhead, the view of Little Bear became clear. I was at the trailhead, my objective was clear, now all I needed to do was plan, rally, and wait. Like so often in the military, this was a "hurry up and wait."

Often there are no available helicopters or the weather won't allow helicopter use, so in these cases the response is ground based, with 4x4 teams being deployed in a staggered manner getting medically qualified climbing techs as close to the subject as possible. Like the risks of using helicopters as mission insertion methods, the Lake Como Road has been fatal historically. More specifically, many vehicles have rolled off the Jaws 2 ledge, which have resulted in people being ejected from the vehicle and killed. It is advisable that passengers disembark from vehicles while the driver carefully negotiates Jaws 2 especially.

The highly modified, personal SAR team members' vehicles designed to negotiate the potentially deadly obstacles slowed their average speeds to that of a fast hiker. In other words, it would take approximately three hours to get the teams formed, up the road, and to Lake Como even using our fastest, most highly qualified personnel and methods. From there, it would be another strenuous thirty minutes to an hour of hard, steep, scree and talus scrambling and then a near technical ridge traverse before being able to make contact with the subject.

In cases of teams being lifted in via helicopters, the helicopter could cut the three-hour 4x4 drive time from the trailhead to the highest landing zone (LZ) from three hours to approximately six minutes. Even taking an additional three hours to fuel up and reach our isolated trailhead LZ, the army Chinook would be able to respond, winch a rescuer to the subject, stabilize the patient, winch the rescuer and patient back to the aircraft, and be back to the command post and an ambulance all quicker than we could get personnel just to Lake Como in the same time. That being a fact, it's counterintuitive and a challenge for first responders and highly trained mountain rescuers to have to "standby."

AVSAR responders at the trailhead on standby during the Kevin Hayne rescue mission. One can see the Crestone Mountain Group in the background (author photo).

As personnel began to respond to the command post at the Lake Como 4x4 road trailhead, I started a roster listing responders' names, times in, roles, notes, and eventual times out. This roster eventually became a minute-by-minute handwritten log of operations and radio communications. What follows in this story, I based on my copy of this log's transcription.

As people responded, I received a text from the captain aboard the inbound Chinook asking us to have a litter and medical equipment ready. I figured maybe a team of air force PJ's (pararescue special forces) would be flying in with the Chinook; I hoped they had crampons because even from the warm dusty desert valley floor, it looked icy and cold higher up.

I texted that we had the equipment ready, and I wondered who I'd be briefing about our Stokes litter filled with our expeditionary EMT packs. I told everyone to be prepared to stand by and watch as hopefully some military specialists took care of everything, and all we would need to do is stand by in case they needed response to a crash or some other contingency. As the AVSAR team volunteers continued to respond en masse, I put on some sunblock and felt content pondering the possibility of none of us AVSAR personnel even deploying. The response to Kevin Hayne would put few folks at risk, and it would be over before sunset.

A few minutes later, the captain texted back that he wanted five ground personnel to go with the litter as attendants.

Damn. In one short text, my expectations of keeping my teammates out of harm's way were extinguished. I replied for clarification—I thought there was a response crew already onboard, and we were providing support?

Negative, Chinook has just a flight crew, no ground crew. AVSAR will need to provide five personnel for the medical response.

Well, I guess we'd have to be our own special forces team. Time to adapt, improvise, and overcome. I told everyone AVSAR would be providing the medical responders, and I asked all the members present who were up to it, qualified medically and technically, and who possessed crampons and ice axes to grab their gear and get ready to deploy into the field. "You guys should feel honored, these Chinook's are what the special forces guys like SEALs and Rangers ride into battle. A Chinook is like the Cadillac of helicopters—big, smooth, powerful."

Out of a group of forty of southern Colorado's most courageous expeditionary medical SAR responders, these five AVSAR volunteers got prioritized to get aboard the giant helicopter (ultimately it was the crampons and axes that filtered the pool of candidates to just a few alpinists): 1. Mick Daniel, an experienced Wilderness First Responder (WFR), local university outdoor program instructor, and professional mountain guide; 2. Mike Henderson, a WFR and proven mountaineering partner of Mick's; 3. George Rapoza, a WFR, local mountaineer, and team vice president; 4. Jess Caton, former team president, local mountaineer, hunter, backcountry enthusiast extraordinaire (a "mule" capable of hauling immense amounts of medical equipment at altitude quickly); and 5. Mark Martinez, a WFR and young stud/"mule" who could provide the strength along with Jess to move powerfully and single-handedly a patient in emergencies.

Around this time another AVSAR leader, the "second in command" acting as the operations manager, John Gilmore, an off-duty senior paramedic with Flight For Life out of Pueblo, began chatting on his radio with the inbound FFL Lifeguard Four helicopter pilot, Dale Geanetta. "Lifeguard Four, I'm at your ten o'clock about three miles out."

"That's affirmative, I've got a visual."

I was happy that John was acting as ground eyes for Dale, a colleague who he often flew with on duty. The camaraderie and trust of small elite teams is an asset beyond value. Seeing the orange A Star ambulance making a beeline to our sandy, rabbit brushed LZ gave me a sense of comfort.

At the same time, the Chinook pilot gave me the heads up text that he was now just twenty minutes out, and soon I should be able to hear and see him. I passed along to the team that the pilot wanted everyone in their climbing harnesses for a possible hoist operation. I grabbed Chris Lavery, one of the team's young leaders, and told him to meet me out in the field to help land the inbound Chinook. Mick walked up to me and gently offered a protest, "I don't think we can do this without you." He looked serious.

I prompted him for more, "What are you talking about Mick?"

"Well, we're headed into a technical environment to provide medical aid to a highly traumatized patient, or more likely to recover a deceased subject, we're getting a lift from a bunch of hardcore military guys ... frankly, I'd just feel more comfortable if you were going into the field with us." I nodded my understanding and wondered if passing incident command to the operations manager would be what was best for the entire team. Would such a move help us safely attain our objective, or would it potentially make things worse?

Mick and I conferred with John Gilmore. "John, you mind if I pass over incident command to you and jump on this Chinook to act as a field lead? The guys on the response team want a vet like me with 'em who can speak G.I. Joe."

"Yup, I've got this." I handed the roster over to John and nodded, "I'll be right back."

I walked over to Mark Martinez, a young athletic rising star who had taken my Intro to SAR course at the college, had gone on to be a student assistant in the course, and then had risen quickly in the ranks of AVSAR. He was dutifully going over his gear, and I could tell he was disappointed as I explained that I was going to take his place on the ground team. I told him the truth that I would have preferred it were him, but with the complexity of the situation, his place would now be on the contingent team.

With some all-around nods reinforcing an understanding of the changes, I ran toward Chris who was posted about a hundred yards out away from all the vehicles. His bright fluorescent orange jacket stood out from the background exactly as it was designed, and he made an excellent LZ marker. As I jogged up to Chris, I could hear the distant, deep, heavy thumping of giant military rotors beating the air.

As it slowly came into view, the Chinook was even larger than I remembered. Like all field helicopter landings, the pilots circled the landing zone several times, spiraling in their proximity every circle. By the last circling, one could easily make out crew members in the various windows and doors of the helicopter. Chris did as I instructed and held his arms up in an easily visible "Y" indicating to the pilot that everything was okay to land. As the

Chinook helicopter landing at the Lake Como trailhead landing zone June 15, 2010 (photo by John Gilmore).

massive helicopter's ground effects came into play and the leading edge of the air cushion hit us, I took cover behind Chris, avoiding the pea-sized rocks and debris. As soon as the wheels touched down, I patted Chris on the shoulder, "Outstanding job," and I jogged back to the four members of the team huddled and ready to board. I put on my harness, lifted my pack, and was the last of the five of us to walk toward the massive helicopter. We were doing a "hot load," meaning we were getting aboard the helicopter without stopping its rotors. We all innately ducked as the massive rotors circled overhead.

Approaching the rear-loading ramp of a Chinook helicopter is an intimidating, loud, obnoxious experience. The Chinook is enormous, and the scale of the fuselage and loading ramp seem more like the back of a C-130 cargo plane than a helicopter. The screaming whine of the twin turbines is literally deafening; not only is all other sound completely lost in the high-pitched roar, the volume is so great that it physically hurts the ears. The rotors swooping overhead, as well as the rotors' shadows, have an effect not too unlike being a small rodent under a giant raptor's ensnaring talons. The smell of jet fuel and its exhaust flashed me back to my time in the military; it was a good visceral reminder of the risks of aircraft and their potential crashes. I was the last AVSAR member to board the craft, so I followed my crew up the ramp where we were split into two groups: George and Jess sat on the left side of the craft, Mick, Mike, and I sat on the right.

Two crewmen dressed in flame retardant Nomex uniforms and helmets boarded the aircraft, and one raised the ramp. As the turbines wound up to an even higher, less bearable pitch, I noticed in between George and I was a four by four foot open square hole in the floor through which I could see the native grasses of the San Luis Valley. Suddenly it made sense why the two boarding crewmen attached themselves via whole body harnesses and carabiners to webbing leashes. It also made sense why, as they came and sat next to us, they emphasized secure seatbelts. Like very succinct, nonverbal stewards of a military airline, they indicated tight secure belts as well as stowing our packs under our seats, seats that were nothing more than canvas stretched over a metal pipe frame bolted to the aircraft wall.

Inside the Chinook there was a lot of space. I thought it similar to the size and dimensions of a bus, though one can usually hear on a bus. As the turbines reached a full crescendo of sound, the rotors changed angle, and we slowly began to roll forward. We accelerated on the grass for a bit, taxiing horizontally like a plane, and then unable to tell the difference between the wheels bumping along the ground and the shudder of the engines and rotors, we lifted from the earth. I knew when we went airborne—the four-foot hole in the middle of the aircraft's floor suddenly became a window.

As the Chinook banked and ascended, the horizon vanished from the rear view, and from my perspective I could see the command post twisting and disappearing. After we leveled off a bit and started our approach to Little Bear, my attention turned to our objective: Kevin Hayne.

I had been given exact GPS coordinates from Deputy Chacon regarding Kevin's location. I also knew where he was from a detailed description given to me by Travis, Kevin's hiking partner. In this search and rescue mission, there would be little searching; I knew where to expect Kevin; this was a rescue, at this point most likely a recovery.

The helicopter was very powerful and quickly entered the gorge containing Little Bear Lake, above and at the headwall of where Kevin was. As we neared the head of the gorge, the crewman next to me screamed at the top of his lungs just a few inches from my ear that the pilot was going to fly around the peak to do a "powercheck." I was happy that the pilots were going to get familiar with the current air density, their current load, the current weather dynamics, etc. I screamed back inquiring about, "Insertion? How?" The crewman motioned at my harness and the hoist poised above the four-foot hole. At the moment, the hole was simply a portal to thousands of feet of air. The crewman tapped my helmet and did the military hand signal to be on watch for our subject.

Photo taken by author with cell phone while on board the Chinook searching for Kevin Hayne, June 15, 2010.

As we circled the peaks of Little Bear and Blanca, we hit a couple pockets of turbulence that resulted in stomach-lurching drops. It seemed a little unexpected that any winds would be affecting us. Being pushed around by wind wouldn't be desired as a crewman hoisted us to the talus below. I briefly turned my attention from the small bubble portal window I was using to observe the peak and I saw Jess Caton, my friend and teammate, unbuckled, kneeling in his chair, excited as a school boy, peering out his bubble, just feet from the four-foot portal to the void.

I motioned to get Jess' attention. George finally tapped him and pointed in my direction. Everyone in the back of the aircraft, army and AVSAR personnel both, watched as I threw my hands in the air and mouthed, "WHAT THE FUCK?!"

I motioned for Jess to sit down and buckle his seatbelt. I pointed at "the hole" and motioned my hand across my throat. With everyone watching, Jess rolled his eyes, shrugged off my concern (I think he mouthed back something about me not being his mother), but he sat and buckled his seatbelt.

As we circled the peak closer, we came around the west face of Little Bear Peak from the north. As we passed to the side of the Hourglass Couloir, I saw a tiny red dot, farther below than where I expected to see it. I pointed it out to the crewman sitting next to me, and I mouthed "Kevin's helmet," and I pointed at my red helmet. I watched as the crewman keyed his mic to the pilot, and the aircraft changed its vector, so we slowly closed the distance between us and the red dot.

Knowing we were closing in on our target, my heart rate increased and time began to slow. In slow motion, the red dot slowly resolved to be Kevin Hayne's helmet, still fastened to his head. He was head down the slope, arms out, and he appeared motionless, but we were too distant to know anything.

At our closest proximity, Kevin's skin color did not indicate life to me, he looked too pale, but there also weren't any absolute signs of death, such as skin discoloration from blood pooling. As we were all watching Kevin intently, surprisingly to those of us without any communication (all the AVSAR personnel), the helicopter started moving away from Kevin's position. I motioned to the crewman next to me, and he screamed that one of the aircrew saw one of Kevin's arms move. I wondered if it was an effect of the rotor wash and mountain winds. Either way, it was impossible to tell from the hovering aircraft. We had to get to Kevin on foot. I would be the first out, and I eyed the hoist with scrutiny.

I looked down and triple checked my harness. Nothing appealed to me about hanging from a tiny steel cable, being lowered onto a 40-degree talus slope, being set up potentially to become an anchor between the earth and a 25,000-pound aircraft. I started mentally focusing on detaching from that cable as soon as I could.

Suddenly a crewman motioned at the hoist and shook his head no. He motioned at the rear ramp and used his hand to communicate that the pilot was going to back the aircraft up to the top of a cliff ledge and let us simply "walk off" the back ramp. This protocol was being employed more and more in Afghanistan by special forces, a method called the Pinnacle maneuver, in which troops are delivered directly (rather than by rope) to the top of a building or mountain top. My mind went from being focused on the hoist to the edge of the ramp. The edge of the ramp that was now slowly approaching the top of a cliff ledge as the Chinook pilots gingerly inched the aircraft backward, like bus drivers backing up a Greyhound.

I had heard about the Pinnacle maneuver, but I hadn't been part of any mission, military or SAR, which had executed one as part of an insertion. I mentally thought about what I should focus on in the next couple steps of the maneuver. As we inched our way backward, the distance between the rotors and the mountain slope became an acutely small space. The crewmen approached the ramp, and on their knees they looked out keying their mics and communicating with the pilots the proximity of the rotor blades to the slope. I knew my job would be to get off the ramp first, and then stand at that spot and direct the SAR personnel sideways, along the top of the cliff, so they wouldn't accidentally ascend straight up the slope into the rotor disk and "burger" what was in their helmets. We would need to disembark quickly to be safe—"safe" being a relative term.

The pilots took a long time hovering and backing up the Chinook, but I figured docking such a massive aircraft with such a small target at 13,000 feet, in reverse, probably rivaled international space station docking skills, so like the aircrew, I focused all my attention on the decreasing distance between the rotor disk and the mountain side. As the edge of the ramp finally contacted the top of the cliff, it appeared to me that the rotor disk was within inches of rock.

As I leaned forward and prepared to unbuckle my seatbelt, getting ready for the signal from the crewman to disembark, I had a powerful intuition wash over me—something was very wrong. Looking around at the crew, I made an assessment of my feelings: I motioned a question to the AVSAR crew—thumbs up or thumbs down. Mick must have been sensing the same negative intuition I was because he almost instantly shook his head no, and clearly mouthed, "FUCK THIS." I began to reach down to tug at the leash of the crewman next to me. I was content thinking "Abort, abort ..." and just then, a chinook wind hit the helicopter's nose and it rose up.

Ironically, one of the definitions of a chinook is a warm, dry wind that descends the eastern slopes of the Rocky Mountains. The same winds that had knocked the aircraft around as we power-checked the air density created a current of warm air that blew up the cliff face over which we hovered, pivoting the nose upward causing the rear rotor blades to seesaw into the mountain.

In an instant, the fuselage filled with fine dust and debris, and the helicopter began to shake violently. Like a movie scene plane crash, I could clearly hear the warning klaxons sounding from the cockpit.

The two crewmen instinctively turned and, like climbing a rope, hand-over-hand followed their leashes back to their seats and buckled their seatbelts; as they did this, I looked around at my teammates' faces. Like me, it took them a bit to recognize what was happening. In the fraction of that second that felt forever, Jess screamed, "IS THIS REAL?"

I couldn't believe it either, but I nodded an affirmative and looked over at Mick and Mike sitting next to me. I motioned and modeled the "crash position" by tucking my torso downward onto my lap; as my Vietnam combat vet dad would say (he had survived a helicopter crash in Vietnam), this was the position of bending over and kissing your butt goodbye.

I tucked my head as deep into my knees as I could. I looked at the metal pipe framing of our seats, being held to the aircraft by small machine bolts; I wondered how little force it would require to snap the bolts. I also noticed my pack, as well as Mick's and Mike's, underneath our seats, packed efficiently, ice axe and crampons strapped to the exterior. I pictured the recent media footage of a Blackhawk helicopter crash on Mount Hood, but we weren't over snow. We were over a massive cliff at the base of which was a high-angle talus slope. I pictured us rotating into the cliff, crashing and falling to the base of it, and then rolling down the talus slope. I thought of rolling in the fuselage, our bodies being punctured by our ice axes and crampons, and I thought about burning. For a few seconds, which under the circumstance felt like much longer, I waited for an already violent scene to escalate.

The aircraft was vibrating like a massive jackhammer, but I could sense we were in a very fast descent, probably out of control. We were obviously going to crash. For the second time in my life, I expected to die. Like the first time, I had a deep, content sense of gratitude for my existence, and simultaneously I felt regret for the effect of my death on my loved ones. I lifted my head to reposition my chin and I observed George and Jess. George was angrily screaming, "I'm never going to see my son again!"

Jess was laughing hysterically; he looked like he was in disbelief and like George, his face had a hint of anger at the situation. An aircraft crash was about to rob us of the rest of our lives. I tucked my head back into my lap. The crewman next to me turned and in a hug-like shield he covered my body with his.

In the embrace of the crewman, I recognized the soldier was providing cover for me. I was wearing insulating mountaineering clothing made with polyester fiber fleece and nylon. The crewman was wearing a Nomex flight suit, material designed for pilots and aircrew, fire resistant and specifically designed for fiery crashes. In an extreme demonstration of compassion, he was shielding my life with his. I was extremely comforted by the act and of dying in the embrace of another, even if it were a complete stranger.

As the helicopter shook, I could sense the rock walls passing by the windows, and our ground speed was rapid. With the taste of the disintegrated rotors and granitic powder filling my nose and throat, I was riding a wildly bucking horse, most likely into a fiery hell. At least I would burn in the embrace of a fellow, compassionate human being. I didn't even know his name, but he was the hero who stands with you in the battle for life, even during the battle in which you're both going to lose.

Years previously I had nearly died in a crevasse incident on Mount Rainier, and for several seconds after one teammate had punched through a snowbridge, I helplessly watched the second on rope be pulled toward the lip of the void. As he slid toward the darkness, I knew there would be no way I could arrest both of my teammates. In that moment facing death, I was hit by a sensation of emotion—it wasn't fear or sadness at all, it was pure gratitude. I felt an *extreme* amount of gratitude toward the universe. And then very surprisingly, my partner arrested on the edge of the void. In a split second, I went from being deeply grateful for my entire existence to being shocked that we lived.

I envisioned us hitting and rolling like a room-sized tumble dryer. I figured at impact or while rolling, the fuel tanks, basically rubber bladders tucked into the fuselage all around us, would burst, splashing and saturating the aircraft and its contents with jet fuel until a spark from the electrical system or heat from the turbines ignited the vapor. From my service in the air force I knew all too well the outcome of such burn victims. I looked at the aircraft floor and I wondered how long I would be conscious. I thought of my fellow rescuer, shielding me as best he could; I thought that maybe my body would save his if we impacted hard and I absorbed energy from below. As I believed my last conscious moments were occurring, I became hyper-focused. Time seemed to slow to a stop.

I thought of my family and I hoped they would understand my desire to help others, and I prayed, "Please let it go black. Please just let it go black. Please let it go black," With that, I relaxed and released, and I awaited the inevitable.

I was expecting a massive explosion to envelop me in an instant, but instead I experienced a sudden and violent force from below. My knees and thighs slammed into my chest with a force that took my breath away. I realized we had impacted something, we were still conscious, and we were not burning alive. How was this possible!

In the fraction of the second that it took me to comprehend what was happening, Mick and Jess had already unbuckled their seatbelts, stood up, and looked as if they were about to bolt out the back ramp. I knew that Chinook engines would often flare out after such an impact, so I knew we had to wait to bail out. The crewman that had been protecting me simultaneously stood with me, we both held up our hands, and we stopped them from exiting out the back. Over the high-pitched scream of the turbines, the crewman yelled and motioned to everyone that we would wait for the pilot's order to abandon the aircraft. He yelled that the pilots were radioing our location and status before the radio cut out. The two rear crewmen grabbed fire extinguishers and began emergency shutdown procedures.

Jess yelled, "I want off this helicopter!" Mick was nodding enthusiastically in affirmation.

I reinforced the crewman's order, "Just wait for the signal from the pilot!" I could tell that soon there'd be nothing I could do to stop Jess from leaving. The five of us AVSAR crew visually assessed each other, and I grabbed my pack readying to disembark from the Chinook asap.

In about thirty seconds, the lead crewman motioned for us to exit via the rear ramp. We wasted no time and with the turbines still whining we bailed off the rear ramp into a flat, grassy marsh. As we walked away, upslope from the Chinook, I took in our location.

Miraculously, the pilots had managed to continue controlling the aircraft and hard land us in an extremely small, flat, grassy marsh at the head of Little Bear Lake at the floor of the gorge. Not a pilot, I didn't know the details, but it seemed amazing that the rear rotors had impacted the mountain around 13,100 feet elevation, and a horizontal half mile away, we hard landed at about 12,100 feet. Intuitively, that glide slope seemed impossible, especially considering the mountain had shredded the rear rotors, literally. The tips of the blades were all short several feet, and all ended with a hairy, frayed look; one blade was broken off where it attached to the rotor shaft. The aircraft's fuselage was crumpled—torqued and bent like a banana (as the army recovered the aircraft they found a large boulder beneath the center of the helicopter, causing its ends to "wrap" and twist around the boulder). The bottom of the aircraft had done what it was designed to do—crumple. One of the massive rear wheels was completely separated from the aircraft and sitting in the marsh several feet from the helicopter.

Us five AVSAR crew ran uphill to a snowfield positioned north and above the helicopter, while the four rear crewmen ran with us but rallied just a bit west of our position. As they gathered, all the army guys started screaming and jumping up and down, "WE'RE ALIVE! Hoo yah!"

Jess was equally enthusiastic to get away from the helicopter, "Let's get the hell out of here. I want as far away from that chopper as I can get." I agreed, but I explained we had to wait for the pilots to shut down the turbines, find out what their plan was, and I wanted everyone to take some time to let autonomic stress responses decrease (in case any of us were injured and the adrenaline was hiding our symptoms).

Chief Warrant Officer David Carter immediately following the Chinook's hard landing on Little Bear Peak, June 15, 2010 (author photo).

The shredded rear rotor of the Chinook following the June 15, 2010, hard landing (author photo).

Mick agreed with Jess, "We should be dead, and we still need to get to that kid, who most likely has passed. Let's climb that face, make contact with the subject, and hike out."

I agreed and explained my reasoning for waiting thirty minutes to assess for injuries and readiness to continue the mission.

Mick hesitantly nodded in agreement. I asked the AVSAR guys to try and calm themselves down and pay attention to any indications of pain or injury. As the deafening whine of the turbines finally began winding down, I told the crew that I was going to speak with the pilots and figure out our next action.

I walked back toward the aircraft as the pilots jumped out. One made a satellite phone call, presumably to a supervisor to pass along the news that we had just demolished a $32 million aircraft.

I automatically began taking digital pictures of the aircraft as I walked around it and made contact with the pilots. The first thing out of my mouth I wanted to ensure was gratitude for their skills. "Gentlemen, I'll be naming my first born for you two. Thank you."

One of the pilots, an older chief warrant officer, CWO David Carter, re-plied, "Don't thank us. That was all about a higher power. I don't know ex-actly how we made it."

I responded, "Well, one of us is going to have a grandkid who's going to win the Nobel Prize in the future." This was a joke poking fun at a mystical reason why we would be alive after something that should have killed us. My joke made the pilots smile, and we chatted about our next steps. They ex-plained that two Blackhawk helicopters were already inbound to evacuate us all, as well as leave a security detail at the Chinook until it could be recovered.

That would mean we'd have to jeep in via the Lake Como road the next day and climb Little Bear Peak's west ridge from the canyon to the north of our present spot. I thought about how nice it would be to get on a Blackhawk and head back to the command post, but I knew that wouldn't be the case. I responded that we appreciated the offer for the lift out, but that we still wanted to get to the subject as soon as possible. Although so remote it was virtually impossible, I had not yet verified Kevin's death, so I had to assume a very slight possibility that Kevin was still alive.

Both Captain Rota and CWO Carter understood. Carter was very re-spectful, "You guys have my respect. After what we've been through, to be headed back up there with the temperatures dropping, it's an honor to be working with you. Good luck."

"It's an honor to be working with you. Thanks for the lift in, and sorry for this," I said, motioning to the helicopter and mountain. "Be safe."

Deep in the gorge, out of sight of any cell towers or radio repeaters, I tried the sheriff's radio to no avail. I found the same with the cell phone. I was able to get out a couple texts that briefly explained the situation and plan. In addition to getting a text out to one of the AVSAR leaders at the command post, I also sent a brief message to my parents, the people I knew who would be most affected if they heard via the media that there was a crash in my county during a rescue.

As I couldn't get a voice call out and the phone was continuing to use up power as it roamed for service, I turned off my cell to conserve my battery for potential emergency use later. I would later learn that my parents had received my text, but upon sending replies never got word again, so I had only lessened their worries, not vanquished them altogether.

I returned to my guys and quickly assessed them for any serious injuries. Mick described pain in his chest, especially when he breathed deeply, but after some palpation, I figured he had bruised his sternum from the sudden impact. As we gathered our packs, medical equipment, and the Stokes litter, an army crewman yelled, "Hey, there's movement up there. Near the subject!"

Sure enough, we looked up and were surprised to see, especially this late in the evening right before sunset, a lone individual slowly traversing the ridge making his way to Kevin's location.

"Oh damn. We're going to have to get up there in a hurry. Whoever that is up there, they're alone. They won't be in any position to provide any treatment, and if Kevin's passed, I'm not comfortable with some lone civilian in proximity to his body. Let's make this ascent stat." We divided up the team gear, decided upon our route up Little Bear's west face, and began our ascent from the crash site.

As we walked away, one of the army crew spoke, "Damn if y'all aren't hardcore. It's going to be rough," he paused, and looked me in the eye, "We'll see y'all when you get back to the command post."

"Thanks. You guys have a safe flight back. We'll see you soon," I said, and as the army personnel continued to scan the cliffs above, the five of us set out.

The west face of Little Bear Peak is fundamentally a 2,000-foot slope, angled between 30 degrees and dead vertical cliff bands scattered between the gorge's floor and Little Bear's summit. Although it is very dangerous third and fourth class terrain because of the slope angle and continuous rock fall, for the five of us experienced rescue mountaineers, the face was terrain we could negotiate off belay.

As was the plan, even loaded down with his pack, some medical gear, and the entire Stokes litter (broken down into two segments), Jess was off like an Arabian thoroughbred mountain goat hybrid, quickly putting distance between himself and the rest of us. Within a line of sight of each other, Mick and Mike teamed up and ascended beneath Jess, and George and I teamed and followed last.

I watched Jess quickly pull ahead of us as I also watched the person up near Kevin make contact with the subject. The individual was so far away I couldn't tell what color he or she was wearing, but I could tell the tiny moving figure made its way to Kevin's location, stayed near Kevin without moving for several minutes, and then they slowly started descending toward us. Without too much deduction, I figured this indicated Kevin was no longer alive.

About half way between the Chinook and the subject, George and I paused for a break. Almost on cue, a Blackhawk flew into the valley from the west. Far below us, the Blackhawk landed near the Chinook and it began to shuttle away personnel. At the time, we couldn't understand why, as we continued to climb the face, that the Blackhawk made several runs. Later we learned that the air's density was so low, even the army's most powerful Blackhawks could only pick up a few people at a time, otherwise there wasn't enough lift to be effective.

As we got closer to the subject's ledge system, I watched Jess ascend the canyon's encircling cliff band to the right of where the lone hiker was descending it, so unfortunately, Jess would not be able to make contact with the descending hiker. Below Jess, Mick and Mike were also not on a line that could intercept the descending individual. George and I changed our course to intercept, and at the base of the canyon's cliff band, we met up with the lone hiker.

From my field notes, it was 7:23 p.m. when I contacted a young male named Warren, from Denver, who was visiting the area to climb Little Bear Peak. Although Warren looked like he had been crying, very weary, almost in shock, I wasted no time in acquiring vital information about the subject.

"Warren, I just watched you make contact with a subject we're trying to reach. Can you tell me his status?" At first Warren could barely speak. He had difficulty making eye contact, and he seemed disoriented. "Warren, can you tell me if the subject, up there, was alive?"

"I'm …" Warren paused for a long time. "I'm pretty sure he was dead."

"Pretty sure? What do you mean? How do you believe that he's dead? I need to know for sure Warren. I need to call this into the sheriff so we can adapt our plan and either put more or fewer people at risk." Warren just stared blankly at me. "Warren, you okay? What's up?"

"How many people are dead on the helicopter?"

"What? What do you mean? No one's dead on the helicopter. We're all okay."

"I saw the crash. I was up in the notch on the ridge above Lake Como. I videotaped the crash using my digital camera."

What? From my experience in the military and working with law enforcement investigators, I knew that video would come in very handy for the FAA's and military's investigations of the crash. "Warren, would you mind showing me that video? There's no one dead from the crash. We're all okay, and as you can see the military personnel are being shuttled out now." My statement seemed to bring Warren back from his thousand-yard stare.

"Yes. Here it is." Warren pushed a couple camera buttons and on the tiny screen I watched our Chinook's rotor blades disintegrate. Warren shot the video from the ridge west of us, above the cliff where the Chinook was trying to insert us. It was surreal to watch the Chinook slowly back up to the ledge, and then sit hovering for a few seconds, until suddenly the nose lurched upward, and the rotors made contact with the slope. In the video, I could see chunks of rotor and rock being thrown hundreds of feet from the cliff top. Instantly, the helicopter lurched off the lip of the cliff and began a nosedive down into the gorge. Then the video abruptly ended. "I'm sorry, the camera only takes one minute video clips. That clip just happened to end right there."

"No worries. This is an outstanding video, Warren. The army and FAA investigators are going to be very interested in this. It can help them prevent something similar in the future. Would you mind if I took the memory card from you and provided it to investigators? They'll return it to you as soon as they've copied it."

"Sure," and Warren turned off the camera and handed me the small memory card.

"Thanks. This will help keep people safe in the future. Now I need to call in our status to the sheriff. Can you please tell me why you believe the subject is deceased." I watched as Warren's expression went blank again and the thousand-yard stare returned.

"I know he's dead."

"Yes. I just have to make sure. Can you tell me why you believe he's dead?"

"You'll see when you reach him."

"Okay, Warren I believe you. Just a quick question, did you touch the subject?"

"Yes, but only to put pieces of the rotor under him."

"What? You put broken helicopter pieces underneath him?" He looked up at me, and for the first time made sustained eye contact. He looked confused and sad. I knew his response indicated that he was in a lot more psychological shock than he initially let on. I figured he was projecting what his mind was processing, what he had seen, not what he had done.

"Warren. Was the subject warm?" This question helped break through Warren's fog, and he slowly shook his head back and forth, "No, no, he's no longer warm."

"Okay Warren, here's what needs to happen. We still need to make contact with the subject, so we're going to continue climbing. It's sunset, and you're solo, in shock, and near 13,000 feet in a very isolated area of wilderness. All of southern Colorado's search and rescue resources are focused on what's already happening. If anything happens to you, there will be no personnel available to help. You cannot have an accident because you will be on your own. As soon as we process the scene up there, we're headed out hiking back to the command post, and I'd like you to accompany us."

Warren shook his head no. "No. There's NO way I can go back up there. It's horrific. I CANNOT go back up there."

"Warren, where else are you going to go?"

"Down. I'll bushwhack out of here if I have to. I'm not going back up THERE."

For a few seconds, I reasoned through Warren's and my options. "Okay Warren, I don't have the energy or the will to convince you otherwise, but you're in a bit of a predicament here. If you won't go back up with us, then your option is to continue descending into the gorge. That'll put you around the crash site at dark. Camp there, but don't get too close to the site, as a security detail is there and won't take kindly to you surprising their position or requesting help. In the morning, you can decide to walk out of here via the Little Bear Lake gorge, which will take you a very long day or two of bushwhacking, and because it's isolated, if you vanish down in that gorge, you'll likely never be found. On the other hand, I suggest you ascend the ridge, and avoid becoming involved with the security detail. You got this Warren?"

Upon hearing the news that he wouldn't have to expose himself to the scene again, Warren seemed extremely relieved, and much of his shock sloughed away, "Yes. Tomorrow, I'll hike back out over the ridge to the Lake Como road. Thank you."

"Be careful. I'm not exaggerating when I say there will be NO ONE available for search and rescue for several days." Warren nodded, and he continued his descent. I would have rather he simply stayed with us, but at least I could keep a visual on his movement within the gorge until morning.

After Warren was out of earshot, I keyed the sheriff's radio and communicated that the subject was a "Code Frank"—a sheriff's radio code for a fatality. This would change the whole mission's tone, from that of a time-dependent rush to get to the subject, including taking bigger risks "so that others may live," to that of a non-time-dependent recovery, taking far less risk with SAR personnel. No body recovery is worth SAR personnel risking their lives or serious injury.

I thought of Kevin's mom, who I had spoken to just hours before while still on ASU's campus. I thought of Kevin's climbing partner, Travis. I imagined all of Kevin's family and friends, and I was saddened thinking of them receiving the official news. At least the dozens of SAR personnel responding from all over the state would slow their response times and be safer.

Because of our different line of ascent, George and I had to traverse a snowfield, but this late after the whole day's insolation and heating, the snow was loose, and our legs easily popped through the thin layers of water ice within the snowpack, giving us secure footholds without running the risk of falling and requiring a self-arrest. I looked up the slope at the position of Kevin's body and I mentally mapped the area in case in the morning the snow returned to water–ice-like hardness on its surface. It would behoove us techs to know which route off the face would entail as little exposure as possible. As I scanned the face, I watched Jess, now about twenty minutes ahead of George and I, reach Kevin's position. Not knowing that I had already made the radio call informing the sheriff of the Code Frank, Jess verified what George and I already knew by crossing his arms in an "X" over his head. George and I continued slowly ascending.

As we got higher and closer to our objective, the slope steepened further, and the snow and ice became more of a challenge. From the command post's communication log, at 1854 hours "Search One" (me) contacted "Base" (the command post) and communicated that we were crossing low-angle technical terrain (this is terrain that requires litters and patients to be on a roped belay, but isn't dead vertical, and the litter attendants may not have to be on belay to operate safely). The angle of the terrain is also reflected by my request at that time to have a medevac ready if necessary for any of the SAR responders. I also communicated that if medevac became necessary, at that elevation the winds were too high for anything but a ground evac.

Four minutes later, at 1858 hours, I radioed that all five AVSAR members were at the location of the subject. We now faced a major body recovery operation with limited personnel, so at 1903 hours, I requested the help of all available Colorado SAR teams through COSAR (the organization made up of all the SAR teams in the state, who when necessary coordinate mutual aid missions—missions that require the aid of other SAR teams or other external organizations). Unlike in too many Hollywood films, moving a body over technical terrain takes many highly trained technicians. Had Kevin survived, the five of us could have potentially stabilized Kevin's condition until the rest of the team responded, but it would take many of southern

Colorado's SAR volunteers to move Kevin's body out of such isolated, technical terrain.

As George and I finally reached Kevin's location, Jess, Mick, and Mike were already sitting down, packs off, donning more layers and preparing headlamps. All three were watching down the valley as the last of the Blackhawk rescue sorties flew away from the Chinook site. I was relieved to see that Warren, even in his shock, had successfully descended almost to the hard landing site and was erecting a tent nearby. As I watched the last Blackhawk flight descend the gorge, I also took off my backpack and put on a couple more layers. In addition to no longer building heat from the hard labor of ascent, the evening winds were picking up and the temperature was dropping quickly.

After preparing for the oncoming cold, I took out my digital camera and GPS, and I began the difficult task of documenting the details of the fatal scene. I started by carefully taking pictures of Kevin's body from far out—about thirty to forty feet from the subject. If possible, and it was possible in this case, an investigator will take pictures of the subject from 360 degrees, usually from the four cardinal compass directions (at a minimum). Then one moves in for close photographic documentation. This includes taking overlapping pictures from all sides, as well as close-up shots of injuries to the subject's body, photos of any of the subject's equipment, of detached clothing or tissue—spots with blood or tissue above the subject's final resting position usually indicating a major impact.

In the far-out photos I tried to capture Kevin's position in relation to the bigger scene. On the near 40-degree slope, beneath the Hourglass Couloir, there were three snowfields, one above the other, each with a small rock band between them. Below the third snowfield, a hundred-foot cliff, then another snowfield that went nearly to the cirque at the bottom of the gorge.

Kevin's body was located approximately two hundred vertical feet below the base of the Hourglass Couloir in the rock band between the second and third snowfield. Although the heat of the day had eradicated any trail Kevin left on the snowfield as he fell, there were many pieces of equipment that indicated his fall line. Kevin's fall ceased about half way through this rock band, head downhill. Kevin was on his back, chest up, head turned to the right. I could see that the forces involved in his fall were considerable—this was not uncommon for a several hundred-foot fall (I estimated his total vertical descent was around 500+ feet). His total distance traveled on the slope was the hypotenuse of the vertical and the horizontal distance, even longer than the approximate 500 vertical feet. From the positioning of Kevin's clothing, I knew he had begun spinning very fast, as the centripetal force of such movement had moved all his clothes to the ends of his body—his upper torso (under the arms) and his feet. I could see that Kevin's boxers had been put back in their proper position after the fall, as it was easy to match a blood pattern on his underwear with a significant abrasion to one of his thighs. I figured that this had been done by Travis or possibly Warren for the sake of Kevin's dignity.

Thinking of Travis here with Kevin earlier in the day, all by himself, my heart ached. The mountain had significantly abraded Kevin's body, including his hands, torso, and legs. He had evidence of profuse bleeding from his nose, mouth, one ear, and his eyes were swollen shut. Although the macabre scene indicated Kevin was alive long enough following his fall to incur swelling and such profuse bleeding, I also knew Kevin hadn't consciously suffered. Upon speaking with Travis earlier that day, he had said that after Kevin's fall, he had very quickly picked up speed, hit a rock wall, and ricocheted out of view down and out of the couloir. It was obvious that Kevin was not conscious at the time his body had stopped (the trauma to his head and neck indicated Kevin was near dead and unconscious when he finally reached this final resting spot). I imagined that Kevin was most likely knocked unconscious that first impact into the cliff alongside the couloir.

By the time I finished taking close-ups of all necessary evidence, the sun had set and it was nearly dark. At 1927 hours I radioed base and communicated that we were out of light and would have to finish processing the scene, ascending the fall line and documenting and recovering Kevin's gear and body in the morning. After waiting for necessary communication between the command post and the coroner, at 1950 hours, base replied, "Hunker down, resume in the morning."

The adrenaline from the last couple hours was finally wearing off, and I felt the first indication of fatigue setting in. I thought, *Good, now we can set up a bivouac for the night and rally our strength for the morning.* At 2015 hours, the sheriff radioed and communicated that I had permission to move Kevin's body in the morning, once the scene was properly processed. I figured in the morning that once we finished with the photography and diagramming, I would allow the en route "cavalry" to package and extract Kevin's body.

I began looking around for a nearby ledge under a small vertical cliff face. This would give us a bivouac site that would shield us from any middle of the night rock fall—it would give us a small pocket where granite projectiles would blow over our heads instead of into them. "You guys see any ledges that would make a good, secure bivouac for the night?"

That's when I noticed the look in Mike's eyes—he looked extraordinarily wasted. It occurred to me that since leaving the Chinook site, I hadn't heard Mike say a word. Now that I had explicitly indicated my intention to stay on scene and standby for the night, Mike's nonverbal communication made it clear he had no intention of doing the same. He looked at me as though he were sad for me, shook his head slowly back and forth indicating no. "You're going to stay here with the body? I'm not staying."

There was a part of me that felt similar, but I also felt that it was not safe to be moving around in that terrain at night, it would be much safer to be mobile in the light of day.

"Mike, it's dangerous as hell trying to egress in this terrain at night, and I have to finish processing the scene in the morning. I'm going to stay and I'd like at least one of you to stay with me, or at least one of you to go with Mike." I looked over at George, and I flashed back to the recent moment of crashing to the earth and George's thoughts of his son, Caleb. I felt a little nausea start creeping up my throat. "By our own agreed upon policies, none of us shall operate solo, but I figure it'll only take two of us in the morning to finish photographing. Only one person need stay with me. What are your opinions?"

Mick and Jess both looked relatively engaged still, and both seemed nonverbally indifferent to the choice. Jess spoke first, "I don't care either way. I can stay." I felt both Jess and Mick would be fine staying, but I thought it best that one of the two of them lead Mike and George away from Kevin, and Mike was used to mountaineering with Mick as a partner. It appeared to me that it would be best if Jess stayed with me, and Mick lead the group of three down to the command post. Also, Jess literally grew up playing in this mountain group and was an enthusiastic, regular big game hunter (more desensitized to very bloody, highly traumatized mammal bodies), and Mick, in addition to working at the university, was also a professional mountain guide and was used to looking out for fatigued clients who were nearing their limits.

Mick, one of the most compassionate, sensitive souls I'm blessed to call a friend, must have sensed what needed to happen, "Kev, we've talked about this before. I do this to rescue folks, and I understand the honor in recovering a loved one for their family, but recoveries are hard on me. I think we should all head down and allow the teams responding to us to take care of all this in the morning. I'd prefer to leave." I smiled and nodded.

"I understand and respect your opinion, Mick. You're looking out for us. You're a brother. I, however, feel responsible for getting this scene properly investigated and secure, and unlike you, I hate moving around this terrain in the dark. Will you head down with Mike and George?" I looked over at Jess, "You mind staying with me?" Mike looked at me as if I were crazy.

Jess replied, "Love to. I'm pretty tired and ready for a nap anyway. Do one of you have a sleeping bag I could borrow? Down at the command post I tossed mine out for the extra space for medical gear figuring we wouldn't be out overnight, that we'd be back to the LZ via helicopter by now." As Mick started digging out his sleeping bag for Jess, Mike came over and gave me a hug.

As Mick handed off the sleeping bag to Jess, I dug out the memory card I had acquired from Warren. I explained to Mick that he should hand it off to Sheriff Stong, who could then hand it to the military's investigators. He tucked the small disk into a secure pocket, and we wished each other luck.

As Mick, Mike, and George began traversing the west ridge, Jess and I sought out a secure ledge near Kevin's body. We knew that overnight temperatures would plummet below freezing, causing the slushy snow all around us to freeze solid, water-ice like, thus in the morning making the snowfields around us virtual bobsled runs. At that time, if we fell onto the steep ice-snow, we would quickly accelerate and be launched over the hundred-foot cliff just beneath our location. We jammed our ice axes deep into the wet, mossy mud and anchored ourselves to them with webbing swammy belts and short leashes. After feeling a bit more secure, we took off our boots, slipped into our sleeping bags, and watched as the three headlamps, making their way westerly away from us, disappeared.

My worst fear as a SAR lead was a serious injury or fatality of one of "my" SAR personnel while under my "command." I closed my eyes and said a short meditation wishing the three of them safe passage back to the command post. I figured it would take them all night to negotiate the risky, class three (with a couple class four moves) route back to treeline, and then hike out the 4x4 road to the command post.

The mission log indicates that at 2211 hours, base contacted Jess and I for a status check. We explained we were secure on a ledge just northwest of the subject. We agreed for the sake of saving radio power to skip the usual protocol—comm./status checks every couple hours until first thing in the morning when we were active again.

I turned the volume of the radio down so we could conserve the battery, but still listen to radio traffic overnight. As we settled in, the first real waves of freezing air surrounded us. The melt-out water all around us began slowing and freezing, and the thought of the snowfield just beneath our ledge freezing solid seemed to slowly increase the slope's pitch, its ominous presence, its liability. "Jess, if that snow right below us freezes up solid, and we accidentally fall onto it wrapped in these sleeping bags, we're dead the same as Kevin died this morning."

"Yeah. I've been thinking that same thing. Plus, look at how shallow our axes are in this mud. I wish the mud would freeze up. If we roll or fall, our axes will likely just pull out. Do you roll around a lot when you sleep?"

"No." After a pause and some consideration, I continued, "I think it best we avoid testing our anchors. We should probably not fall asleep, or at least take shifts staying awake letting the other one sleep lightly."

"Good idea."

With that, Jess and I sat back against the rock face and listened to a small stream of water trickle between us. Eventually Jess got out his smart phone, a relatively new technology that was a small touch screen computer. He joked, "I wonder if we've got service this high up?"

"We might. We do have a line of sight to the cell tower from up here."

"Well, I'll be damned. It just connected. Now I can get word out to Tish." Over the next few minutes, Jess typed out a message to his wife communicating what we'd just been through, and what we still faced. "Check this out. We're on the news—9News is reporting the National Guard has said a Chinook helicopter was involved in a hard landing trying to rescue a climber on Little Bear Peak."

"Hard landing, eh? I'd call it more of a CRASH, but I suppose in the air force we learned the difference was how much control the pilot had coming in. No control equals a crash, a little control equals a hard landing. Either way no matter what you call it, the mountain had totaled the thirty-two million dollar aircraft. They're going to have to bring in another Chinook to fly it out." Jess was half-listening, reading other news. "It's amazing to me that we can get updates from the media on the incident we're currently still involved in. Anything else interesting in the news?"

"The Broncos' contracts are being drawn. Demaryius Thomas just got offered a contract for an unknown amount. Estimates are between ten and fifteen million for five years."

"Are you kidding me? That sounds outrageous and ironic from this perspective. He gets ten million to play a game, and we're here sitting on this ledge, doing what we're doing as *volunteers*. Makes me think of all the volunteer firefighters here in the valley who go out in the middle of the night, night after night, so they can scrape folks out of car wrecks. Good thing Thomas is getting paid what he's worth," the last part emphasized in my thickest tone of sarcasm. "In a perfect world, you'd think it'd be different."

"This sure isn't a perfect world."

"Indeed." I looked over at Kevin's body, just discernable at the limit of my headlamp's beam, "Anything but perfect."

Over the next few hours, Jess and I vacillated between periods of meditative silence and telling jokes or engaging in other superficial conversation with the intent of keeping each other awake and mindful of our risky situation.

Around 0100 hours, we noticed an almost imperceptible strobe effect lighting up the entire atmosphere. The flashes slowly became more and more frequent, as well as more and more easily perceptible. Eventually, we could sense the far-away rumbling of thunder. I don't recall which one of us finally said it, but we both realized that a large, uncommon middle of the night thunderstorm was off to our east, on the other side of Little Bear Peak in the Wet Mountain Valley. A few wispy clouds ghoulishly floated over the ridge and summit above us.

"What kind of rain gear do you have, Jess? We may be in for a hell of a storm at thirteen thousand feet."

"I'm good, but it's not going to be comfortable."

"I'm not too comfortable anyway. My back's starting to seize up, and I'm just about soaked from the misty splashes of cold water dripping down this wall we're leaning on. You wet too?"

"Yeah. My bag's slowly soaking through. And I'm getting cold. It sure will be excellent to see the light of sunrise."

"It's only a few hours away now. It sure would be a blessing if this storm would miss us."

I imagined how amazing the first light of sunrise would be. I loved alpine starts, getting up and starting to hike before sunrise. I imagined the first rays of light illuminating our location, the moisture in our clothes steaming off, our bodies warming from the energy of photons. Having gone through many difficult situations in which I had been extremely cold and uncomfortable physically (I started my adult life as a "northern tier" security specialist with the U.S. Air Force), I had learned to cope with extreme cold, and in this situation, I meditatively remained in my imagination, putting far less emphasis on the cold, wet reality, and more on the imagined place of warmth in my mind.

An hour later, Jess and I were relieved as we perceived the distant thunder sound get farther and farther away until it totally vanished, and the strobes of light slowly decreased in intensity until they also vanished. From my midnight shifts in the military and working in a hospital in college, I knew the time between 0300 hours and sunrise would be the most challenging to stay awake.

We had heard several rockslides crash down the cliff faces about a half mile to our southeast, but between 0300 and 0400 hours, the rock fall became much larger and more frequent. On occasion, I could smell the burnt fireworks-like scent produced from the rocks as they smashed down the giant faces. In between slides, the silence was comforting.

Then I heard what sounded exactly like a horse whinny. Logically I knew there was no way there was a horse within miles of us. Maybe I was hallucinating. "Damn Jess, if I just didn't hear what sounded like a horse."

"You heard that too?" Jess was surprised, "What the hell was that?"

"I don't know, but it sure wasn't a horse."

"Sounded like one."

We both got silent and listened out into the darkness, the void, for any sound. All we heard was wind. We could hear its waves blowing around the cliff face and mountain.

I broke the silence. "I figure it was the acoustics of this gorge. I don't know how, but I'd bet a rockslide ended up sounding like a pony whinny. Pretty damn weird. It's just after three, just a couple more hours 'til first light."

"Thank God," Jess murmured almost imperceptibly. The long hours and cold were taking a toll. Jess and I were exhausted.

Even though we had very luckily avoided riding out a thunderstorm, at freezing temperatures in the middle of the night at 13,000 feet, we were both wet, cold challenged, fatigued, and our brains were starting to interpret sounds in creative ways. I was eager for warmth, my bed, security.

I was tired of such an insecure place.

I couldn't tell well how much time had passed, but in the midst of awaiting the first morning light I heard something, or someone, moving above us. I turned to Jess, "What is that? There's someone above us, on the summit of Little Bear? What the fuck?! This time of night."

Jess responded, "How is that possible? Who'd be climbing right now, here, in these conditions, having seen what's been going on below them? Maybe it's a bighorn or a goat?"

Then, I heard what confirmed my worst fear—the start of a massive rockslide and someone screaming, "FALLING!"

I screamed, "Jess, get up against the rock, the slide's going to pass next to us!" Through the sleeping bag, I pushed my feet against the edge of the ledge and tried to back myself against our small rock face for protection. As the slide got larger and closer, I could more clearly hear the falling climber screaming.

"FALLING! FALLING!" The climber was somehow still conscious for what seemed like hundreds of feet. How was that possible? It was such brutal, sharp, rock hard, deadly terrain. How could this be possible?! Two deaths on the same mission! As the slide began to rush past us, in the same location as Kevin Hayne's body, I thought I saw a body bouncing and cartwheeling down the ledges.

I felt frozen up against my tiny muddy ledge. I wondered about Kevin's body and the new fatality being washed down the rocky cliffs. I wondered what would be left of them at the base.

The feeling of powerlessness was overwhelming and terrifying. I saw a figure cartwheel past us. I could see the body was disfigured, limbs misshapen, face unrecognizable, and yet still conscious and screaming. I was frozen in terror.

Suddenly, the rockslide, the falling climber, the sound, the chaos, it all disappeared. All was black, and I was awakening on the ledge I had just been on in the chaos, but instead of the chaos, it was serene. I was on a small muddy ledge, Jess quietly, lightly sleeping next to me, stars lighting up the sky all around me.

I had awakened from the nightmare with a bit of startle. I was confused at first, although all the action in the nightmare had vanished, I had awakened from the dream, but it was still the same setting.

I turned on my headlamp, looked to my left about a hundred feet, and there at the limit of my beam was Kevin's body, in the exact same position as it had been when we sat down on the ledge hours prior.

I consciously tried to get control of my quickened breathing and reminded myself that the key to survival in such situations is maintaining a positive mental attitude, and not allowing emotions to hijack my reason.

The falling climber and rockslide had all been a figment of my imagination; however, my fear from an imagined tragedy quickly focused to our real world liabilities—falling asleep and the hardened, icy slope just beneath us. I turned to Jess, and as my labored breathing settled, I could hear Jess' deep, long respirations. He, too, had fallen asleep.

Gently, so I wouldn't startle him, I began in nearly a whisper, "Jess. Wake up. We've gotta stay awake. We're almost there."

Groggily, Jess came to, "Yeah, yeah. It's cold. What time is it?"

"I just woke up from a hell of a nightmare. My heart rate's about 150."

"Great place for a nightmare. What was it about?"

"Tell you about it some other time."

"Sounds good. What time is it? How much longer 'til light?"

"It's just about four. I'm guessing an hour, maybe hour and a half 'til first light."

"Thank God."

If I had been groggy and sleepy before, the nightmare had awakened me with such a force, I was now very awake. The adrenaline was being well distributed throughout my body, and I was grateful for it. I knew the biochemical high would keep me awake and safe until Jess and I were up and working to vacate the scene. The hardest memory from the nightmare to lose was the screams I had heard. Several times I turned on my headlamp and peered over at Kevin.

When one's sitting on the edge of the void, battling real-world risks as well as ghosts, it's a blessing to have a battle buddy, a war companion, a brother. Jess leaned over and said, "Kev, there's no one I would rather be sitting here with." I thought of Jess' wife Tish, and that you'd not wish for your spouse to be exposed to the level of risk Jess and I were battling.

"Jess, you are the most hardcore, bad ass mountain man I know, and I hope it never comes to it, but if we're facing the end of the world, you're the brother I'd want at my side." I couldn't see it because it was still too dark, but I sensed that Jess had the same grin on his face as I did. In the coldest, darkest time of the night, I was warmed by brotherhood.

Finally, the first ultraviolet of sunrise began illuminating the surroundings. Color began returning to our world. I was cold, near shivering, and I wished I could do sun salutations until I was warm; instead, I began flexing every muscle I could muster and then releasing, flexing, releasing, over and over again. This was a trick I learned while enlisted, posted in the Upper Peninsula of Michigan, guarding nuclear weapons. My specialty, like other elite roles in the service, was one of the few that was operational at all times, under any circumstances, in any temperatures. I had spent many midnight shifts, out in the elements of the northern woods, coping with ambient temperatures of negative 40 degrees Fahrenheit and colder. On some nights the windchill dropped to negative 70 and lower. By flexing and unflexing, I was fundamentally synthetically shivering.

As the sky and the San Luis Valley turned pink, I could see where water had splashed and turned to ice all around us. A small splash of water had covered, with a thin layer of verglas ice, my shoulders, back, and boots (placed next to me). The splashing had covered Jess with the same glaze. I wondered if I looked as discontent as he did—hunched over, staring out over the valley through squinty, tired eyes, stoically passing the minutes in a semi-conscious state. He looked about as motivated to get out of his bag as I felt about getting out of mine. For a few more minutes, we patiently waited for more light and the motivation to begin the task ahead of us.

According to the mission log, at 0535 hours, I contacted base and communicated that Jess and I were awake and readying to finish the scene's processing. Base requested that we relay coordinates and equipment we already had at hand. At 0536 I replied, "North 37 degrees, 33 minutes, 51.9 seconds by West 105 degrees, 29 minutes, 58.3 seconds, elevation 13,060 feet. We have a Stokes litter, two two-hundred-foot ropes, minimal rock anchors. Personnel inbound should be ready for low-angle, technical snow and ice terrain, 30+ degree angle slopes."

I made that call from my sleeping bag, but within a minute or two, Jess and I emerged. The air temperature was below freezing, we could see our breath, and we both continually moved "with a purpose" to build up warmth. Although the light was now good enough to continue the operation, the hulking summit of Little Bear would block direct sunlight for hours.

I found it difficult to break the ice off my leather mountaineering boots and laces, and it was near painful to slip my already cold feet into the frozen boots. Once we got over the initial shock of the cold, Jess and I worked quickly and efficiently to pack our personal gear and begin our last tasks before vacating the difficult scene.

We started by retaking the photographs from the night before, which were all slightly blurry from lack of light, or in the case of flash pictures, they were too focused on just the foreground. I wanted to ensure that the pictures properly reflected Kevin's positioning in relation to the entire mountainside.

After retaking the photos, we moved up Kevin's fall line and documented and collected the evidence that the fall had strewn all over the slope. This included a lot of what had been in Kevin's backpack.

I recalled the previous day's conversation with Travis, in which he explained and apologized several times for having to move Kevin to attempt first-aid. He had been very worried about any further damage he could have caused his friend by moving him. Travis' mom was a nurse and had taught him how dangerous it was to move a patient with a potentially injured spine. I had hoped to reinforce for Travis that he did everything he could, and he should be proud of himself for having such discipline in such a horribly challenging situation.

Now remembering that conversation, I saw with my own eyes the evidence of what Travis had been through, and the fact that the situation was completely out of his hands. The moment Kevin's handhold failed, there was nothing anyone could have done to change the outcome. As Jess and I ascended the fall line, we found Kevin's cell, Camelbak, SPOT device, a stuff sack, jacket, and a few other odds and ends.

Overnight the freezing temperatures had returned the slushy snowfields to near water-ice hardness, and with carefully placed steps, ready to self arrest with my ice axe, as I got to the highest piece of evidence, I looked up the slope. From that point, the route increases in steepness. No other evidence remained on the steep ice above that point.

As Jess and I finished gathering evidence and securing it near Kevin's location, I radioed that we were nearing completion and were intending to leave the site.

Rather than the quickly expected, "Good copy," what Jess and I got was a request to "Stand by." According to the mission radio log, at 0610 hours, Mike Adcock came back over the radio. Later, he said it was one of the harder radio calls he has made. "Base to SAR One."

"Go for One."

"Kevin, this is Mike Adcock. I'm so sorry to make this request, but as the regional teams are rallying and heading out they've asked that to save time, and because this is our jurisdiction, you guys package the subject and have him ready for technical extraction by the time they get there." Jess, standing next to me clearly overheard the request. We were both surprised and a little demoralized.

I couldn't help but voice my frustration to Jess. "Really? After yesterday and last night, we've got to do the packaging."

Jess was all business, "Oh well, we're here, and we're probably the most qualified to do it anyway. Let's just finish it."

By qualified, I knew that Jess meant that preparing rigor mortised bodies for transport in litters generally affected a small set of us the least. I briefly recalled a previous body recovery in which overcoming rigor mortis had required Jess and I to do some "noisy" joint manipulations. A couple team members reported they were haunted by the sounds for weeks.

Jess was right, we might as well be the ones to give Kevin closure. I reminded myself of the honor to be a body's first "pallbearer"; it was a deep honor to return a loved one's remains to his/her family in whatever shape those final remains may be.

"Good call, Jess. Let's finish."

I keyed the radio mic, and called back, "Affirmative. Subject will be ready for extraction upon personnel reaching this location. Will radio when finished and descending."

In a focused, efficient manner, Jess and I respectfully laid Kevin in a cadaver bag, and in the process I could sense crepitus in Kevin's extremities, including his neck. Jess and I gently secured Kevin in a Stokes litter. We built a small, level rock ledge on which we securely placed the litter, ropes, anchors, and other extraction equipment.

At 0729 hours, I radioed base to inform them that Jess and I had completed packaging, and Jess and I were beginning our descent to Lake Como. As we left the site, I turned around and took several pictures of Kevin's body, secure on the platform we built, to show his relation to the large face. By the time we traversed the face and intersected the top of the west ridge where we

Picture of Kevin Hayne's body above Little Bear Lake. The Chinook is at the head of the lake below (author photo, June 16, 2010).

could look down into the Lake Como valley, the sunlight finally touched us. We welcomed the rays, but Jess and I were already warm from our efforts to descend.

In the bright, warm sunlight, route finding became easier, and I couldn't help but wonder what the egress, in the middle of the night, had been like for Mick, Mike, and George. On a couple occasions overnight I had envisioned their progress. Even in the daytime, people had fatally mistaken a nearby couloir for the correct route and fallen to their deaths.

In the middle of the night in such terrain, to say route finding was a challenge is an understatement. Fatigued, sleep deprived, eager to descend and feel safe, in the middle of the night any small mistake could easily prove deadly. My biggest fear had always been, and remained to be, one of my teammates being seriously injured or killed while trying to help others. Upon checking in via radio, no one had communicated anything about any emergencies or contingencies overnight, but to satisfy any doubt, I radioed and inquired whether the sheriff had received the memory card with the video of the helicopter's rotors disintegrating. An "affirmative" let me know they had made it.

As Jess and I picked our way through the talus at the top of the ridge, we took time at several spots to take pictures of the broken Chinook far below us in the Little Bear Lake valley to our south. We also took time to stop and look down the chutes and ribs that were especially exposed or where we knew people had fallen to their deaths. At one especially exposed spot, the top of a steep couloir on the ridge's south side, I remembered the last time Jess and I had been at that location together. "Jess, you remember the last time we were here?"

"Yup, I was just thinking the same thing. Isn't this where we set Jim Cornwall down to dab the blood out of his eyes and one of us dropped the gauze roll, and we all listened to its plastic packaging bouncing. It seemed to bounce forever until its sound vanished. It was like we were over a bottomless abyss."

"Looking down it now in the light, had any of us fallen here, for all purposes it is bottomless."

"Tish almost fell here. As we were pushing the litter around, it knocked her off balance right here. She barely recovered. It's amazing none of us were hurt."

"You can say that again. How do you think the three musketeers fared last night? They made it back, but I wonder if anything happened?"

"Yeah, I'm a little surprised they preferred hiking out over this shit at night. Sure, we froze our butts off, but traveling here at night? After Cornwall's rescue, I'd rather not."

"Indeed. That Cornwall rescue taught me an invaluable lesson though."

"Which one was that?"

"Remember that all the couloirs on the north side of the west ridge that link the lakes with the ridge? They all basically look the same, especially looking down into the valley from the top of them, but the actual route, the safe access couloir is the *only one* that isn't solid rock and talus at the top. It's the only one that has sandy soil, dirt. How many souls could have been spared over the years had everyone known this?"

"Probably a lot. Knowing that would have likely saved David Boyd."

"That's who I was thinking about, too. How many total lives have been lost over the years on this north side access because of that mistake?"

"It's not the numbers that make me wary. It's David Boyd that makes me think. He was a brilliant medical doctor, experienced in extreme endurance athletics. What was he, some global adventure racer?"

"Yeah."

"Well, here's a super smart doctor, capable of the triple slam, having just completed all three fourteeners in the group in *one day*, and because he mistook the proper exit, he died. I feel like if it can happen to him, it can happen to *anyone*."

I recalled all of Boyd's gear. "The moment we found his body and started taking inventory of his equipment, a lot of it was the exact same as what I carry. I very much identified with that. It shook me up a bit. Actually it still does. Speaking of which, let's remember we're totally wasted from the sleep deprivation. It's like we're drunk. Let's make sure we stay mindful of every step."

Staying focused on every step along the ridge, pushing ourselves through an intoxicated-like blur, we came upon the top of the access couloir seemingly quickly. In the daylight, we could easily verify it was the proper route. Not only was there a gravel and dirt path marked by a cairn, one could see the dirt "trail" begin zigzagging down the couloir and descending along the sides of the couloir where the scree aprons met the surrounding cliffs. Staying close together so any rock we released would fall away from us rather than onto one another, we continued our descent. Because of the steepness of the gully, we lost elevation very quickly. At 0927 hours the first vehicle transporting the cavalry made a radio call to the command post to notify them that they had dropped the first group of SAR personnel at the base of the access couloir and had made contact with Jess and me.

At the base of the couloir, the last glaciation of the valley left a talus moraine, a large heap of rock, so Jess and I could not see the 4x4 road and were very pleasantly surprised to see a vehicle and a group of AVSAR folks waiting for us as we came over the moraine's rise. Mick, Mike, and George had been picked up here, sometime around 0100 hours, eight and a half hours earlier, and they had been driven back to the command post, arriving around 0300. All three had then driven themselves home, thus avoiding contact and long debriefings with anyone but the middle of the night incident commander.

All the folks meeting Jess and I were eager to hear about the hard landing in the Chinook. Jess and I couldn't express to everyone how happy we were to see people—seeing everyone's loving smiles and eagerness to reach out, welcome us, literally hug us.

At 0943 hours, after taking off my helmet for the first time since getting on the helicopter the previous day, I radioed the command post asking for total numbers of SAR personnel currently en route to complete Kevin's recovery. With Jess' and my knowledge of the scene, we were trying to help them prepare and plan for the last steps to complete the mission. It was an immense relief to learn that multiple agencies were sending SAR and other first responders, including Rio Grande County, Custer County, El Paso County, and Gunnison's Western Mountain College SAR team. After providing the first relief team (comprised of AVSAR personnel) with information and a list of recommended equipment still needed to complete the objective, Jess and I planned to continue our descent to the command post.

As we concluded our field briefing, neither Jess nor I could have seen anyone descending the access couloir. From our perspective, it was hidden by the rocky moraine. All of a sudden, a familiar face presented itself—Warren, the young man who had videotaped the Chinook's rotors disintegrating upon contacting the slope, had successfully gotten over the ridge and to our location looking no worse for the wear. I called out, "It's good to see you! What route did you take over the ridge? Did you pass by any of the Chinook's security personnel?"

"Nope. I got up this morning at first light, saw you guys moving around up there, and decided to stay as far away as possible. I ended up ascending almost directly straight north from the Chinook."

"How'd you get past the cliff band that circles the gorge there?"

"There's a couple little, very steep gullies that one can use to get up over the band. It was good to be alone though. I released a couple small rockslides ascending the scree."

"It's good to see you're out. Now it's just a downhill hike from here. You want a ride out?"

"No, thanks. I'm good. You guys take care."

"You, too."

Having a sense of closure knowing Warren had escaped the valley to our south, I reciprocated much love and support to our fellow SAR brethren, now gearing up to ascend the access couloir, and Jess and I loaded our packs into the modified 4x4, one of the few vehicles in the region capable of reaching such a remote location. The driver, Steve Morrison, was a local 4x4 enthusiast whose hobby was welding, machining, and working in his personal auto shop. The Frankenbeast of a 4x4 he used to negotiate the Lake Como road was an old full-sized Chevy Blazer that he had lifted considerably, modified with specialized rock-crawling features such as independent locking wheels. The back top of the Blazer he cut off, so that the beast looked something like a

Tonka Big Foot truck, but whose cab was open to the flat bed where we could work on patients or transport bodies. During many SAR missions there were few vehicles as ugly, or as welcomed and loved, as Steve's Frankenbeast. This moment was one of those very appreciative times. Jess and I were very happy at the thought of moving over the land by something other than our own power. The drive down would be technical in the sense we'd have to get out and portage the most deadly "Jaws" obstacles, but for the circumstances, this was the equivalent of a limousine offering us a ride to home, our beds.

Descending the obstacle known as Jaws 4 (the steep rocky wall above Lake Como, near the waterfall), the vehicle felt as if it were doing a headstand, nearly vertical as it slowly scratched down the smooth rock faces. There were times when even totally braked, Steve had to negotiate carefully sliding and skidding until the vehicle came to rest.

I felt secure in Steve's hands, and I was beyond exhausted. I felt pretty disassociated with reality as we passed Lake Como. In one sense, everything felt cartoon-like, but in another it was super vivid.

No longer at treeline, but solidly in the montane zone, the trees and vegetation were as green and vivid as anything I had experienced in tropical rain forests in the past. The smell of the pines, the lake, the soil was so delicious. I could hear every thrush's song, every cricket's chirp distinctly. Everything had a sense of "jamais vu," the opposite of déjà vu. How many times had I heard a hermit thrush's song or a cricket's chirp, and yet right then, I had this impression as if I were hearing and seeing things for the first time.

Steve negotiated the tight woodsy bypass of Jaws 3 as if he were driving around a suburban cul-de-sac, and as we approached Jaws 2, the deadliest of the road's Jaws obstacles, we rounded a corner and came upon a large group of SAR responders, ascending the road on foot. Simultaneously, Steve, Jess, and I looked at each other and nonverbally nodded an understanding of what needed to happen.

Before saying anything, Jess and I jumped out of the beast and grabbed our packs. This group of SAR folks was made up primarily of college students responding from Gunnison. As Jess and I disembarked from the vehicle, one of them said questioningly, "Did you guys talk to the guys in the helicopter crash yesterday?"

"Yup, as a matter of fact we are those guys." Several of the group were guessing as much by the way they were sizing us up.

"Wow, we didn't think you guys would be this far out this quick."

"We got an early start. And thanks to Steve, here we are." As if on cue, Steve began the sensitive maneuvers required to turn around his beast at a spot that was just a few feet wider than the usual two-track.

One of the college students, looking exhausted already, asked, "What are you guys doing?"

I responded for Jess and me. "We're getting out and walking from this point. It's far more important you all get up there as fast as possible to get this recovery done than we get a ride out. It's all downhill for us from here. You guys on the other hand, take your time."

Jess and I briefed this group similar to the first. We passed along the scene details and what awaited them, focusing on safety considerations, and then we wished them all good luck as they slowly drove away. We listened to the low, powerful growl of Steve's beast as it ascended back into the gorge east of us. "Jess, you want to wait for the next time Steve passes?"

"You're kidding, right? I'm getting back to the command post as soon as I can. I'm walking out of here if I have to."

We shouldered and adjusted our packs, and having been freed from them for a bit they felt exceptionally heavy. Slowly, we continued by foot. As tired as we were, we were happy, and our morale was high. At 1058 hours, I radioed base to inform them that Jess and I would continue descending on foot. If possible, we'd look forward to an intercept.

At 1139 hours the radio log indicates that an Alamosa SAR member, Mike Maier, who was also a volunteer firefighter with the local Mosca-Hooper Fire Department, radioed that he had made contact with Jess and me at the Jaws 1 obstacle. To Jess' and my surprise, standing at the top of the obstacle's granite dome, we looked down upon a nearly brand new, personally modified, bright yellow Hummer.

Not only was Mike Maier there to greet us, so was John Gilmore, the Flight For Life paramedic who was the incident commander the day before. The last time I had seen John was when I boarded the Chinook.

With giant grins on our faces I said, "You guys have no idea how good it is to see you."

John responded with eyes welling up in tears, "You guys have no idea how good it is to see *you*." I gave John a long hug. "I've been very eagerly looking forward to welcoming you guys back. It's so good to see you. I don't know what to say really," John said.

Jess laughed, and I nodded, "Indeed. It's been a hell of a time since the last time we all saw each other."

John summed it up, "As a flight medic, after what you guys went through, I don't know if I could ever go up again. How are you guys?"

"You nailed it, John. I don't know if I'll be jumping aboard any aircraft soon. For a few scary moments, I was convinced we were dead, and that's not even what bothered me. It was the idea of burning. You should have seen the army guys jumping up and down, laughing, crying. I don't know if a couple of our guys appreciated how close we were."

"We in the air ambulance business well appreciate it. As far as I'm concerned, from the sounds of it from the army guys, you guys are nothing short of miracles. Let's get in, and on the way down tell me about what it was like."

Jess and I threw our gear into the back of the Hummer, and jumping in shotgun I realized that it was a mere distant cousin of the Humvees I had spent much time in patrolling Saudi Arabia's capital, Riyadh, and surrounding deserts in the mid '90s.

Like Steve in his Frankenbeast, Mike gingerly turned the Hummer around and began the slow, skilled descent back to the command post. Having been in the elements for nearly a day, it was surreal for Mike to roll up the windows and crank on the A.C. Although just a few hours prior, Jess and I had been battling the cold, we had now descended to an elevation at which the warm, desert temperatures were becoming a challenge.

Cruising along in a vehicle, I was amazed at how quickly we transitioned from the high altitude sub-alpine environment to the San Luis Valley floor's hot, dry, desert environment. As Jess and I relayed our experiences to John and Mike, I watched vividly colored swallowtail butterflies flutter through the aspen groves passing by just outside my window. The swallowtails always hung out at the mouths of the canyons and gorges. We would be back to the command post shortly.

Now in much closer proximity and direct sight of the radio repeaters, as we descended we listened to the clear radio traffic summarizing what was occurring on the mountain above us.

At 1151 a new group of army Blackhawk helicopters arrived. This group included an army colonel, Chinook specialists, crash investigators, and a full security detail that would be assigned to the Chinook crash site until it could be recovered. John mentioned that because of the low air density, the Chinook would have to be dismantled and flown out in sections rather than all at once. The process could take weeks.

As we neared the trailhead, John said we probably wouldn't recognize it as our usual command post—multiple army helicopters, army personnel everywhere, Alamosa's Sheriff Stong, the extra-large mobile command unit RV, not the usual using one of our trunks as a desktop. I looked forward to seeing how many folks could rally in such an incident.

We listened to the communications as we descended the road's last traverses. At 1157 hours the first team, comprised of some Alamosa and Custer County personnel, radioed they had a visual on Kevin and were safely making their way to the body's location, albeit slowly. During the same communication, they also radioed a request, a request that I felt very appropriate but unlikely to be granted. Having seen the remote location of Kevin's body, and understanding the extreme energy and risk it would require to extract his body by moving it along the west ridge, down the exit couloir, and back to the rendezvous just above Lake Como, the request was that they be allowed to technically lower, via rope, Kevin into the basin near the broken Chinook. Then they asked if he might be flown out via the Blackhawks about to start sorties into the valley.

Knowing that military and FFL protocol fundamentally forbid the use of air support in body recoveries, I was certain the request would be denied. I had a whole new personal understanding for the reasoning for such protocol—the use of aircraft in mountainous terrain is *extremely* risky. It is such a high risk that it should only be employed to rescue patients still alive. Their use and high liability factors *cannot* and should not be justified in body recoveries.

I was a bit more than surprised to hear base come back two minutes later at 1159 hours and give permission to the crew to change plans. I thought, must be nice being a colonel. They were told to lower Kevin straight into the Little Bear Gorge where he and whatever associated personnel would be airlifted out by Blackhawk. Later during our after action review (AAR), it was proposed that the army had okayed such a change because security of the crash scene included evacuating the body and civilian personnel.

At 1201 we heard Sheriff Stong arrive at the command post and transfer possession of the memory disc to the army colonel. At 1216, the initial team moving in on Kevin's location radioed that they were about thirty minutes from the scene. They estimated that it would require an hour and a half to lower Kevin to the LZ from his current location once they were on scene. At 1228 the first Blackhawk flight to the crash site from the command post took off. At 1239, base radioed they had a visual on the descending yellow Hummer.

The first (or last) section of the Lake Como road as it ascends from the sandy parking lot/trailhead out on the valley flats, SAR personnel and locals refer to as the "baby heads"—so named for the size of the rock that's been exposed by decades of 4x4 vehicles that have driven up and down the enormous alluvial fan. The rocks' sizes, named in the macabre spirit of a baby's head, are the perfect size to constantly challenge and roll the ankles of anyone hiking over them (especially tired folks with heavy backpacks). Jess and I couldn't express how joyful we were to not have to walk out the last two miles of the dreaded "baby heads."

At 1245 hours, just shy of twenty-four hours from the start of the mission,

Jess and I rolled into the command post, having been warned but still surprised at the number of personnel, vehicles, Blackhawks, and general busy tone of the place. Unlike our welcome at the Lake Como rendezvous point, as we got out of the Hummer we were greeted more formally by the sheriff and army personnel. The sheriff and an army colonel shook our hands and welcomed us back. They explained that before we did a debriefing with investigators, we should head over to the Red Cross vehicle, clean up, and get re-hydrated and fed. Jess and I couldn't have agreed more, and we quickly walked to the Red Cross vehicle and a face we knew well, Adeline Lee's.

Adeline had been a consistent, very supportive Red Cross leader who we had learned to call at the beginning of any long, involved mission; we knew she would be there for the SAR folks giving the support they needed coming out of field deployments. In this instance, her face was like that of a battlefield angel. After Adeline and I hugged, I consumed about a liter of Gatorade and a half dozen granola bars. During this process, several beloved Alamosa SAR personnel approached us and began asking questions about our experience. Before answering their questions, I had one myself, "You guys know why all those army personnel over there are looking at us so strangely?"

"Yup. Go get debriefed, and you'll find out why."

After a briefing in which Jess and I relayed our experience to investigators, I thanked them all with as much grace as I could muster for being so tired. Sitting in the mobile command vehicle, another camouflaged soldier climbed the stairs and I immediately recognized him as one of the pilots I had spoken to the previous day, Chief Warrant Officer David Carter. I greeted him very happily, "Hey it's good to see you again. I kind of wish I had taken you up on that Blackhawk ride offer yesterday. It's been a long night."

Author speaking with AVSAR technicians after returning to the command post June 16, 2010 (photo by John Gilmore).

Stoically, Carter just grinned and nodded an affirmation. CWO Carter and I spent several minutes recollecting the prior day, the flight around the peak, the time just prior to the rotor strike, the hard landing, the night, the extraction. I was beginning to fall asleep talking as we ended our conversation.

As I walked back to my car, I passed a couple soldiers who were looking at me in a manner that was a bit nerve wracking, "Hey, why are you guys looking at me so intensely? It's a little unnerving."

"We're looking at a ghost. For several reasons y'all should be dead. Didn't they tell you the statistics?"

"No. Isn't that shit classified? I'm a civilian remember."

"Well, between you and me, you've got one of the world's best Chinook pilots on scene. Carter's a pilot instructor, who's one of the best Chinook pilots in the world. As he and a couple other investigators said earlier, they've never seen the kind of rear rotor damage like you guys incurred, and not had the front and rear rotors disintegrate on each other and cause catastrophic failure."

"Catastrophic failure? As in plummeting directly to the ground?"

"Exactly. Plus, that's just one of three mysteries. It's also nearly as amazing that with the forces you guys experienced hitting the deck, you didn't burst the rubber fuel bladders and go up in a jet fuel fire. You realize you guys put enough energy into the aircraft's frame to bend it like a banana, as well as torque it like a twisted piece of licorice?"

I was speechless.

"And lastly, the glide slope, from the point of rotor impact to the point where you hard landed, it seems that it would have been impossible with the amount of damage to the rear rotor and loss of lift. You guys are now all part of a very elite club. That's why we were looking at you like that."

"Thanks for the insight. You guys be careful up there securing the scene and recovering the helicopter. At night there's still sub-freezing temperatures and the possibility of storms."

"That's a good copy."

Feeling some closure, I returned to Adeline's station and chugged a caffeine-laced Coke. It would see me through the forty-five-minute drive home. It would be a bummer to have to pull off and sleep if I started nodding, but I also promised myself that I would do exactly that at the first hint of drowsiness. As I had trained all my team members, after being awake for twenty-four hours, especially on a taxing mission as we had just experienced, people act as if they're legally intoxicated, and they will even fail driving tests that assess such.

Many, many injuries and deaths to SAR responders occur on their drive home after a taxing mission; they fall asleep behind the wheel, crash, and never awaken again. I thanked Adeline for hers and the Red Cross' deeply appreciated support, I quickly shook a few hands, and I said thanks to Jess, "I'll see you at the AAR at the next monthly meeting. Let's hope to God we don't have another call out 'til then."

"Amen brother," and Jess and I headed out the dirt two-track back to Highway 150 and our long awaited beds.

A couple weeks later, the team met for our monthly administrative meeting, and we used the gathering as an opportunity for an AAR (after action review meeting). AARs are used by teams of first responders and military teams as an opportunity to be honest about what was done well on a mission, and also to be self-critical and discuss what can be done better in the future. It was at this meeting that I finally heard about the mission's ultimate conclusion, with which I wasn't directly involved.

Andrew McClure, a young amazingly skilled rock climber and mountaineer, explained to the group the final part of the mission to recover Kevin. He explained that he had been part of the first group that had met Jess and me as we returned to the Lake Como rendezvous point. He, the other AVSAR members, and the members of the Custer County SAR team took their time safely negotiating the west ridge route to Kevin's body's location. Andrew mentioned that the visiting team members were especially grateful that we had packaged Kevin.

Andrew detailed for all of us how upon reaching Kevin's location at 1255 hours, he built snow anchors in the snowfield above Kevin, as the scree around the body was too loose to even imagine setting solid anchors. Andrew said that to save time, while he built the snow anchors above, SAR responders from Western State simultaneously built rock anchors below, located at the top of the gorge's cliff band. Custer County personnel simultaneously downclimbed the cliff band and then waited at a point under the cliff band ready to receive Kevin and continue immediate transport from there to the LZ near the Chinook.

Andrew said that at 1357 hours (according to the radio log), the first of two four-hundred-foot low-angle technical lowers began. Upon Kevin's body and a couple attendants reaching the rock anchor point at the top of the cliff band, Kevin and the attendants switched from the snow anchors to the rock anchors and continued their descent. He said they were a little concerned to hear a weather forecast and the following transmission (noted to have occurred at 1330 hours):

"Teams on the mountain should prepare to stay overnight. Current conditions at base 86 degrees, hot, dry low air density conditions, high wind gusts likely." They, like most rational people, were not looking forward to a cold night in a remote location with the body of a young man who most likely subconsciously reminded all of us mountaineers of the potential consequences for taking such risks.

· At the base of the cliff, Custer County took over transport, and they carefully escorted the litter over the steep talus all the way to the Blackhawk LZ near Little Bear Lake and the Chinook. The radio log notes that at 1626 hours, Kevin's body and accompanying attendants were a hundred yards from the LZ.

By this time, Andrew said the army personnel had set up a large canvas tent for the security detail, and seeing the damage to the helicopter with their own eyes was eerie. It was like visiting a historic ghost town, the scene was quiet, but one could sense the recent high levels of energy and activity—*eerie indeed.*

Everyone was very happy to learn that even with the gusty, hot winds at the command post, two Blackhawks were planning on coming in and picking up the body and SAR personnel, leaving only the Chinook's security detail behind.

Via the radio log, at 1630 hours the first Blackhawk took off inbound for the Chinook's location. At 1634 hours, the second Blackhawk disembarked. At 1638 hours the first Blackhawk landed, and this is the last entry in the radio log.

At the AAR, Steve Morrison, the driver of the Frankenbeast, explained that after their last trip up to Lake Como to deliver personnel, they stopped on descent and recovered Travis and Kevin's tent and gear at their camp adjacent to Lake Como (they radioed this information at 1441 hours), and then they carefully continued their descent to the command post. Steve approximated his return to the command post around 1730 hours, shortly after the two Blackhawks landed at the command post with Kevin's body and all the SAR responders.

Around the same time as the AAR, after nearly two weeks of watching Blackhawk and Chinook sorties in and out of the Little Bear Lake gorge, we learned that the army had completed their aircraft recovery.

A couple months later, after several people referred me to it, I watched a video in which an interviewer, documentary style, interviews Kevin Hayne about his recent experience being rescued from the Maroon Bells by Mountain Rescue Aspen.

The video, still available on YouTube as of the time of this writing, titled *Kevin Hayne What Faith Can Do*, details Kevin's uncontrolled slide down the Bell Cord Couloir. It is a haunting foreshadowing. In the interview, Kevin explains that in the midst of the slide, he felt a sense of peace come over him as he released his fate to God. Since then, I have chosen to believe that Kevin's last moments of consciousness were of peaceful surrender.

Personally, this was the second to last SAR mission in which I participated. I, too, was beginning to surrender peacefully.

Jesse Peterson
Willow Lake, May 25, 2012

"Many miles away there's a shadow on the door of a cottage on the shore of a dark Scottish lake."
—Sting, from the album *Synchronicity*

When my father was a young man in his late teens and twenties, he backpacked solo throughout Colorado's mountain ranges. He and my mother passionately loved the mountains, and we spent most of my childhood vacations in Rocky Mountain National Park. Longs Peak was my first fourteener, which I climbed for the first time at the age of twelve; my younger brother was just nine on the same trip. Up to the third grade, I grew up in the suburbs of Denver, Littleton, and Englewood. After I turned nine, we moved up to the foothills west of Denver between Evergreen and Conifer, and after playing in the backyard mountains all afternoon, I would listen to my dad's stories about hiking and fishing.

For my sixth-grade graduation present, I asked my dad to take me on a several day backpacking trip. I was only twelve, but we successfully hiked from Echo Lake to Bear Track Lakes. There, we fished for trout, and then we backpacked back to Echo Lake. It was on these sacred trips that Dad passed along the finer points of mountaineering, as well as what he knew of the state's different mountain ranges.

Of all his numerous, fascinating personal narratives of Colorado's mountains, the most entrancing were those of the Blood of Christ Mountains, the Sangre de Cristos.

Like *Indiana Jones*, who as a child ventures into his father's study and finds him on a search for the Holy Grail, my own father's mountaineering adventures had included stories of youthful expeditions to seek evidence of a lost treasure. My father told me it was likely conquistador gold. Like Indiana's fictitious Gold Cross of Coronado, the Sangre de Cristos are shrouded in a mythical air.

In my father's stories, I learned of his understanding of the legend of the Caverna del Oro. He described to me in mythological-like stories his youthful experiences looking around his campfire at night with his flashlight and seeing a plethora of sets of animals' eyes reflecting back toward him. He would remark, "I had never seen such a density of wildlife in any mountain range. Although the range is a long thin spine, the wilderness in that spine is rugged and primal. I saw things there I saw nowhere else."

To his young son, in his own early days of exploring the local foothills for nearby adventure, the stories of Spanish conquistadors being pursued by local Native Americans and ditching a significant amount of gold in a mountain cave were worth more than the literal gold had it been in my father's closet.

Like the fictitious Indiana Jones character, I strayed from my father's fascination with a specific treasure and I became fascinated with mountaineering in general. Like the fictitious Indiana Jones, fate led me back to the sphere of my father's interests years after I had forgotten about them.

The vast majority of my youthful Colorado mountaineering occurred along the Front Range, occasionally venturing as far southwest as Aspen and the Elk Range. It wasn't until I began working as a teacher and had summer vacations to explore more distant, isolated mountains did I venture into the Sangres and San Juans for the first time.

In my late twenties, while still living in Denver, I began ticking off fourteeners from my "list." Remembering my father's story of reverence for the Sangres, I put extra energy and time into researching the range, studying its topo maps, reading the guidebooks. After careful pondering, I set my sight on my first summit in the Sangre Range—Kit Carson Peak.

My first solo attempt was unsuccessful (although I did successfully ascend Challenger Point on that first round). On my second attempt, a year or two later, I returned with a proven mountaineering partner, and we were the first team on Kit Carson's summit for the day. My initial experience of the Sangre de Cristos through the "portal" of Crestone and Willow Creek met and exceeded every one of my boyhood mythological-level expectations. The first time I ascended past Willow Lake and came around the corner looking south toward Kit Carson, I'm quite certain that had a character such as Dr. Jones actually existed, as he made his way past the obstacles in the cave that held the grail, Jones would have felt exactly as I did looking up the east-facing slopes of Challenger Point and the north faces of Kit Carson.

A friend of mine is a dual American Pakistani citizen. He grew up in the Pakistani Himalayas, and of all the mountain ranges in the United States that remind him of his boyhood home and the Karakoram-Hindu Kush-Himalayan Mountain ranges, the Sangre de Cristos are his favorite. This is one reason his home is in Crestone, at the western base of Challenger Point. We've spoken in the past about Pakistan and the legend of Shangri-La, originating from the Hunza Valley region of the Karakoram. The term Shangri-La was coined in the 1933 novel *Lost Horizon* by British author James Hilton. Hilton spent time in the Hunza Valley a few years prior to the publishing of the novel. For these reasons, I think of the mountain valleys of the Sangres, especially those leading up to the Kit Carson and Crestone Mountain Groups as America's Shangri-La.

In 2010, I was involved in a helicopter incident while trying to rescue Kevin Hayne, and a couple months later my father unexpectedly passed away. Both events took a toll on my ability to lead AVSAR properly, and in the spring of 2011, I resigned from the AVSAR team. I also resigned from my part-time teaching position at Adams State University.

Since my resignations, I have remained a consultant to active duty SAR leaders and personnel. I continue to seek opportunities to serve and train the public and SAR personnel about mountain survival and SAR skills.

One late spring weekend in 2012, while I was visiting friends in Fort Collins and sitting at one of the coffee shops grading a pile of papers, I logged online and read the local news from Alamosa. It was the first weekend in June, and an article explained a tragic incident that had resulted in a fatality the previous week.

"Man lost in lake canoe accident," was the title. Directly quoted from the online version of the paper:

> Posted: Wednesday, May 30th, 2012
> CRESTONE—A canoe accident at Willow Lake near Crestone on Friday resulted in the presumed drowning of Jesse G. Peterson, 28, Alma.
> According to a Saguache County Sheriff's Office press release, at approximately 8:43 p.m. on May 25, Outward Bound Program Manager Joann Yankovich contacted the office to report a missing person in the area. The report came after one of her coordinators learned of a canoeing accident on Willow Lake.
> The reporting party stated Natalie Brechtel, 28, Carlsbad, Calif., was rescued and treated for hypothermia after the canoe she and Peterson had been floating on flipped, according to the press release. Peterson, who allegedly did not know how to swim and allegedly was not wearing a lifejacket, was then nowhere to be found.
> According to the press release, Saguache County Sheriff's Deputy Dan Warwick interviewed Brechtel and she said that she and Peterson had set up camp for the night when they saw a boat near the lake's shore. She stated that Peterson had experience in boats, canoes and kayaks regardless of his inability to swim. Once in the boat, the pair could not maintain control because of winds, which eventually turned the boat over.

After Brechtel swam roughly 15 feet to the shore, she looked back and could not see Peterson, according to the press release.

Two Outward Bound team members treated Brechtel for hypothermia and the other 12 team members conducted a search for Peterson, according to the press release.

A Saguache County Search and Rescue effort took place on Saturday, which did not produce a body dead or alive, according to the press release. The Colorado Search and Rescue Board was notified to request a helicopter for aerial search; however, high winds stopped flights on both Saturday and Sunday. Dive teams were also requested, but altitude, water temperature and depth would have required acclimation. If they had responded, divers would have only been able to stay in the water for approximately 10 minutes.

Search efforts were discontinued on Sunday and, with concurrence of the family, will not continue, according to the press release. The lake will be monitored in case the body surfaces.

One reason I was visiting "FoCo" was to visit a woman I had recently begun dating. As part of my courting process I decided I'd introduce her to my love of search and rescue through immersion.

I crossed my fingers as I asked, "Would you be interested in going on a hiking date? One with a little search and rescue twist?"

"Maybe. What are you thinking?"

"Well, a young man just tragically passed away in a canoeing accident. Take a look at this."

I showed her the article. "My thought is that we take a hike up to Willow Lake and see if we can't locate Jesse?"

"What makes you think you can find him any more easily than the Saguache team?"

"Because of something I know about cold water and bodies from my days in the Upper Peninsula of Michigan. There comes a time of the season in which bodies that have gone into the water when it's cold finally warm enough that decomposition will finally occur. That's when a negatively buoyant body will suddenly start to float. I think I can gauge the time Jesse's body will rise based on experiences with seeing other mammals' bodies rise at treeline in the spring and summer. I think we should 'take a hike' the last week of June."

I didn't mention that this was the anniversary of the time of year that the mountains gave up Lygon's body just a few years prior. I thought maybe the end of June marks the time when the last remnants of Hades' seasonal underworld breaks, and Persephone is free.

If Persephone freed Jesse to rise, I'd want a good pair of binoculars to scan the depths of the lake from the precipices of the cliffs on the eastern side of the lake.

My date admitted, "I'll hike to the lake with you, but I don't want to help search for a body."

"No worries. From your perspective, it would only be a hike up into a magnificent mountain valley. Wait until you see this view of Kit Carson Peak from the north. It's more like something you'd imagine in Patagonia than Colorado. We'll have a picnic, enjoy some sunshine, and recon the east side of Challenger Point for an ascent later in the season. In the most 'successful' scenario, I'll leave you alone at our lunch spot for a few minutes to sunbathe while I secure Jesse near shore. Ultimately, all we can expect to do is report whether or not he's visible and ready for recovery. It'll take a team to bring Jesse's body back to his family."

"I know how important it is that his body is recovered, but I don't want to be personally part of it."

"Most folks don't. I understand you not wanting to be involved with looking for a body. How about we just look at it like an early summer hike. I'll just happen to look at the lake with some binoculars." I looked at the calendar, "Let's hike up to Willow on Friday, the 29th. The binoculars might come in handy for watching the bighorn sheep up near Willow Lake. There's a pretty sizable herd that has become quite comfortable with people. Maybe you can get some good photographs of a full-curl ram."

I was leading our conversation away from the idea of finding a water-logged decomposed human body. Although I've searched for, rescued, and recovered many people in various dangerous environments, such as on cliff ledges, I also train so that each professional rescuer knows his/her personal preferences and limitations. Many people's limitation is water.

I am a pretty solid swimmer. My mother grew up in Wisconsin, and she felt teaching her children to swim proficiently was a basic survival skill. I started swim lessons at the same time I started school. The summer of my junior year in high school, I attended a party with friends in a secluded mountain valley containing a large lake. Even though it was summer, the day was cool, the elevation was around 9,500 feet, and clouds punctuated the sunshine with dark shadows passing overhead. Most likely an excuse to get everyone to strip down to their "swimsuits," we all dared each other to race across the lake, a distance of only a hundred and fifty yards. I stripped down to my nylon shorts, and we all waded into the water. Out of a couple dozen kids, a half dozen of us began the swim across the lake.

Half way between the two shores of that cold mountain lake, one of my hamstrings painfully cramped, completely seizing in motion. I immediately stopped my strokes, turned over, and innately began kneading the painful ball in the back of my upper leg. Everyone had turned back to shore but a friend who was on the swim team. He slowed, turned, and asked if things were okay. I told him, "Keep going, I'm headed back to shore." I was happy to see him turn and with even more vigor and strength make his way into the wind. As I continued kicking one leg while kneading the other, I looked into the water below me and I saw nothing but blackness, but I was nowhere near the bottom. For a split second I imagined my other leg cramping, or accidentally inhaling water, and I imagined how quickly my lean, dense body would plummet to the bottom, and then my mom came to mind.

"Don't ever panic in water. You know how to dead man float, and once you know how to dead man, you should be able to survive in water until you become hypothermic or fall asleep." With that thought, I put my face into the water and floated peacefully kneading my hamstring. What I didn't know at the time, which I know now, is that putting my face in the water probably triggered the mammalian dive reflex; it slowed my heart, slowed my breathing, and helped me regain some composure in a potentially dangerous situation.

Every once in awhile I would raise my face to orient myself, and I was surprised how quickly the wind blew me back toward the shore from which I had embarked. In a short amount of time, I felt more relaxed with my eyes closed, face down in the water, the sound of the wind and chaos blocked by the peaceful quiet of underwater.

Nearing shore, my charlie horse finally dissolved, and I slowly breast stroked back to shore near where the crowd had gathered to cheer on my middle of the lake compadre, now emerging on the opposite shore. I was exhausted by the time my numb fingers and toes touched the muddy lake bottom, and in the few feet it took me to crawl up to shore, several small high altitude leeches hitched rides on my legs. I couldn't blame them, something as large and warm as me in this frigid water? As I peeled them off my ankles and calves, I threw them back into the lake, rather than onto the rocks to dry out. My mother's swimming lessons served me well.

After I had enlisted in the air force, I was asked if I'd be interested in attending the army and air force elite Special Operations Dive School, at the time located in Panama. After talking to several specialists who had attended "Drown Proofing School," and learning that some of that training would fundamentally include drowning, as well as finding out that this qualification would lead to me diving into lakes to help the state police look for the bodies of airmen and soldiers whose cars went through guardrails into Lake Superior. I respectfully turned down the training. I told my supervisor and commander that I'd do anything they needed accomplished above the surface of the water, but I'd prefer not to be qualified to operate under it.

About a decade later the same offer would be made to me after joining the AVSAR team. The local regional dive team captain, Harry Alejo, was also a full-time sergeant and investigator with the Alamosa Sheriff's Office as well as a deputy coroner. Harry was also a Vietnam War veteran; he had been a marine recon diver. Harry reminded me very much of my father, and I saw him as a mentor. After working together on a couple SAR missions, Sergeant Alejo explained to me his leadership role on the dive team and that he was looking for recruits with military backgrounds, people who exhibited a lot of mental discipline.

"I like your hook, Sergeant, and I'm all about being on a team led by you, but you've got to be straight with me."

"Of course."

"Gimme a run down of one of your most difficult civilian SAR underwater missions. I might as well ponder the most extreme if I were to begin training and join the dive team."

"A few years ago, I was called out to a drowning at one of the lakes. We all responded code three, were in the water within an hour, but she was gone. She had fallen off a canoe, lost her breath in the cold water, and vanished under the surface without a trace. The dive team had raced to the approximate location of her submersion and immediately gotten in the water and searched the base of the lake in that area. As you may know, people have been known to live after being in cold water for more than an hour, but in this case, the hour turned into hours, and we declared the subject deceased. Our rescue turned into a recovery. One of the hardest parts of this mission was getting *to* the water, as I had a personal relationship with the subject. She was the daughter of a friend."

"I'm sorry. Those personal connections happen more often in our small interconnected towns."

"It's always been an honor to recover anyone and provide that physical and spiritual closure to their families and friends. It's even more important and honorable when it's someone close, whom you've known and cared for."

"When I was enlisted in the air force, we were often responding to the suicides and car wrecks of our fellow airmen. I'm sorry."

"It took several days to recover her. Ultimately, I was on the bottom of the lake doing a patterned search, and I had kicked up a lot of sediment into the water. Visibility dropped to just a few feet, sometimes just inches in front of my dive mask. The water temperature was cold, and the light from above was dim and opaque. I was slowly swimming along when out of the murk the body emerged directly in front of my mask. I bumped her, and in the cloudy light of my dive lamp I instinctively reached out to stop her from floating away. I didn't want to lose her into the darkness after days of searching.

"She was neutrally buoyant, darting around like a missile between the lake's surface and floor. Unfortunately, she was also beginning to show the effects of long-term water submersion. As she floated away and I reached out and grabbed her arm, the tissue of her skin around her elbow ripped, and I degloved the tissue of her lower arm and hand."

I looked lovingly toward Sergeant Alejo. I have a profound respect for souls who've spent their entire existence so altruistically giving toward others.

He continued his story, "I forgot one of the most basic rules of recovering a body at that stage of decomposition—push, don't pull. Even with all my years of experience with repulsive scenes, I vomited into my regulator. This is not good at a depth of more than fifty feet under water, especially in those circumstances. You understand why I look to recruit people with extreme attention to detail and high levels of discipline?"

"Makes sense to me. What did you do?"

"I calmed down, pulled the regulator out of my mouth, cleared it, cleared my mask of puke, and slowly moved forward into the murk until I had caught her in my arms and was slowly pushing her through the water, *not* pulling. If you join, don't forget that lesson."

"So you're just slowly swimming along, but you can't surface quickly because of the bends, right? How long did it take you to surface?"

"On that one, I think I got her just below fifty feet, and as I ascended, I spent about ten minutes at ten-foot intervals. It took about an hour for her and me to rise to the surface and get her in a Stokes litter in a boat."

"And that entire time you're virtually alone, cut off from the world? No radio, no comm.?"

"You've got your dive buddy, and you can communicate with Morse Code via your dive lamps."

"Indeed." It didn't take long for me to ponder his offer. "Sergeant Alejo, I said this same thing to a master sergeant in the air force years ago. I'll make you a deal. I'll be about as good as anyone you've ever known at rescues and recoveries above the surface of the water. I'll help you guys search for suicides and fatalities along the shores of the Rio, but SCUBA and deep, dark, cold, water … I'm honored by your request, but *no* thanks."

"At least give it some thought, and let me know if you ever change your mind."

I've never changed my mind.

***

The morning of Friday, June 29, 2012, I received a text from a friend in the sheriff's office, "R u still Willow bound today?"

"Affirmative."

"Did you hear news about j peterson?"

"Neg."

"Recovered by Saguache SAR last week."

"Tango."

My date was relieved that our hike up to Willow Lake would be free of SAR moonlighting in the form of searching for a body, and I relaxed seeing the day as an opportunity to enjoy the trail with a Zen "new mind." I'd approach the trail like I had never been there previously, even though I had hiked it many times.

I decided that this time I would hike into a gorge that had a violent, gory history, and I would try to detach from the negative emotional attachments that had occurred historically and through my own experiences. To override my memories of past missions, I prepared some research about a geophysical feature I found fascinating that was located just south of Crestone on the northern boundary of the Great Sand Dunes National Park.

On the two-lane highway that leads into Crestone and the trailhead, I pointed in the direction of the Crestone Crater, an unusual feature on the north side of the park where many believe a meteorite or comet impacted in the late 1800s. I also pointed out the small white Buddhist stupa at the very southern edge of Crestone. "That's very close to where the nearly invisible trail begins that accesses Cottonwood Lake and the Crestones from the west. In the past I've visited it, left offerings, and it has very much reminded me of my time in the Buddhist Solo Khumbu of Nepal."

My date and I left the trailhead relatively late (at least from the perspective of an alpinist accustomed to leaving the trailhead at 3:00 a.m.), after the sun had risen. It was still cool, and as we sauntered past the trailhead sign following the creek, and then up the initial thirteen switchbacks, we enjoyed the smell of the blooming Indian paintbrush and columbines. In addition to the flowers, there were seemingly endless varieties and colors of alpine butterflies and pollinators.

The sun hit us for the first time as we topped out on the ridge that looks southerly down on an enormous, peaceful, flat green pasture, the remnants of a glacial-age lake. The trail traverses east into the canyon and quickly gains elevation in a series of steep switchbacks that end with a last few, rocky, exposed ledges through a series of large "boilerplate" rock features.

Beyond this the trail's steepness eases, and it meanders through a subalpine forest before a last steep rise that includes a picture-book waterfall just below Willow Lake.

Since Saguache SAR had recovered Jesse a few days prior, my goal for the day was to hike to a point above the lake where we could see Kit Carson Peak, as well as Challenger Point's eastern slopes and standard route.

As my date and I sat and ate our lunch, I found a pocket in the rock that allowed me to sit back and enjoy the vista. I scanned the standard route for any sign of people or movement. I started at the tops of the cliffs above the lake, and then I slowly scanned the scree and talus slope as it rose steeper and steeper, turning into a high-angle snow-filled couloir.

The standard route went to either side of the snow chute, topped out on the 14,000-foot ridge called Challenger Point, and then traversed nearly a mile to the notch between it and Kit Carson Peak. I admired the enormous cliff

The eastern tip of Willow Lake, looking south toward Challenger Point's eastern slopes and the north face of Kit Carson Peak (author photo).

band that stretched the length of the ridge from the slopes between Challenger's standard route and the Kirk Couloir of Kit Carson. That cliff band and the Kirk Couloir were areas of high probability of injury or fatalities, as well as the Outward Bound Couloir, the chute that is northeast of Kit Carson's summit. In the summer of 2006, when I moved to the San Luis Valley, Douglas Beach, an experienced climber, outdoorsman, firefighter, search and rescue volunteer, and former navy SEAL, fell from the northeast face of Kit Carson and was recovered at the base of the Outward Bound Couloir. Beach, from Wyoming, left behind a wife and five children.

When I taught survival and SAR at Adams State University and to members of the county SAR team, I would often emphasize that the Sangre mountains can kill anyone including characters like Douglas Beach.

My date asked, "Where are most people hurt or killed on this peak?"

I pointed up to the notch, where Challenger's ridge intersected Kit Carson. "Most accidents occur up there, usually after the person has summited or turned around. On the way up, beyond that point, one must traverse a ledge that wraps around the top of Carson's summit. Although the actual ledge is anywhere from twenty to ten feet wide, as long as one takes his time and places every footstep on the inside of the ledge, there's no real risk of injury or death unless a storm and lightning come in. The mental exposure as one navigates the ledge is *huge*. Similar to Longs Peak's "Narrows" section, very few people fall from the ledge, but many are extremely psyched out by its airiness. Beyond that notch and on the way back to that point, people get anxious and make every step count; this equates to few issues except for storms trapping or killing subjects, or subjects getting off-route in cloudy conditions and falling. The big generator of SAR business here occurs once people get *back* to that notch. At that point they feel they're safe from the exposure. They're tired and they begin letting their guards down. They forget that they crossed the entire Challenger ridge on the way up and they try to descend directly down the Kirk Couloir, or they fall on the very steep, loose rock of Challenger Point's east slope cliffs."

"Most accidents occur on descent right?"

"People let their guard down, they relax, they forget that the summit isn't the end, it's only the half time show. I wish I could ingrain in mountaineers the lesson my dad ingrained in me—saunter a bit on your way up—stop and turn around, enjoy the view, and *visually memorize* the route back. Tell yourself little stories as mnemonics to help guide you on the way down. Once you're tired, racing a storm, eager to get down, that's not the time to be wondering which way the route is. It's best already to know the route back down. That's also why circuits are more dangerous than the same route up and down."

"That makes sense."

As my date and I hiked out, I stopped and took a picture of the canoe. Just a month prior Jesse had fallen out of this canoe and vanished. Just a few days prior, the canoe had been implemented in recovering Jesse's body.

As we hiked through the enchanted subalpine forest just below Willow Lake, we passed a couple with a young black lab and I thought of my rat terrier Freckles, who we had left at home on this hike.

I thought running into the dog was a good excuse to teach my date an important lesson about dogs on big mountains. "The first time I was up here before I lived in the SLV and I was just visiting the region, I encountered a couple with a black lab high up on the Challenger ridge. The dog's pads were beginning to crack and bleed from the constant rock hopping, and he was showing signs of distress. I remember sitting and taking my hourly five-minute break, rehydrating and eating an anti-bonk snack while watching the

The author's hiking partner looking down on Willow Lake from the top of its eastern cliffs. Jesse Peterson's body had been recovered from the lake just days prior to this picture (author photo, July 29, 2012).

The canoe stowed along the shore of Willow Lake, Crestone, Colorado (author photo).

couple deliberate about what they were going to do. At one point, they desperately looked around and asked me what I thought."

"What did you say to them?"

"I told them they really didn't have any options. They'd have to carry the dog out."

"That was their only option? Search and rescue doesn't rescue dogs?"

"No. The AVSAR team has approximately thirty to forty active duty members, about twelve to twenty-five of which can make any given call-out. If the team gets consecutive call-outs, the numbers of available responders quickly drop. The additional time it takes neighboring counties to answer mutual assistance requests, at the absolute bare minimum, is six hours, and more realistically, neighboring teams usually respond the day after the incident begins once they're requested."

"Wow."

"Because of the potentially risky position that rescuing a dog puts the SAR team in regards to taking away its ability to serve humans, I ensured that my SAR personnel were very clear on what my official response was to dog rescues—no dog rescues by county personnel. Dog rescues had to be organized by unofficial private parties."

In a sarcastic tone, I joked that in an extreme case I would take my time getting to the location of the canine, and then I would humanely euthanize the dog so as to not allow it to suffer, and to not expend very finite resources making up for a human's very bad decision.

"That's a bit extreme. You're joking?"

"Yes, of course. In this case I notified, unofficially, one of the cavalry heroes, Steve Morrison, that moron owners who were at risk of me assaulting them needed Steve's assistance in getting a dog out to safety. I reminded Steve to put forth as little effort as possible and figuratively beat-down the dog owner as much as possible. I wanted my heroes' energy saved for people. I wanted to rescue the dog, but I wanted the owner to learn a lesson. As a leader of a rescue team whose priority has to remain people over dogs, as much as I personally deeply love dogs, people have to be prioritized. Period."

"It's common sense that you wouldn't risk people's lives and safety over a dog's."

"And yet a lot of people bring dogs into the high country and end up in situations where the dog gets injured or its paw pads get damp in a storm and they rip off leaving bloody paw prints easily tracked for miles. Eventually the dog refuses to move. Then the owner can either carry it out or abandon the pup."

"Does that happen?"

"Sadly, yes."

A couple months later, in August of 2012, a man would abandon his female German shepherd mix, Missy, in the Mount Bierstadt–Mount Evans wilderness area west of Denver. After eight days, a group of volunteers (truly self-organized, non county-insured individuals) rescued Missy from the peaks.

"Honestly, there's one more scenario I've run into in SAR involving horses that's as heart wrenching as an abandoned dog is—horses are too big to carry out."

"Oh no. What?"

"Well, right about here in this beautiful little enchanted forest, a friend of mine, an off-duty Department of Interior BLM ranger was on his way down this trail tracking a blood trail from higher in the gorge when he encountered so much blood he knew an animal was dying. Sure enough, he finally encountered two men and two horses, one of the horses had a badly compound open-fractured leg. My friend said they were transferring their gear to the single horse, and a rifle was propped up on a nearby tree. He left the scene knowing how it would climax."

"I never even thought about an injured horse."

"It's easiest not to ponder these things, as animals are innocent and rarely have any say in getting themselves in the situations in which they become injured or dead. Unlike most people. I was on a mission that occurred on the northern tip of the Sangres involving a very loyal companion."

"Tell me that one."

"An AVSAR teammate, Jim Coulson, who was an army ranger and prisoner of war in Vietnam, was on a hasty team searching for an overdue retired air force colonel. The colonel had gone out on an exploratory 4x4 drive with his mixed breed medium-sized dog on the roads and trails in the vicinity of the northern Sangres, on the Wet Mountain side. A week after being reported missing, Jim's team found the colonel. He had rolled his vehicle, dragged himself to a nearby tree, and passed away. His uninjured dog, with no access to food or water, was loyally sitting there with his master, slowly starving and dehydrating to death. Jim said he has no idea how that dog survived for a week without access to any water. When I think about how dogs give everything they've got to us, I don't understand how anyone can be so selfish as to put their best friend at risk. If you bring your pup that's too big to stuff into a fanny pack in a moment's notice, my rule is to be very careful going above treeline. Even the cadaver dogs I've worked with are usually smaller labs. Small's just easier to manage in highly weight sensitive situations like talus rock that's wet from a rainstorm."

"I understand why rescuers get really, really pissed off when innocent dogs pay the price for ignorant, inexperienced masters."

"It's one reason I have a small dog. If I bring Freckles along on a long hike, I expect to be carrying him in the end, usually between mile ten and fifteen for the day. Around the time he's spent, he pulls up alongside me and sits *on* my feet. Soon after that, he refuses to move at all, and allows me to walk quite a distance away before whining and slowly trying to catch up. That's when I toss him in the pack. That way I'm not slowed down by a canine, but I can still enjoy his companionship if I want it. Plus, he's a convenient size for the tent.

The author with his rat terrier, Freckles, on the summit of Ellingwood Point looking south toward Blanca Peak (left) and Little Bear Peak (right). (Photo by Adam Wright with fish-eye lense.)

"My general rule is that if I'm going higher than treeline, traveling over rock for any length of time, or can't afford the extra weight at the end of the day, I don't bring a dog. I'm not a sadist, I'm not cruel, and to subject a dog to long distances over rugged, rocky, above treeline terrain is sadistic and cruel."

As my hiking date neared its conclusion, in the near darkness of sunset we returned to the trailhead and walked up to the car. As I opened the trunk, I took in the moment and I thought of another date ending, about a month prior. I thought about Jesse Peterson up at Willow Lake.

We put our packs in the trunk, and for a few moments I looked up at the stars just beginning to twinkle. I thanked Jesse for reminding me that for all the tragedy, the flip-side to existence is love. Spending the day enjoying the mountains, seeing the trail and views from the eyes of someone who associates nothing but wonder, I fell in love with the Sangres again.

I watched the stars twinkle and I thought of Jesse's last moments before the canoe tipped and he plunged into the near freezing water. He had been enjoying a wondrous afternoon, on a date with a young woman, likely feeling engaged in life and love, feeling very similar to what I was at the moment—contentment.

Two months later I read a letter to the editor in *The Crestone Eagle* and it reminded me that although I am no longer active with SAR, I am grateful for the time that I was active. It reminds me that no matter who we are, however we may help, support, and show compassion to others in times of need, it is heroic when we do.

August 29, 2012
Small community over hundreds of miles
Dear Editor,
Thank you so very much to all who sent cards, called, emailed and contacted me in person after our beautiful son and beloved brother Jesse Greye Eagle Peterson tragically drowned in Willow Lake on Memorial Day weekend.

Your outpouring of love and true caring show again what it means to live in this incredible small community spread over hundreds of miles. Jesse will be missed every day and every night, and only with your love and support will that reality be bearable.

Thank you all for your offers of help, food, and support in general. It means more than I can ever express in words. Thank you so much to both Saguache County offices of Clerk and Assessor for your compassion and understanding.

Thank you to all involved in the search and eventual recovery—you know what your work means to all of us.

Thank you to R. for your strength and to J.H. for your continuing guidance.

With deep gratitude and love,
Peter Peterson

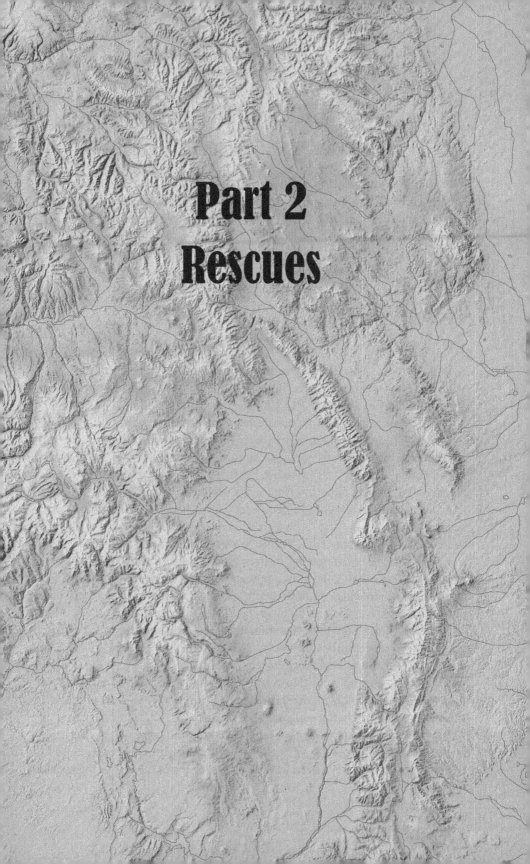

Part 2
Rescues

James Cornwall
Little Bear Peak, September 10, 2009

"I found the tales of rescue in the high mountains the most har-rowing to read about—my palms grew sweaty and I experienced sensations of vertigo as SAR teams tie themselves to sheer rock faces and rappel down to climbers stranded on ledges only a few feet wide."

—Joseph Cummins,
The Greatest Search and Rescue Stories Ever Told

At 1:23 p.m. on Thursday, I was in the midst of teaching a middle school grammar class when my phone began vibrating. I took the cell from my belt and looked at the caller ID, "911 CSP Regional Dispatch."

We had only been in school for a few weeks that year, but I had already trained my students, as part of my emergency drills, that I might receive calls from people in desperate need in the middle of the wilderness. They had already been told about 911 patches in which I may be acting like a 911 dis-patcher, giving life-saving instructions. I reminded them it might be one of their own family I'm trying to help, and that if there was a classroom man-agement issue during the time I took such a call, they could be affecting someone's ability to stay alive. Eighth graders, for all their angst and reputa-tion, still know rare interesting moments when they occur. When they saw me take this call, they knew it was serious and for an extremely rare moment in a middle school classroom filled with students, one could hear a pin drop. "Yup, it's dispatch calling—you guys stay quiet." I accepted the call.

"Kevin, this is Kate with Colorado State Patrol dispatch. I need to patch you through to a climber up on Little Bear Peak. He says his partner fell about fifty feet, has a head laceration and is unconscious."

I looked around the classroom full of students and mentally ran through the emergency medical directions I might have to start giving over the phone. CSP patched the climber's cell phone call to them directly to me. I knew the climber may have a very limited amount of battery; this might be the only time I would have the chance to talk to him. This class was full of eighth graders—they could handle whatever trauma I was going to treat over the phone.

I looked at my watch. In two minutes, at 1:25 p.m., the bell would ring and my afternoon planning period would begin, free of students.

The students couldn't quite hear what Kate was saying, and they leaned forward in their seats as I replied, "Did he indicate his location?"

"It sounds like they're near the top of the peak."

"Probably near the Hourglass?"

"I think he mentioned something about an hourglass. Alright, I'm going to get his climbing partner back on the line. His name is Bill."

"Thanks Kate."

"You'll be on hold for a bit. Bill will be on the line with you soon."

Perfectly timed, the class bell rang, the kids flinched instinctively, and they all got up and began filing out.

"Goodbye, be safe, always wear your seatbelts." This was my routine way of ending class, indicating to the students it was time to move along. As the last student walked out the door, I gently shut and locked the door behind him. I sat down in the front row in one of my student's desks, and I closed my eyes imagining the scene miles away, far above treeline, near the summit of a deadly mountain.

Kate's voice came back on the cell, "Kevin. I have Bill Schott on the line. Bill, this is Kevin Wright with Alamosa Volunteer Search and Rescue. Are you there Kevin?"

"Affirmative. This is Kevin. Bill, can you hear me?"

"Yes."

"Bill can you describe to me your immediate surroundings? Can you tell me where you are?"

Bill described the base of the Hourglass, on the "standard route" of Little Bear Peak. "My partner Jim fell, and we're both now just above a cliff that drops off into the valley."

"Okay, Bill. I know where you are, and I want you to know there's a team of us coming for you and Jim. Now I'm not sure how much phone power you have, so let's make as much use of it as possible. Tell me what happened and the condition of your partner. Can Jim speak to me directly?"

"No. Jim can't speak. Jim's barely conscious. He's lost a lot of blood."

"Bill. Can you describe to me what happened and how Jim is doing now?"

"Yes. We were just descending off the summit of Little Bear Peak. We had just completed the down-climb of the steep, roped section near the top."

"Yes. I know where you guys are located. Please continue." I wanted to give Bill any reassurance I could.

"We had just taken our helmets off and were traversing along the slope back to the west ridge. That's where one of the rocks under Jim slipped, and he lost his footing. He started falling, and he couldn't stop. He kept falling, cartwheeling, I'd estimate fifty feet, and right before the top of the cliff he stopped himself. I'm sitting next to him now. Jim's bleeding badly out of several cuts on his head. He's barely conscious. He's murmuring, not making sense sometimes."

"Bill. You're doing a great job, and we've got a team coming for you as fast as they can get to you. Do you see anywhere else that Jim's bleeding? Is he bleeding primarily from his head? Describe his breathing to me."

"He's not bleeding anywhere but from his head. His hands are black and blue and they're starting to swell."

"How is Jim lying? Is he stable? I'm worried he might have a spinal injury. If possible, he shouldn't be moved. We're coming as fast as we can."

"He's laying on top of a big rock. We're pretty close to the edge of a cliff. He's bleeding a lot from his head. He's got big gashes all over the top of his head."

"The top of his head? Bill, are the wounds open? Are there flaps, can you see tissue under his skin?" Suddenly, I felt better to be in an empty, echo chamber of a classroom, void of middle school ears.

"Yes. There are flaps of skin and hair, and I think I can see skull. He's lost so much blood."

"Okay Bill. Listen to me. Can you access Jim's helmet?"

I could hear things scratching on Bill's cell speaker. "Yes, I've got it."

"Okay Bill. I want you to close the flaps of skin on the top of his head. I want you to put the flaps of tissue back in place over Jim's skull. Then carefully, I want you to place Jim's helmet back over his head and evenly apply pressure over his cranium. At the same time, be very careful of a possible broken neck. Put on enough pressure to keep the flaps closed and stop the bleeding, but not so much as to move his neck. Does that make sense Bill?"

I heard more scratching on Bill's cell speaker. Bill was doing what I had just described; he was doing everything he could to save his climbing partner, his friend. I could hear Bill talking through a muffled cell phone.

I spent the time waiting for Bill by mentally going through trauma checklists. I started with the standard ABCDE's: Airway, breathing, circulation, disability, exposure. Jim's airway and breathing were stable, at least since the incident. His circulation, however, required immediate field treatment. In rare cases, patients have bled to death from relatively small head lacerations. Jim's profuse cranial bleeding needed to be addressed for him to live long enough for rescuers to reach and evacuate him.

In trauma, even though the initial medical assessment follows the ABC acronym (airway, breathing, circulation), a trauma responder remembers that the D of disability is really being taken into consideration from the A of airway. I knew that putting pressure on Jim's head could exacerbate a cervical spinal injury that could result in Jim's paralysis or death, but Jim's life was currently more at risk from bleeding to death than from a small bone fragment slicing through his spinal cord. That considered, I was very, very concerned about moving Jim's neck or spine. I envisioned Bill putting Jim's wounds together as well as he could and then very gently applying pressure, just enough to cease the bleeding, but not enough to palpate Jim's spine.

In my mind, as the muffled scratches continued, I got through the ABCD's and finally got to E, symbolizing "exposure." In trauma, this is a reminder to do a complete assessment of the patient's body, exposing them completely, cutting away clothing so that any disfigurements or small bleeds can be easily identified and managed. I imagined Jim at 13,000 feet, well above treeline, high up on Little Bear Peak's west face. Indeed, in Jim's case, the E of "exposure" made me think of the literal meteorological context of the word. It was only 1:30 in the afternoon in early September, and afternoon storms could still develop into formidable monsoon cumulonimbus incus thundersnow monsters.

Bill finally came back on the cell phone. "Kevin? Yes, I think that the pressure of the helmet is helping. The bleeding is slowing."

"Bill, you're doing a great job. Make sure you're very careful of Jim's neck. I'm afraid he may have broken it, so we've got to be very, very careful of any possible fractures. Try not to move Jim unless you have to in aid of his breathing. You're doing great, and we're heading to you right now. Bill, it's going to take us some time to get to your location. How's the weather? What's the sky look like?"

"Right now, it's sunny and warm."

"Okay Bill, that's good. When Jim's bleeding stops, and you get a chance, you get out all your jackets and wind and rain gear. Get ready to put it on Jim." I explained to Bill that I suspected we could get some afternoon storms, and we went over what Bill needed to monitor in his friend such as respiration, heart rate, consciousness levels, and exposure to the elements. At their elevation in mid-September, simply the sun setting could change the environment from a radiantly warm, summertime-like greenhouse to a near-freezing, brisk, windy, hypothermia-inducing winter-like scene, and that's not describing what happens when a late season, late afternoon thunderstorm rolls in.

"Bill, it's going to take us around four hours or so to reach you, and that's if everything goes well. At the longest, it could be six to eight hours before we can get to you. You've got to be ready to sit tight through potential afternoon storms. Try not to move Jim unless you absolutely have to. If you need anything, any medical directions, anything changes with Jim's vital signs, call me back directly at this phone number or call 911 again. You've done really well stabilizing Jim. You're saving his life. We're on our way as quickly as we can."

"Thanks. See you soon."

"See you soon, Bill."

I stood up, grabbed my jacket and briefcase, shut off my classroom lights, closed my locked classroom door, walked to a classroom across the hallway, and I asked one of my trusted co-workers to cover my last few classes. She knew I would owe her, and she was eager to help anyone in distress. I notified the secretary and principal that I was responding to an emergency and had my classes covered, then I jumped in my car, its trunk already containing my 72-hour SAR pack, including my clothes and boots. I turned onto Highway 160 and headed east out of Monte Vista bound for the Lake Como trailhead about one hour away. On the way, I called our executive secretary, Suzi Rasmussen, and she began an all-team callout.

I followed the speed limit until I crossed the county line; as soon as I was in my home county of Alamosa, I knew all the police and they knew me; additionally, they knew that I was responding (as several of them were, too), so I sped up to about 80–90 miles per hour. I was careful to be mindful of all the high-speed driving skills I had learned years prior while training at a military police academy. In between Monte Vista and Alamosa, I called the sheriff on speaker phone and requested he call Flight For Life. I asked him to request their "Lift Ticket" service. I wanted a lift into a landing zone (LZ) as close to Jim as we could get. I also called the team's other leaders and let them know FFL was on its way.

Flight For Life's Lift Ticket program pairs one of the Lifeguard helicopter teams with the corresponding regional county SAR teams. SAR techs get certified for the program by training with one of the Lifeguard teams. The helicopter comes in on a training day, lands (usually behind the Alamosa Sheriff's Office building), and techs are cycled through the basics—how to use the restraints, what to do in an emergency, what systems to shut down immediately upon crashing (if one is still conscious and can do so).

In addition to buckling in and plugging in the helmet to learn how to "comm." with the pilot, the SAR team sits through a short FFL video and briefing by the aircrew. Upon completion of the half-day training, Lift Ticket certified techs receive a bright orange or yellow card. This card, carried in the wallet, equals a "lift ticket" so that during a SAR mission, if need be, the tech presents the lift ticket to the aircrew of a Lifeguard helicopter and can then jump aboard and be lifted as close to a medical patient as possible, thus considerably speeding up the response time to patients. Upon being delivered via the Lift Ticket as a SAR hasty team, the tech's job is to reach the patient as quickly as possible, stabilize, and then wait for others to show up to transport the patient back to the field LZ and Lifeguard team waiting to transport the patient to a major trauma unit asap (Pueblo).

As I was cruising at a smooth 80 mph across a straight flat desert highway, I called the sheriff and he said that he had already called Flight For Life. They were inbound at the trailhead LZ a short time after I'd be arriving. My plan was to fly in our fastest, most capable medical and technical climbing SAR personnel, stabilize Jim, and then await a large contingent team of ground-based techs to perform the carry-out of the patient to the helicopter LZ. I hoped that we could pull it all off in time to save Jim's life. In the military I learned the motto, "Hope for the best, but be prepared for the worst." I hoped we could save Jim, but I prepared for him dying while we were en route or dying while we tried to evacuate him.

I followed traffic law to an obsessed perfection as I buzzed through Alamosa, and I figured that with the volunteer team's staggered response times, many teammates had probably stopped to grab their 72-hour backpacks, and now we were all getting on the highway heading out to the trailhead at about the same time.

As I passed the last residential homes along Highway 160 just east of Alamosa, I floored the Corolla until its governor kicked in around 95 mph. Statistically, the most dangerous thing SAR responders do is to drive to and from the mission, especially driving home after a long mission and falling asleep at the wheel. Danger and risk-taking is relative, so to help maintain a calm Zen focus and to support an operational planning state of mind, I played classical music in the background.

Although there are a couple dead spots between cell towers along the route, I continued to receive text updates from Suzi, the team's executive secretary, which team members were responding to. Suzi was also a reserve deputy with the sheriff's office, and she often acted as incident commander. She probably sensed that although I was helping to get things rolling, she was coordinating the operation, and I would likely be one of the first responders sent to the patient. She would be the incident commander and operations manager for the mission.

I arrived at the trailhead after at least a dozen other SAR responders. I walked around and tied long fluorescent surveyor's tape tails to the tips of several car antennas as impromptu windsocks for Lifeguard Four, inbound from Pueblo, now just minutes from landing. To increase our visibility as SAR personnel, we were encouraged to wear bright fluorescent clothing. In my case, I had acquired a bright orange jacket with reflective strips sewn all around the exterior. I was visible from a distance, and I grabbed a radio so I could act as the ground comm./support in the field landing.

I asked several techs to help me check half a football field-sized chunk of rabbit brush desert for FOB (foreign objects/debris) and removing it so that it could not be picked up in the helicopter's rotor wash and recycled back into the helicopter and damaging it. We especially were eager to clear out things such as chunks of barbed wire, a chunk of rusted out car panel, jackets, hats—all things that could easily go airborne and cause havoc.

As the helicopter circled and used me as their landing guide, I put my back to the wind, that way the aircraft would have a slight headwind as it would land in front of me. The pilot watched my hand signals in case I saw any FOB get picked up or any other reason to abort a landing, but in this case, everything went textbook perfectly.

Flight For Life's Lifeguard Four crew meeting with the author just following their initial landing on September 10, 2009, at the command post for the mission to rescue James Cornwall (photo by Don Thompson).

Everyone on scene circled up and I briefed the group. The plan was obvious and a "standard textbook mission." We would follow our standard operating procedures for our given personnel and resources. With over twenty personnel en route to the trailhead, the SOP was to assign several techs as a hasty team. We prioritized the most technically capable medical personnel, and via Flight For Life, those techs would "lift" up to the closest LZ to Jim, stabilize him, and then standby while everyone else responded via modified 4x4s, as the contingent "muscle," the carry-out team.

Lifeguard Four swapped out their flight nurse and flight medic for two of our SAR personnel. These two would be the first to embark on the race to the patient to save his life. Then two more flights of two persons each would follow the first flight. In all, six techs would be lifted to the closest LZ to the patient, and then everyone else would race to the scene via ground transportation (the 4x4s and their feet). As soon as everyone was on scene, we would carry the patient back to the LZ, and get the patient to a trauma unit as fast as possible.

I had designed the AVSAR team roster to be a spreadsheet of the official volunteer team members and their qualifications information. Included were columns that indicated each team member's skill sets. I listed the skills if the team member had consistently demonstrated them to the team during training. Some volunteers were more proficient with horses, horses being very helpful in extracting bodies from isolated wilderness areas where mechanized vehicles are forbidden. Other team members were highly qualified medical specialists: EMTs, paramedics, nurses, physician assistants, medical doctors. Another group of team members were the 4x4 "gearheads." These were the men who had their own personal auto shops, garages capable of advanced machining and welding. Their highly modified vehicles served as the specialized, modified rock crawlers that served as the most badass, special operations-like ambulances one may ever be graced to be transported in. Another group of techs included the technical mountaineers—the riggers and climbers; then there were the skiers, the snowmobilers; the hunters, the ATV enthusiasts, the Civil Air Patrol pilots/liaisons, the law enforcement officers, and the SCUBA divers. Everyone on the team had a skill set they brought to the rescue table. With the team's master roster, the incident commander quickly prioritized who should be on the initial hasty teams, inserted two at a time via the FFL helicopter.

Mick Daniel and Mike Henderson, two skilled mountaineers who were also medically experienced and certified Wilderness First Responders, would be the first two flown in. Next it would be Chris Lavery and Andrew McClure, two young, fast mountaineers who were also certified in wilderness first response and wilderness first aid. The third and last flight would be Don Thompson and myself. Don was older, seasoned, and an experienced veteran SAR team member. He had run races such as the Hardrock 100, had previously proven himself cool-headed and capable in the midst of chaos. I was an experienced mountaineer and emergency medical technician. After us six, the vehicles driven by Roy Hood, Jess Caton, and Steve Morrison would shuttle people up to Lake Como where the vehicles then needed to be cached so the team could ascend the west ridge, traverse the ridge easterly for about a half mile, and rendezvous with the patient at 13,000 feet just below the Hourglass. The vehicles' cache would be right next to the LZ where the FFL helicopter would drop the hasty team members. The plan was that once everyone returned to the LZ, loaded the patient on the chopper (that would then go directly to the hospital), the vehicles would be on location ready to ride back to the command post.

I asked the incident commander, reserve deputy and AVSAR executive secretary, Suzi, to remain at the command post, and I asked Jess to lead the team of ground pounders (everyone in the vehicles). Jess and I agreed it was going to be a long night.

I helped the Flight For Life pilot land near the command post, radioing and hand signaling ground conditions. The aircrew joined us for the last summary of the plan. The briefing ended with weather predictions and communication contingencies, in case any radio communication failed us, a common occurrence in the mountain valleys without line of sight to repeaters. Because it was already late in the afternoon, we all agreed that the most likely scenario was that we wouldn't be able to fly FFL at night in such treacherous mountain terrain. We would be awaiting a Flight For Life extraction at least until morning. Depending upon the patient's condition in the early morning when we were likely to return to the LZ, we could re-assess what the mission required—extraction via the ground vehicles because the patient's condition was stable and good, or possibly a body recovery via the ground because the patient had expired. If the patient was still requiring critical life-saving procedures, Flight For Life could come in at first light if conditions were safe (a high enough cloud deck for visibility of the ground and no wind).

Mick and Mike loaded onto the small orange helicopter and lifted off very quickly after the pilot had sparked the powerful turbine engine. The time it took to deliver the hasty responders and return to pick up the next group was just ten minutes.

Next flight in was Chris and Andrew. By the time the helicopter was returning for the third set of hasty responders, Don and me, those ingressing via the ground vehicles were ready to head up the road. I followed the directives of the pilot (given in hand gestures), and Don and I mindfully walked up to the aircraft and got on board.

As we plugged in our helmets' communication systems and reviewed what to do in the case of an emergency, the second the review was over, we lifted off and very quickly gained altitude. I watched the vehicles leaving the command post, small clouds of dust rising, and because of the nature of the modified 4x4s, I thought they looked like a Mad Max convoy. Indeed, our mission was primal and apocalypse related—like the hero Mad Max, we were trying to save a life, to delay the apocalypse for one soul.

As the pilot flew into the western entrance of Chokecherry Canyon, my attention turned 100 percent to the massive rock walls, cliffs whose scales were in the thousands of feet, steep snowfields, couloirs, talus and scree aprons surrounding the small craft. Flying in certainly saved an enormous amount of energy, but even at the helicopter's speed and perspective, the mountain was dominant and dictated everything we did.

Feeling some light wind nudge the helicopter side to side was more than enough for me to look forward to being under the power of my own locomotion as soon as possible. As we landed, the pilot wished us luck, explained it was a hot offload (the turbine and rotors weren't shut down), and his compadre would see us in the morning. The next pilot would already have the LZ's GPS coordinates, so the next day and in the future, like breadcrumbs, any of the FFL pilots could follow the track to this exact spot. Don and I thanked him, departed the helicopter, took refuge a few hundred feet away, and took a couple pictures as the orange flying chariot lifted off and graciously turned and descended the valley. The stark contrast of the helicopter's loud, whining turbine with the sudden silence of treeline as its rotor beats vanished into the light breeze was a shock, and another shock was the near instantaneous transition from 8,000 feet elevation to 11,000 feet.

Author securing backpack after being dropped off at the nearest LZ to the patient on Little Bear Peak (photo by Don Thompson).

I looked up the west ridge's access couloir, and I could see the team ahead of us. Chris and Andrew were about halfway up the ridge. Each of the six of us carried something very helpful in the medical stabilization of the patient. In my pack I was carrying an inexpensive sleeping bag that we used as "hypothermia bags"—disposable sleeping bags that we could layer as seasons got colder and warmer.

It was near sunset, clouds had covered the sun on several occasions, and the cool 11,000-foot elevation breeze reinforced that the patient, Jim, would be needing the layers of external warmth as soon as possible. I started heading up the scree-filled couloir, and I asked Don if he had anything critical to the initial care of the patient. "Just extra water. Get going, I'll be behind you," he replied. Knowing that within about an hour to an hour and a half the ground crew would arrive in this spot and be ascending right behind us, I figured it would be okay to put some distance between Don and I as we ascended the standard west ridge route of Little Bear Peak.

About half way up the ridge, I caught Chris. Seeing that his partner Andrew was at the top of the ridge starting the traverse and out of sight, I asked if Chris wouldn't mind me leap-frogging him, switching partners, and if he would accompany Don to the accident site while I caught up with Andrew. Chris nodded and gave a thumbs-up in affirmation, the altitude taking its toll on longer dialogs that would rob us of oxygenation.

By the time I gained the ridge and started traversing easterly along the ridge's crest, Don and Chris were three-quarters of the way up the ridge from Lake Como. I looked down the route, very clearly burning the image and details of the route into my senses and memory. I had been here so often it seemed second nature, but even with experience one wants to be attuned to details that can mean the difference between staying on route and getting off route in highly technical, dangerous terrain. In this case, I memorized the fact that this route never went out on hard rock, no boilerplates. The route, as steep as it was, was scree over hard soil. Several people had lost their lives by descending the wrong couloir; from high up on the ridge, Blue Lake looks similar to Lake Como, and too often people have tried to descend a chute that's too far easterly on the west ridge. As they descend into farther and farther steepening terrain, by the time they realize their mistake, for many it has been too late, and they've fallen and died.

In this evening's case, I was making fast time. I had set a pace that kept my heart rate around 150, and I was sweating heavily. The strong, consistent breeze skimming the ridgetop felt especially refreshing. The breezes also foreshadowed the cooler, denser, humid air of the night. It would get cold later, as soon as the sun dropped behind the horizon, something that would occur within a half-hour or so by my estimation. I could use the last sunlight of the day to spare my headlamp and much more quickly cover the ground between the notch at the top of the Lake Como access couloir and the base of the Hourglass Couloir, about a half-mile east where the end of the west ridge intersects the northwest and west faces of Little Bear Peak.

I could no longer see Andrew, as the ridge rose from the notch I had just gained, thus producing a false summit perspective and Andrew was well beyond the terrain where I could see. I thought I might be able to catch him by the time we reached the patient. I knew we were all racing as hard and fast as we could push our bodies, but the thought of Jim, the patient, suffering and so desperately needing our assistance made a slight sense of panic creep in, and my heart rate rose a bit.

It was just a small rise in the rate of my pulse, but it was too much at such extreme limits—the thin air, the aerobic challenge, the physical pushing. I had to stop and catch my breath and slow my heart rate. I put Jim out of my mind and focused on being mindful of every step. Even though the refrigerator-sized talus boulders were mostly solid, a path even worn into the rocks from years of use by peak baggers, there were still the occasional smaller talus blocks and shifting terrain that would cause the foot to move or worse, roll. As I traversed the ridge and continued ascending gradually, I caught glimpses of Andrew. He and I were about paced—as fast as I thought I was covering ground, I wasn't closing the distance between us as we moved. Coming over one final rise between the west ridge and the mountain's west face, I could see the patient, the patient's hiking partner, Mick, Mike, and Andrew. The sun had just set, and the three SAR personnel were getting out their wind layers and headlamps. Drenched in sweat and suddenly stopping, the breeze would chill all of them quickly, and they were all instinctively taking precautions to guard against anything that could strip their bodies of energy.

As I walked onto the scene, Mick approached me and pulled me aside. "Jesus, Kevin. I just got here a few minutes before you, and I've just started assessment. Look, there's blood everywhere. He's barely responsive. I can't find a pulse anywhere—his blood pressure is so low. He's murmuring gibberish when I stimulate him. We may lose him on the way out."

I had prepared myself for the worst, so I was expecting an unconscious patient, near dead, agonal gasping. Learning that Jim was still responding, albeit barely, to verbal stimulation was profoundly boosting to my morale. Maybe this patient would live? Most likely not, but maybe.

I began going through my mental EMT's checklist. Number one was always the safety of the scene. I had surveyed the scene as I approached it, and what jumped out at me regarding safety was that the group was precariously located beneath a loose rock face with lots of potential for rock fall. The group was also located just thirty or so feet from the top of a hundred-foot vertical cliff.

I introduced myself to the patient's hiking partner, Bill, the gentleman who I had spoken with hours before on the phone. It felt like days ago. "Bill, hi I'm Kevin Wright. We spoke on the phone earlier. Sorry it took so long. We got here as fast as we could. We're the first responders who flew in via Flight For Life, and there's a lot more coming up behind us via 4x4s. Would you do me a favor?"

"God, it is so good to see you guys!" Bill said, looking very tired.

"Indeed. Now do me a favor please, Bill. Put your helmet back on and sit above Jim here. Provide a bit of a shield in case any rock fall bounces down from above."

"Good idea."

"If we hear any rock fall coming from above, do *not* look up to see if you can see it coming. Instead, just hunker down into the boulders the best you can and shield your head and Jim's head if you can."

I threw off my pack and immediately donned my windproof jacket. The sweat on my back felt cold without the pack insulating it. I asked for the wilderness first responder (WFR) pack, which one of the first two SAR techs had carried in before me. I opened the bag and I prepared to do what I could to stabilize the patient and prep him for evac.

I put on exam gloves, prepared several rolls of gauze, and asked Andrew to fire up a pot of hot water. I asked Mick to be my assistant. As our head-lamps' light began competing with the ambient light of the high-altitude sunset, I got down close to Jim and started assessing him for injuries. As I crouched down, a small rock got in my way under one of my knees. I tossed it downhill out of the way, and I was surprised to watch it bounce over the edge and disappear into oblivion. There was no sound of impact. A fall here could have catastrophic consequences. I began speaking loudly so the patient could hear me through the shock, "Jim? Jim, can you hear me?!" There was no response at first, just the slow rise and fall of his back indicating respirations. I tried again, "JIM. JIM CORNWALL, can you hear me? Say something JIM."

This time Jim responded with a clearly audible moan. He was semi-conscious and reacting to the verbal stimulus. This gave me hope. As I knelt down very close to him, I took note of how his body was wrapped around over the top of the boulder. He had come to rest face down, wrapped around a refrigerator-sized boulder. I was very concerned about Jim's neck and spine. It seemed that with the amount of energy that his body had sustained while falling, he very likely had broken his neck. As I continued my assessment, I noticed that in the process of falling, Jim had severely lacerated the top of his head, and now these injuries were slightly lower than the rest of his body, his feet being about the same height or a little higher than his head. His injuries and his body positioning had resulted in a great deal of blood loss. On the rock on which he fell, the nearby rocks surrounding his head, and the rocks beneath Jim's location, I estimated there to be at least a couple liters of blood.

Andrew mentioned that it was surprising how much the metallic smell of the blood would still linger so richly in the mountain breeze. I wished that someone on site was certified to put in an IV so we could raise Jim's blood pressure, unfortunately, none of us who were on site were IV certified.

At first Jim's and my communication occurred in the form of me loudly barking questions or directives and Jim moaning in response. Mick, the second most medically experienced person on the scene after myself, acted as my assistant in stabilizing Jim. I looked up at Mick to make sure he was ready as I loudly said, "JIM, I'm going to take off your helmet and see what's going on with your head injuries."

Jim moaned in response. "Mick, let's get this bleeding stopped, and then we'll stabilize the C-spine." C-spine stood for cervical spine—in the case of a broken neck, it is imperative that a cervical collar (C-collar) is used to stabilize the injury to avoid fractured bone severing the spinal cord and killing the patient. I was amazed that even after the approximately six hours it had taken to respond, which for that location was an amazing speed record made possible by a helicopter insertion, that Jim's head lacerations were still weeping, enough that a drop of blood was still consistently dropping from his helmet every minute or so. The mixture of old blood and fresh blood was a scent that would challenge anyone's resolve, even those of us who were well desensitized to it.

Bill told me that he had done as I instructed and used Jim's helmet to distribute universal pressure all around Jim's head, thus helping put pressure on the wounds and stopping the bleeding. Being very careful of Jim's C-spine, I slowly withdrew his helmet to examine what the injuries looked like (now six hours following the incident).

I was not surprised to find that Jim's head was not simply lacerated (slices in the skin), but there were large avulsions (flaps) to significant areas of his scalp. In his sixty- to seventy-foot tumble down the steep slope, Jim had impacted his skull on the razor sharp rocks and split the tissue into several large flaps. Most people know how injuries to the head bleed profusely, even from a small gash. The size of the avulsions and Jim's positioning, head down, explained the profuse loss of blood on scene.

As the last ultraviolet light set on the Blood of Christ mountain tops, I thought it ironic that in the deep purple-red glow, actual sangre spilled in the Sangre mountains appeared black, its metallic odor and syrupy viscosity being more significant than its color.

Jim's blood continued to ooze from a small weepy point where two avulsions met, where the flesh had retracted a small amount, exposing a quarter- to a half-inch of Jim's deeper skull tissues. The blood was still doing its job trying to fill the gaps, to clot, to protect from infection. Some of Jim's hair had gotten caught in the closing of the flaps, but the wound edges had begun to fuse and close, so I used some warm water and an iodine solution to disinfect topically the wounds and the top of Jim's head, and then Mick and I carefully bandaged and dressed Jim's head, one of us manually securing Jim's C-spine and the other replacing the helmet to continue providing universal pressure all around the top of Jim's skull. The next challenge was going to be stabilizing Jim's cervical spine (his neck).

I asked one of the techs to get the cervical collar out of the medical bag, and as he handed it to me, something was wrong. It was in two separate pieces in its plastic bag. I took it out of the bag and noticed that in multiple times of being taken out and repacked in the backpack, it had become creased at one of the least reinforced junctions in the plastic, and it had broken into two pieces. "This C-collar is worthless," I mentioned to Mick and the other techs. "We're going to have to improvise with a SAM splint." Mike, who had flown in initially with Mick, unrolled a SAM splint and began fashioning it as a C-collar. Slowly, deliberately, while Mick placed a small amount of traction on Jim's neck, I secured Jim's cervical spine with the modified SAM splint. Upon fitting it, the chin cup was a little small, but with a quick adjustment of the malleable styrofoam-covered aluminum, the impromptu C-collar was working as good or better than the actual medical splint would have.

I started to become haunted by the idea that none of us medical personnel were currently certified to put IV lines in patients, so even though Jim would have significantly benefited from the additional blood pressure and hydration an IV line and solution would provide, there was no one nor the equipment for such a treatment. Instead, like the SAM splint, I adapted to the situation and what we had available. I diluted Gatorade with some warm water, sucked up about 60 milliliters of solution in the syringe usually used as a field vacuum for the airway, and I slowly began dribbling electrolytes and water back into Jim's body.

About the same time that it had taken me to bandage Jim's head wounds and stabilize his neck, the remaining team members who had come in via ground vehicles began walking into the dark scene by headlamp. As Mick and I slowly dribbled Gatorade into Jim's mouth, he became more responsive and lucid. Out of the dark, more and more equipment appeared next to us. I was happy to see the litter, a two-piece Stokes model, now buckled together in the single piece by which we'd carry Jim out. Using multiple assistants with lots of hands, we carefully log-rolled Jim into the litter.

As I started securing Jim to the litter via a spider web of tubular webbing, I thought about what we had in store. We were going to have to traverse along the west ridge for about a half-mile and then drop a couple thousand feet down a scree-filled chute that was about a 40-degree slope. We'd have to belay the litter over the tops of some very steep ribs, all in the darkness of night. As I finished tying Jim in, he started moaning loudly and cursing, "MMMM-mmm, please don't tie me in. Please don't fucking tie me down!"

This was the first time I'd heard Jim curse, and I was a bit wary as increasing combativeness and change of character was something I was on the lookout for—a sign of intracranial pressure (ICP) building up. This far in the wilderness, with as much time as Jim had between dropping his first F-bomb and an operating room that could relieve pressure building up on the brain, Jim would pass away long, long before we flew him out on board Lifeguard Four. I asked Bill if Jim's cursing was normal for him.

"No, but I think he's just really, really angry about being tied into the litter. I think he's claustrophobic."

"I know this is going to be hard on him, but for his security, we have to tie him into the litter. Tell him to stop fighting."

Bill and I took turns forcefully telling Jim to relax and stop fighting us. We had to get him secured in the litter to begin the evacuation. At one point, Jess Caton's wife, Tish Caton, the only woman on site, tried to help Jim stop fighting. He responded far more to her voice than any of the rest of ours. I couldn't blame him, Tish's voice was soothing compared to the rest of our gruff barks.

"Go to your happy place Jim. Go to a place where you're relaxed, a place far away from here," Tish said over and over to help ease Jim's pain and anxiety. Finally, Jim was ready for transport.

With Jim securely tied into the Stokes litter, we began our carry-out. I told the SAR members to keep an eye on Bill as we made our way out. He had already experienced an extremely long day, and he was at risk of complicating the mission by having an accident. We were in no position to render aid to two patients.

As we began making our way across the slope, the nighttime darkness slowed our progress, and we all became acutely aware of the danger we were in and the danger of what we planned to do. At this point, only the light of the stars and our headlamps illuminated the route.

There were a dozen people on the scene. Bill was exhausted from providing Jim company and aid during the day, not to mention Bill and Jim had successfully summited Little Bear that morning. I didn't count him as part of the carrying crew, and I asked him to follow along carefully watching his footing. A total of a dozen people may seem like a lot; however, if possible, such a carry-out calls for twenty-four rescuers. With twenty-four, eight rescuers can carry for twenty minutes and then be relieved for forty minutes as the other two groups of eight rotate carrying. In this case, not only were we twelve folks short of the ideal twenty-four, a couple of the techs present were suffering from acute mountain sickness and nearly worthless when it came to carrying a patient; I could hear one occasionally vomiting out in the darkness, and the other was nursing a headache that was causing him ataxia. The remaining ten SAR personnel began switching off spots on the litter—six people grabbed hold of the litter and walked carrying it at their sides. Eight people could fit had we also not needed to carry our large 72-hour SAR packs. Out of twelve, two sick, six on the litter, the remaining four divided into two teams of two.

One team of two went ahead into the darkness and scouted the route by headlamp. The effort it required to move Jim even a few feet in the talus was enormous; having to backtrack because of route finding errors would waste precious life-saving time and energy. In addition to the two people who went ahead and scouted, the remaining two hung around the litter and assisted in really tough spots or relaxed their arms, preparing to rotate into one of the six litter carrying roles relatively quickly, after maybe a twenty-minute break. This simply was not enough time for muscles near failure to recover between hour-long carrying sessions. Sometimes the scouts or the two others recovering from carrying acted as body belay anchors and belayers as Jim's litter was carefully passed from attendant to attendant over exposed sections at the tops of rocky ribs.

Often the team would be able to cover only a few feet before the boulders would rise or fall considerable distances for a litter. Class three terrain becomes the equivalent of class four, and class four becomes class five. A small obstacle, such as an eight-foot sheer wall, is a fun, short bouldering problem when encountered on a route using ridge-top talus as a boulder field maze, a "choose one's own adventure" to a mountain top; but, trying to negotiate a litter with a man-sized patient through such terrain was exhausting, back-breaking work.

In the cases when we'd encounter a small obstacle, such as an eight-foot wall, we'd have to set the litter down on the edge, position half of us at the base, half at the top, and then do a handoff, where all the techs would remain solidly planted and only the basket and patient would move. Every time we set Jim down, he moaned and squirmed and fought, and he cussed in muffled fits, and occasionally yelled out, "Just let me up, I'll walk out of here." It was often Tish who would speak soothingly to Jim, reminding him to relax, psychologically make himself distant from the place where we were, "Go to your happy place, Jim." He continued to voice his discomfort with being tied into the litter.

The trail, marked by cairns that were relatively easy to follow during the day, became a difficult challenge finding by headlamp at night. The scouts, although relieved of their litter-carrying duty, were constantly anxious, moving quickly ahead trying to gauge where the next cairn would be based on the line-up of the team's headlamps. If the trail took a little dogleg or unexpected turn, the scouts got off route and had to search desperately fast to get back on route before the litter caught up to them. On a couple occasions this occurred, and it gave the litter team a chance to set down and shake out their grips, as well as be more attentive to the patient.

At one point we set Jim down on a rock ledge. Our headlamps had minimized the universe's scale down to what was immediately in front of us. We were becoming very attuned to all the small ledges and pockets where our feet would stick as we moved Jim from boulder to boulder, ledge to ledge. On this ledge, those uphill from Jim had good perches, solid ledges, but those of us below him had more precarious ledges to stand on, ledges that had been worn smooth from the years of climbers funneled into this section of the route. Those of us who had been on the route more than once recognized the spot even in the darkness as one of the tops of a rib of rock. It was one of the big ones, one that dropped into an avalanche chute and ran out all the way to the valley floor near Little Bear Lake, thousands of feet below.

I listened to Jim's breathing and took his pulse. At this point, a small pool of blood was collecting at the corner of one of Jim's eyes. As I tried to figure out where the blood was originating, I realized that Jim was bleeding out of his eye, literally. Jim had hit his head so hard during his several story fall that he had ruptured blood vessels behind one of his eyes. Slowly, this blood was working its way forward and emerging at Jim's tear duct area. Over time, as we transported Jim tied down, face-up, blood slowly built up in one eye. On one of the set downs, one of the techs with the WFR bag was getting out a new roll of gauze to hand me to dab the blood out of Jim's eye. As the tech handed off the gauze roll, still in its plastic packaging, I dropped the gauze package. This happened at a time when no one was speaking, no sounds were audible except for the panting of hard work. Everyone's headlamps turned downhill from Jim and searched for the dropped gauze roll, but by the time everyone's lamps had swung looking down the chute, the roll had vanished falling away in the darkness, but we could hear a faint bouncing of its plastic for several seconds. Eerily, the sound quickly dissipated into the pitch black.

I exclaimed, "Well, it's steeper here than it looks by headlamp. Everyone watch their footing and if you lose your balance, recover quickly. Don't build up any inertia on these slabs."

The uphill carriers at least had the added security of feeling that if they lost their footing or balance, the litter would act as a last ditch body belay, stopping their slide. Anyone on the downhill side had no additional security if our footing or balance failed. We simply began sliding downhill away from the group. This happened continuously to those of us on the downhill side.

On another occasion I was downhill of the litter and as it was being moved over the rock it scraped a rock the size of a traffic cone, not too different in shape from a cone, either. As the litter struck the rock, the rock fell and one of its edges slid down the front of my shin, stripping several layers of skin off several inches, even through my pants. I felt a bead of blood build up and slowly run down my leg. "Son of a bitch," I exclaimed to Jess.

"What?!"

"I just scraped my leg and it's bleeding into my sock."

"Well, can you weight it?"

"Sure. It's not that bad."

"Well then it's functional and not a problem. If you can weight it, let's keep going. I can barely grip the litter any more. Literally, I'm losing my grip."

"Me too."

Jim moaned again and blurted out his displeasure at being tied up in the litter. "Untie me, I can walk out. Let me try."

Shortly, the group ran into the scouts. We had traversed the ridgeline to the point at which the ridge and route drops in elevation. The scouts had missed the trail dropping off to the south of the ridge. Although this loss of the trail wasted time, it gave those of us carrying some time to massage our forearms. Mick and another tech agreed to go forward and help get us back on route.

Jim moaned again, "Please let me get up. I have to use the bathroom, and I think I'll be able to walk."

It was now somewhere around 11:30 p.m. The team had all been fighting valiantly to get Jim across the talus of the west ridge. Foot by foot, sometimes inch by inch, the battle to move Jim's litter was extremely hard won. People's grips were reaching muscle failure, their forearm muscles simply past the point of any utility whatsoever.

Since it had been hours (almost twelve) since Jim's accident, and because I hadn't noticed any increasing signs indicating intracranial pressure buildup, I thought I might make a rare, radical treatment call in terms of Jim's medical treatment. I thought that Jim was possibly correct. Maybe with the amount of Gatorade (which was only about 180 cc's of liquid), Jim's blood pressure was high enough that with enough support to either side, maybe he and two assistants could walk very slowly down the class two trail. Everyone could help when we ran into the occasional spots of class three moves. The issue with this plan was that if Jim's back was broken, and I were to take him off the backboard, sit him up to walk, the pressure of movement could exacerbate the injury and paralyze him, or worse, kill him.

I remembered a saying in wilderness expeditionary medicine that only two people in the world are qualified to take a patient off a backboard and clear their spine—an emergency room doctor and a wilderness first responder. Very, very rarely should one ever have to take away a supportive splint outside of an ER (such as a cervical collar or a KED splint for the thoracic and lumbar spine). I would have never expected to be in a situation requiring such a radical option, but here I was, and I had learned that SAR regularly required us responders to improvise in situations we didn't expect.

Slowly I ran my fingers down each of Jim's back vertebrae, palpating each back and forth, up and down with enough force to produce discomfort, especially if I were to run into any tissue that was fractured or inflamed. I ran into no such tissue as I "cleared" Jim's back. I chose not to clear his neck. So much energy had obviously gone into the top of his skull that Jim's injuries and state convinced me that he had significantly injured, likely fractured, his neck, so I left on the improvised SAM splint cervical collar. Jess and I slowly assisted Jim as he sat up. Jim was somewhat lucid and grateful to be unrestrained as he sat up and prepared to rise to his feet, but as we braced him and he tried to stand, his blood pressure changed and Jim slumped over into unconsciousness.

Jess and I carefully laid Jim back into the litter, and re-tied his restraints. We now had no choice—we were between a rock and a hard place, a do or die situation. Either the twelve of us would make the LZ by morning, or we'd have to sit and wait for a relief group to finish the carry out, a group that would take hours to respond from neighboring counties to get to our location—hours that Jim didn't have. If we couldn't keep moving Jim and get to the LZ, Jim would die.

I looked around, and especially in the light of the headlamps, people's expressions and moods looked weary and desperate. As I began to contemplate how long Jim would live if we found ourselves stuck, unable to move any longer, I remembered a trick I had seen a long time ago, either in my youth being around Alpine Rescue Team members or later when I was enlisted in the military. I remembered in long carry-outs that attendants used short leashes of webbing to extend their "grip" from the litter over their shoulders.

I told everyone to standby and fuel up on food, water, electrolytes, and anti-inflammatories. I passed around my bottle of Ibuprofen and modeled an 800 mg dosage. Then I asked for a few minutes to adjust the litter's rigging.

As everyone else chugged water and ingested some "vitamin I," I cut away the unused tails at the end of tie-ins, and eventually what I had was six sections of eight-foot webbing leashes. I tied a loop in one end of each of the leashes, and then I girth hitched this loop on the litter near each attendant's location. Now each attendant could lift the litter and use the webbing strap to distribute the weight across their arms, shoulders, and neck. In the case of any emergency, an attendant nearly had to let go of the strap to disengage from the litter. In low-angle technical litter transport like this, it is protocol that attendants never tie directly to the litter.

After demonstrating how to employ the new webbing straps, and hopefully with a little blood sugar and painkillers kicking in, people slowly roused to their feet and we all agreed to make another go for the notch on the ridge that marked the top of the Lake Como access couloir. If we could make it to that point, the rest of the route was basically setting anchors at the top of the chute and lowering Jim using ropes, the "package" being guided down by a couple attendants.

Mick walked forward and illuminated the next cairn with his headlamp. "We're dropping off the top of the ridge on its south side. We're getting close to the notch where we'll drop to the lake." What would take a strong hiker on a sunny day maybe ten minutes to cover, took us over an hour. The good news was that not only did the webbing straps suddenly give us the power to continue moving the litter, Jim's vocalizing his displeasure with being tied down ceased. It was as if the struggle to sit up and valiantly propel oneself down the trail under one's own power had been absolutely squelched; the will to fight the claustrophobia draining like Jim's brain had drained of blood upon trying to stand.

I had been carrying the litter acting as the primary medical caretaker for Jim. I had been checking and recording Jim's breathing and respirations. I had been wiping away the latest blood to pool on his eye. Mick was helping with route finding, and as we all got to the west ridge notch above Lake Como, Mick said that he would help Andrew, our team's ace rock climber and rigger, in setting up the extensive anchors required to lower the litter with two or three attendants attached. Mick and I agreed I would remain primarily responsible for Jim during this time.

I watched as everyone's attention and headlamps turned toward the top of the access couloir—a network of crumbling fissures and blocks, some of which were surprisingly solid. Solid enough that Andrew, Mick, and a couple others began placing active camming protection and hammering pitons deep into cracks, intent on equalizing the mass placed on them, using them as anchors to lower a crew down the couloir.

I knew my team, some of the most graceful, masterful, rock climbers, mountaineers, medical "renaissance folks" I had ever been blessed to know. I sat back trusting that without me watching each anchor's placement, they would be solid when finally utilized. After taking Jim's pulse and other vitals, I laid down right next to him and shut off my headlamp. I looked up at the exceptionally dark sky filled with billions of stars and the obvious arm of the Milky Way. I relaxed and consciously matched my breathing to Jim's. I listened to his clear, rhythmic breathing and I felt his wrist for a strengthening pulse. I didn't want him to sleep with such head trauma, but I also didn't think that forcefully keeping him awake would be of any benefit. I watched a shooting star briefly flash over our heads and I closed my eyes focusing on Jim's breathing.

From an anxious semi-awake state, I sat upright startled. I must have just started to drift off, as I was briefly confused as to why I was awakening to the smell of rich, alpine grass and earth instead of a comfortable bed and pillow. In the dark, I could hear Jim's breathing next to me, and I looked up into a headlamp that whispered, "Kevin, Kevin, you awake?"

"Yes. Jeez. I must have dozed off while waiting for the anchors to get set up. How long was I asleep?"

"Not long. You were snoring for maybe a couple minutes or so. We thought you might wake up Jim! Andrew just finished setting the anchors. They should have 'em equalized at focal points shortly. Who's going to be lowered with Jim?"

"Let's figure that out when we get ready to start the lowers." I sat up and looked around at my surroundings, reorienting myself after the catnap of just a few minutes. I began the obsessive ritual of taking Jim's vital signs.

Another headlamp voiced, "Hey Kev, how can you sleep at a time like this?"

"Sorry, I didn't mean to. I shouldn't have fallen asleep like that."

"No, not that, I mean I'm so jacked up by all of this, how can you physically be mellow enough to sleep?"

"I've been through a lot of training and experiences that have desensitized me to getting jacked up by stuff like this. If I'm not mellow and thinking clearly, my patient's medical treatment will suffer. That, and I work with a bunch of heroes who I'd trust with my life. There is no substitute for powerful confidence than trust in one's teammates, and I trust you all very much. Sorry that I fell asleep."

"After we start the lowers, when should we call FFL for the rendezvous?"

"When we're about an hour out from the LZ, and we're pretty sure the weather and winds are going to cooperate."

"Will do."

I finished taking Jim's vitals, which showed no significant changes. While Mick and Andrew equalized the mass on all the anchors, I prepared some more diluted Gatorade to carefully pump into Jim's mouth for the slightest additional hydration, blood sugar, and electrolytes. I made a mental note to stop this treatment when we were about an hour out from the Lifeguard Four rendezvous. Full stomachs and surgery anesthetic don't mix—or they mix in the sense that in surgery one vomits the contents of his/her stomach up to aspirate those contents into the lungs. Diluted sugar water, aka Gatorade, would make a very poor substance to aspirate, as the sugars in the electrolyte solution being a prime biotic growth medium. Jim had miraculously survived to this point, and if we could get him aboard that helicopter alive, I did not intend on him aspirating Gatorade in surgery.

Soon Mick announced that the rigging for the litter lowering was set-up and good to go. The rigging was beefy and set up to lower the litter, patient, plus two or three attendants, attached and hanging off the litter's sides. These attendants' jobs were to help guide the litter past obstacles.

I did a quick systems analysis and overall, I estimated the maximum potential force on the system equivalent to four full-grown men, about 3-4 kilonewtons of static force. As I double-checked and went meticulously over each section of rigging, I estimated its weakest point capable of holding at least 20 kilonewtons. The system's expected force to breaking force ratio was about 4:20, or about 1:5.

I knew that according to Mountain Rescue Association (MRA) standards, that ratio should be 1:10 or greater. According to the MRA, we should have been using a main line plus a belay line to provide redundancy.

Unfortunately, we only had 1,200 feet of rope with us, three 400-foot sections. It would save Jim a lot of time getting to the hospital if we could lower him in one initial 800-foot drop, set another temporary anchor system at the base of that lower, and finish up with a second 400–800-foot lower rather than multiple two-line 400-foot lowers.

Several of us carried Jim over to the lip of the chute and tied him into the rigging. Everything was ready except for who would act as the attendants. Unlike the last several hours in which the carriers and attendants did not attach to the litter, this lower would require a couple attendants attaching themselves to the litter so they could use their mass to help guide and manipulate the litter as it glided over the near 40-degree slope. In the back of all our minds, we knew if the anchor system had a catastrophic failure, this would mean a litter, a patient tied in very securely to that litter, and at least two attendants, secured to the patient and litter, would suddenly begin falling, sliding, building inertia in a tight, scree-filled avalanche chute, very quickly becoming the catalyst for a massive rockslide. Even though this type of technical lower wasn't nearly as glamorous as the dead vertical "cliffhanger"-like scenes, they were just as dangerous and potentially fatal. One in ten thousand systems such as this statistically fail. If backed up by a belay line, whose failure is also one in ten thousand, that means a dual line system has a chance of failing ten thousand times multiplied by another ten thousand. A dual line system has a statistical failure rate of one in ten million. If there were enough rope, we would have used two lines, but in these circumstances, I felt the risk was worth it and I'd go with the one in ten thousand chances. I said that I'd act as one of the litter's attendants; without skipping a beat, Roy Hood and Jess offered to be the other attendants. Andrew and Mick volunteered to stay at the top, near the anchors, and run the main line, including the difficult, technical task of passing main line knots, where the team added one rope to another, creating a knot not easily passed through the system's friction devices.

After the three of us tied to Jim, we carefully positioned the litter under the focal point and leaned back, putting significant mass and force on the anchors. We loaded the system gradually, listening and seeking any sensation of anchor failures. In the starry darkness, everyone's headlamps on the spider web of anchors accentuated vibrations in the line. Sounds seemed amplified, as did the dark void below us. The north-facing slope was the least illuminated ground around us, and in its steep recesses, light from the east and west were blocked. Only the faint light from the northern sky gave the steep scree and talus any relief at all. As had been the case for hours, our headlamps would provide the only functional illumination of our worlds, thus limiting our worlds to a very small visual bubble.

To keep everyone as safe as possible from rock fall caused by the movement in the couloir, everyone agreed to move together in one group alongside the litter and attendants. The only people not moving would be the techs left at the top of the couloir. They were the crew who were in control of lowering the litter and attendants. After they had lowered everyone two rope lengths, 800 feet, we'd get out of the fall line and take cover. The lowering team would then descend to us, and we'd continue the litter lowering process.

Jim was quiet as we began the lowering process. From his perspective, it was finally a smooth ride. The litter was being suspended, most of its weight being hoisted by the anchors and rigging from above. The three of us attendants took turns shifting the litter to one side or another to avoid high areas and other obstacles that would snag the basket and make for a bumpy ride for Jim. The team lowered us ever so slowly, just a few inches at a time.

As we got farther from topside, we switched from using voice communication to radio communication. We carried sheriff's office radios, but for this work we used five-watt personal mini radios, the types kids and families often utilize on vacation. They worked perfectly for the "shorter" line of sight work we were doing. Those of us on either side of the litter called for faster or slower descent. At around the 400-foot mark of lowering, the litter descent came to a halt, and the top side team radioed it was time for them to do a knot pass, adding another 400-foot rope's length to the available lowering system. Roy, Jess, and I looked out over the Lake Como Gorge and we could see the first light of dawn illuminating the talus skirts below us. We could see that we were about one-third of the way down the steepest scree and talus. After this additional 400-foot lower, we thought maybe one more 400-foot rope lowering and then we could carry Jim to one of the 4x4s, drive him the short distance to the LZ, just a couple hundred yards up the valley along the Lake Como 4x4 road between Lake Como and Blue Lakes.

In just a few minutes the knot pass was completed, and Jim and the three of us attendants descended the additional 400 feet. The spot where we'd stopped, where we'd need to lower Jim just one more 400-foot section had no solid anchors. It was the spot where the access couloir opened up and the alluvial talus apron spread out in all directions. There was nothing solid to place anchors in or tie leashes around.

Roy, Jess, and I looked at each other, and Jess spoke for all of us, "I'm ready to get this done. With just a little resistance from above, I think two of us could walk Jim out." As Jess finished this sentiment, I was scanning around us for anything large enough to use as a belay platform, and there next to us was a good-sized boulder, about the size of a refrigerator lying on its side. It looked halfway solid, and it was obviously the most solid thing anywhere near us on the slope. I jumped up on it and coiled the rope next to me. Finally, I slung a loop around my back, and I explained the idea of a dynamic belay to Roy and Jess. I wasn't ever going to suddenly stop the rope sliding around my body, rather just speed up and slow down, thus not producing any massive dynamic loads that would shock the system and the rock slope on which I was sitting. I wanted to avoid the whole rock I was on moving down the slope and triggering a much larger rockslide.

I looked at my watch and estimated we were about an hour from FFL being able to land, so I pulled out the sheriff's radio and sent a transmission to the repeater, hoping the incident commander would hear loud and clear. I requested Flight For Life and let them know we were about an hour out from having the patient ready to fly out at the previous day's LZ. John Gilmore, an off-duty flight paramedic with Flight For Life, was down at the trailhead acting as our incident commander, having relieved Suzi who had been IC all night. John radioed back that the FFL crew was in mid-shift change, but they'd be on their way shortly.

I was beyond exhausted, but I knew that our struggle for Jim's life would soon be out of our hands. With the last call made before we'd be transferring patient care to a medical helicopter crew, I felt a last surge of energy.

I began lowering Jim, Roy, and Jess slowly. I ran the rope around my waist, using my body as a large friction device. Since I wasn't holding up Jim's entire weight, rather I was providing Roy and Jess oppositional force for hovering Jim above the rock, I was able to provide a faster descent rate than I thought initially possible. Tish, Jess' wife, stayed up next to me during this last rope lowering. She was happy to see us nearly finished with such an epic, near impossible carry-out. About halfway through the lowering, Jess called up to slow it down. As my gloved hands pinched down on the rope and added some friction to the line and my waist, I felt a subtle shift in the rock I was sitting on. Sure enough, my large anchor rock and the scree around it had begun shifting, descending the slope. Tish instinctively stepped sideways and away from the shifting rock, and I nodded in approval. I thought there was no sense in us both ending up in a rockslide; at the same time, I loosened my grip and allowed the rope to slide more freely again.

As I lessened the force being applied to the rope around my back, the rock beneath me slowly came to a halt. The escalator of rocks around me also stopped moving. After all movement ceased, I looked up and saw that I had drifted ten to twenty feet away from Tish. One more time that night, the team was spared a potentially nasty contingency.

After another minute of lowering, Roy, Jess, and Jim reached the base of the talus apron, the point at which the boulders flattened out into moraines. From there the team would carry Jim to one of the 4x4s parked alongside the Lake Como road. As Jess and Roy unclipped the rigging from the litter, Tish and I began descending toward Jess, Roy, and Jim.

By the time I reached their stopping point, team members who had been descending alongside us had taken up carrying Jim, and someone else was coiling the ropes we had used to lower the litter. I looked at my teammates all working harmoniously, and I had an overwhelming sense of love for them. Who are these crazy heroes who do such things for absolute strangers? I couldn't help but feel I was in the company of some of the finest souls in the world.

As I finally reached the bottom of the scree and the Lake Como road, I sat down next to Jim, now placed securely in the back of a modified full-sized Chevy Blazer with the back top cut off (this vehicle was Steve Morrison's and served as our backcountry ambulance and hearse). In addition to Steve's

Blazer there were two other modified 4x4 Jeeps operated by Roy and Jess. The sight of our "cavalry" vehicles was heartening. They would deliver Bill and us to the trailhead and home soon.

I took my helmet off for the first time since I had put it on getting out of Lifeguard Four the day before. The act symbolized that Jim was soon to be on his way to Pueblo via a very fast moving helicopter. As everyone began to rally around the vehicles and begin stowing equipment for the ride down, I took Jim's vitals again. It was still challenging to find a pulse, but I could watch Jim's chest rise and fall in the brightening 6:30 a.m. light of summer, and I felt confident that Jim would live, at least while under our care. I was relieved that other than a little bit of morning fog, only small wisps of condensation were rising from the evergreens. There was no hint of weather or wind that would hamper Flight For Life making a landing at its first available opportunity. The radio sparked to life and announced that Lifeguard Four was approximately twenty minutes from landing at our location. "Thank God," I murmured aloud.

Steve started his Frankenbeast monster of a Blazer and we slowly drove up the two-track 4x4 road to a grassy, flat knoll located just above and east of the cutoff to climb the west ridge via Little Bear Peak's main route. I suggested to Steve how far away to park the Blazer until the helicopter had landed, and right on schedule we heard the beats of rotors echoing from the cliffs of the gorge.

The cool, dense morning air would aid in the helicopter being more powerful and controllable than it had been the warm afternoon before. As the pilot got within visual range of the LZ, I assisted by lifting my arms in a big, bright orange "Y," with a long fluorescent piece of flagging tape drifting from one of my hands to indicate wind direction and strength. Immediately upon touching down, the pilot cut the turbine and the rotors came quickly to a halt. The pilot and a flight nurse jumped out. The original group of twelve of us, who had battled so fiercely the night before, carried Jim the last few feet from the Blazer to the side of the helicopter.

As we transferred patient care to the air ambulance crew, the flight nurse was visibly shocked and remarked, "What the hell is this?" pointing to our improvised SAM splint C-collar. Most mainstream medical folks, unless they had a special forces military background, didn't have a clue as to what a SAM splint was or how to use it in expeditionary conditions. I explained what had happened and why we had to improvise, but she still looked perplexed. Instead of continuing an explanation, I offered to and helped her discard the improvised collar and put on a properly fitted, brand new, hospital style C-collar. Soon after this, I contentedly watched Jim being administered

AVSAR's "team of twelve" carrying Jim Cornwall to the awaiting Flight For Life air ambulance (photo by Don Thompson).

some long overdue painkillers, and I wished the aircrew luck in flying back to Pueblo.

After Jim had lifted off, the group's sleep-deprived attention turned to replacing some long expended calories and hydrating with whatever water and electrolyte solutions were available. After our breakfast, we all piled ourselves and our gear into Roy's and Jess' Jeeps and Steve's Frankenbeast, and we began the slow, technical drive down the canyon, disembarking from the vehicles, as usual, at the Jaws 2 and Jaws 1 obstacles. Bill was still awake, now after twenty-four hours, and the ride down wasn't very conducive to catching up on some zzz's.

It was nearly noon by the time we pulled back into the trailhead parking lot being used as our command post. Being welcomed back into the camp by the Red Cross volunteers was superb. They gave us snacks, drinks, and most importantly, hugs. They asked us how we were doing, and they made sure each of us was safe getting home.

After a short debriefing, we got word through John Gilmore, the FFL paramedic, that Jim had made it to the hospital alive and was being stabilized in the ICU. Bill looked especially relieved. John said that the hospital passed along that without our intervention, Jim would have died. It was official, at least for the time being, that our hard work had led to a life being saved. Jim

Cornwall would *not* be added to our SAR list of fatalities. Up to this point, he was a survivor. I wished Bill well, and I reinforced the importance of him not driving too long. He was sleep deprived and his reactions would be dulled, similar to being intoxicated. We hadn't battled all night long to lose another to a car wreck.

Several days later, we were notified via John that a neurologist detailed the true nature of how close Jim had been to death. Up high on those cliffs in the middle of the night, Jim had been on a far more precarious edge than any of us had realized.

In fact, Jim had suffered a serious subdural hematoma—a very dangerous brain bleed. The actress Natasha Richardson, Liam Neeson's wife, several years ago had an accident while skiing that resulted in a subdural hematoma. She was assessed, sent home, initially showed little signs or symptoms of such an extensive injury, but then shockingly she passed away several days later. Subdural hematomas occur when blood collects between the tissues that surround the brain beneath the skull. As the blood collects, the pressure on the brain increases causing pressure inside the skull to rise, which can quickly or slowly (over several days) lead to unconsciousness and death. Some subdural hematomas spontaneously resolve, others require drilling into the skull and relieving the pressure surgically. Many subdural hematomas result in death.

The neurologist that examined and treated Jim passed along that it was a blessing in disguise that none of us had been IV certified and pushed fluids into him during the night. Raising his blood pressure to something more normal would have caused the hematoma to become far worse, thus Jim would have most likely died.

A couple months later, the AVSAR team held our annual awards ceremony, and at that year's awards, two very special guests attended: Jim and his wife, Kathie Cornwall. They were both still recovering, but both were very healthy and grateful. It was one of the finest moments of my life, celebrating such a miraculous, positive outcome in such a desperate, horrible situation. Some time later, Jim and Kathie shared a photograph of all their children and grandchildren—a photograph filled with dozens of people, all of whom were deeply and positively affected by Jim's survival.

Years later to this day, on September 11, Jim and Kathie call me, still expressing gratitude for everything Bill Schott and our team did to save Jim. They are deeply, deeply grateful for all the days after September 11, 2009.

All the souls affected by Jim Cornwall's survival. Photo given to the AVSAR team by Jim and Kathie Cornwall.

Elisabeth Perry
Blanca Peak, August 7, 2010

"I wanted you to see what real courage is, instead of getting the
idea that courage is a man with a gun in his hand. It's when you
know you're licked before you begin but you begin anyway and you
see it through no matter what. You rarely win, but sometimes you
do. Mrs. Dubose won, all ninety-eight pounds of her. According to
her views, she died beholden to nothing and nobody. She was the
bravest person I ever knew."

—spoken by Atticus Finch, Harper Lee, *To Kill a Mockingbird*

The use of helicopters in mountain search and rescue operations is a very
dangerous option, and this option is used only when the risk is worth the
potential benefit. There are rare exceptions, but in general helicopters are too
dangerous to justify their use for body recoveries, and similarly they are too
dangerous to use for non-life-threatening injuries, such as injuries that SAR
can evacuate via the ground.

In June of 2010, I had jumped out of a thirty-two million dollar military
Chinook helicopter and turned around to see its rear rotors shredded, one rotor hanging limply along the fuselage, the helicopter's "skin" wrinkled from the
frame being bent and twisted. Next to the aircraft was one of its large wheels.

Although the media reported the incident as a hard landing, after the
rotors had hit the mountainside and I felt the helicopter lurch and vibrate at
the edge of control, I was convinced the incident would conclude catastroph-
ically—I was sure we were all going to die. As we were nearly free falling the
thousand feet between the mountainside impact and the pilots' emergency
landing zone—a small grassy area just above an alpine pond east of Little
Bear Lake—from the back of the aircraft all I could sense was the fight the
pilots were in to remain in control.

As the helicopter bucked off the cliff and descended, I saw flashes of
charred metal, melted glass, barbequed aircrew. In college, I worked security
in the busy ER near the university I attended, and I had learned the lessons of
the burn unit: many burn victims succumb to their injuries days after the initial injury, and for those burn victims who survive the first few days, there is
the hell of the debridement treatments. As the Chinook descended, and I pre-

pared for a crash, I kept hoping that unconsciousness would come before the experience of all of us burning. It remains a miracle, for several reasons, that all of us on board that aircraft walked away without major injuries or fatalities.

Another sad part of the overall mission and story was that by the time we finally reached the subject, he had been deceased for a considerable amount of time. A dozen of us on that helicopter had taken enormous risks to ourselves (and our families), for a corpse.

Just five days after the helicopter crash, I was called out to respond to another mission. One day short of the longest day of the year, June 20, 2010, I went out on my last mission as an active duty SAR volunteer. That mission was a rescue of an injured young woman, Breanna Dumke, a health and exercise graduate student from CSU in Fort Collins. She and her hiking partner, Julie Barnes, were both in outstanding athletic shape and they had begun hiking up Colorado's fourteeners as part of their athletic endeavors.

The women had driven down from Fort Collins and parked their car in the sandy parking lot at the very base of the mountain group; 4x4s can climb much higher on the road, the modified 4x4s and ATVs possibly crawling all the way to Blue Lake, but these women smartly parked their front-wheel drive car below the baby-head rocks, still out in the sandy flats of the San Luis Valley.

From there, they had backpacked into the Lake Como area and spent the night camped near treeline. The next morning they left their camp at first light and began the hike from treeline to the summit of Ellingwood Point, their first objective of the day.

After carefully picking their way to a successful summit of Ellingwood Point, the women traversed the steeply sloped saddle between Ellingwood and Blanca. Breanna was in the lead when she slipped and began "cartwheeling" down a steep talus and scree slope.

Breanna instinctively protected her head during the fall, but upon coming to a stop and inspecting herself, she found that during the tumbling she had lacerated her left knee. The laceration was deep, jagged, and between three and four inches long. They were high up on the mountain and because of that they still had a line of sight to a cell phone tower. Where Breanna had come to rest, Julie had been able to contact 911 and had been patched through to me.

Julie was alarmed that Breanna had "filled one of her hiking boots with blood." I could tell Julie and Breanna were scared by the amount of blood loss. They asked about a tourniquet and a helicopter evacuation. After reassuring Julie that a tourniquet was unnecessary and could easily result in Breanna having her foot amputated, when the situation simply required a lot of pressure initially and later a few layers of sutures, I was also quite succinct about a helicopter evacuation, "For a non-life-threatening injury such as Breanna's, it's much safer that we evacuate you via four-by-four's on the ground."

I instructed Julie in the methods to aid and monitor Breanna during the time it would take us to respond. I assured Julie that we were on our way and that if they could move, they should move down the trail, and we would intercept them as soon as possible.

In our standard operating procedural method, the team responded in our usual staggered timings, and the group of us loaded into the three AVSAR 4x4s.

Even though it was a day prior to the solstice, the first official day of summer, there were still deep mud puddles in Chokecherry Canyon's entrance, and there were snowdrifts beyond Lake Como on the way to Blue Lake. Just before Blue Lake, a snowdrift nearly stopped Roy's jeep in which I was a passenger. I got out and began walking when he punched through the snow in his beast of a machine.

By the time we arrived at Blue Lake, Breanna and Julie had amazingly self-evacuated all the way to the grassy flats east of Blue Lake. I had spoken to Julie on the phone and expected for the two of them to be in the area of Blue Lake, but upon actually being the first to see them huddled in the green grass, it was a relief. I was happy to briefly turn around and wave at the line of responders hiking to my position, indicating to them the subject was very close to the vehicles. This would be a textbook "easy" rescue.

I walked up to Julie and Breanna, and although it was the second longest day of the year, the sun was beginning to set and I wanted to make the most of the remaining light. It was below 50 degrees Fahrenheit, and the temperature would drop with the sun. I introduced myself and a new, young EMT team member, Stefan Ortega, to the women. I directed Stefan to practice aggressive field treatment of a wound that was hours old. We flushed her deep laceration with a iodine solution and bandaged it appropriately. I was glad to see that Breanna bled profusely and covered her sock and shoe in blood; the wound's amount of bleeding helped decrease her likelihood of infection.

As Stefan and I began treatment, I learned that Breanna and Julie had slowly and painstakingly hobbled down the steep Blanca Peak trail, and upon crossing paths with a young backcountry motorcyclist, Rodrigo Lopez, Rodrigo had piggybacked Breanna down the steep "waterfall" section.

After providing some basic wound treatment and a brief carry-out to the 4x4's, we strapped the ladies in and began our slow creep down the mountain. As usual, the vehicles slowly scraped and slid down the major Jaws obstacles; as usual everyone but the drivers disembarked from the vehicles at the most dangerous spots. We portaged patients past Jaws 2 in case the vehicle ever rolled off the ledge. Jaws 2 has killed drivers and passengers when they have been ejected out of their rolling vehicle, and then had the vehicle roll over them.

Creeping along the 4x4 Lake Como road in the dark, the change in elevation was only apparent by the change in vegetation, first from lodgepole pines to aspens and willows, then to piñon pines. I made small talk with Julie and Breanna as we slowly traversed the 4x4 road back to the command post. I slipped into the conversation the team's recent encounter with the danger of helicopters, and I emphasized those risks were unnecessary for non-life-threatening injuries.

Just past midnight, the SAR caravan of modified 4x4s emerged from the piñon pines at the command post. I explained to Julie and Breanna that they could save a few more bills by driving themselves to the hospital (they had relayed it would benefit them to save as much money as they could in the process of patching up Breanna). Breanna opted to ride with me to the hospital with Julie following behind. After the ER and many sutures, I helped check both women into a local, convenient motel. It was a textbook rescue—it was a magnificent rescue that would ultimately turn out to be my last deployment into the field.

For more than a month, the AVSAR team did not receive any emergency 911 calls. At the beginning of August, the weekend of the seventh and eighth, I decided to take a drive up the Front Range to return some equipment to the El Paso County Search and Rescue team that had been used during the recovery of Kevin Hayne's body.

Following a quick rendezvous in Colorado Springs to return their team's equipment to one of their officers, I continued my jaunt up to Fort Collins to visit friends.

I was at a coffee shop in Fort Collins on the morning of Saturday the seventh; it was approximately 11:30 a.m. when the call-out came in. Even though I couldn't physically go out on the call, I answered the phone and listened to the initial call-out information and subject profile.

The subject, Elisabeth Perry, was a twenty-seven-year-old female from outside the San Luis Valley. She was visiting, she had experience hiking and peak-bagging in the Colorado mountains, and earlier that day she had dislocated a shoulder while scrambling up on the saddle between Ellingwood Point and Blanca Peak. After the parallel experience rescuing Breanna just a month before, my first impression was that of relief; like Breanna, the subject was a healthy, athletic young woman with an injury that shouldn't pose a threat to her or anyone else. It would be another textbook rescue.

This early in the day, 11:30 a.m., I thought the team would be able to get her back down and to the medical center before sunset. There wasn't much advice or influence that I had that could help. I reminded everyone to prioritize the safety of rescuers, and then focus on safely rescuing the subject. I hung up the call with a lot of confidence in a team whose mission was a "standard operation." Since everything had started so relatively early in the day, I thought this might be a rare SAR mission in which headlamps weren't necessary. I smiled thinking of the unofficial motto of Colorado SAR, "See Colorado by Headlamp."

A couple weeks later, on the evening of August 24, 2010, the team met for its once a month meeting and we held an after action review (AAR) in which we discussed what went well on the "Perry Mission." As usual, we discussed things we would want to repeat in the future, as well as things that went poorly, that we would want to change or avoid in the future. Andrew McClure, who had been one of the lead responders, led the AAR. The following is a combination of Andrew's verbal and written reports given to the sheriff, and from information gathered from interviews with responders such as Andrew McClure, George Rapoza, and Eric Lutringer, all AVSAR personnel present during Elisabeth's rescue.

From Andrew's report:

> I got the call from George Rapoza around 1130 hours, and I was on the
> road headed to the Como trailhead around noon. I talked with Jack
> Hunt, the president of Rio Grande County SAR, on the way. Jack was
> gearing up and bringing along Marc Syrene, also of RGCSAR. Jack and
> I discussed the Flight For Life Lift Ticket program at that time. I picked
> up George, and we rode together to the trailhead, arriving around 1240
> hours. With the 4x4 personnel response a total of just Roy's Jeep (which
> had mechanical issues on the last mission), I called FFL and asked for an
> airborne standby.

An airborne standby request alerts Flight For Life (FFL) that they're most likely going to be needed for an evacuation very soon, and it's a request that they go airborne and get in as close to the incident as possible and standby.

Andrew's report explained that dispatch patched him through to two bystanders on scene with Elisabeth. They were trying to help her manage her dislocated shoulder and pain. Out of several bystanders who were on scene and offered to render aid, one was a nurse and another was an Army National Guard Specialist, Dwayne J. Enderle. Andrew reported that "D.J." had been an army medic and was not able to reduce Elisabeth's dislocated shoulder. The subject, Elisabeth was in so much pain she was ataxic, unable to walk.

Because of the steepness of the terrain, the best option was for Elisabeth to stay put and wait for AVSAR personnel to transport her out.

From Andrew's report:

Elisabeth was unable to walk and had a recent (that morning and a few days previous) history of epileptic seizures. Suzi requested clearance from the Sheriff to use FFL to insert team members near the subject. Once we had a go from the sheriff, we requested FFL's assistance. With the team fully assembled at about 1400 hours and FFL on the ground, the plans were made to insert who we could and bring extra gear on Roy's Jeep. FFL would insert me, then Stefan, then Jack, and finally Eric. Roy would bring Mark M. and Marc S., George, James, gear and maybe someone else in. At about 1500 I was in first after flying over the subject and attempting to land at Crater Lake, with an eventual LZ below Blue Lakes. Once Jack arrived he and I started up to the subject, leaving Stefan to wait for Eric before continuing. We had just made it to Crater Lake when Marc S. caught us. We checked a possible LZ above Crater, where a couple of the army medic's friends had a fire started for us later when we were descending. We pushed on up to the subject who was at about 13,600 feet, approximately 200 feet vertical from the ridge crest and 400 feet NW from the saddle (approximately 1730 hours).

There were four individuals with her, two descended with Marc S. (who went to get a rope) shortly after we arrived. D.J. was the army medic who had stayed with the subject and maintained patient care. We quickly placed the subject in a sleeping bag in the litter and covered it with a tarp/space blanket. Moments after she was insulated and somewhat sheltered the weather let loose. We threw on our rain gear as it started to drench us with rain and hail. The lightning flashed and boomed so close it made me think leaving and descending was the only sane option. We waited it out and began building an anchor for the initial lowering down a talus-filled gully. I descended with the nurse and went down to the fire to gather the other members for the carry-out. Marc S. had contacted other members who had the rope and webbing and returned with that gear about the same time I had started down.

I started back up with Eric and James, with Mark M. and possibly Roy. When we arrived (2045) Marc and Jack had completed the first lower and the search for the second anchor was underway. The rock is so fractured and questionable, and seems to slope down leaving few horns or other positive natural features. We finally used a four-point anchor to lower down another 80 feet vertical of moderate angle slab and eventual low-angle talus. Just as we were ready to lower, a group of climbers arrived to assist. They greatly assisted in the carry down through the talus and the headwall and down to the fire. There was no more technical terrain after the second lower and it only required diligent footwork and someone scouting ahead to find the route down.

We arrived at the fire around 0100. We rested and discussed our options. The climbers were going to descend. Roy headed down and Eric was battling altitude sickness. Everyone was tired and the helicopter would not come until morning. We stoked the fire and tried to rest a little. The subject was placed in a fresh, dry sleeping bag for the rest of the night. Around 0530 the sky started to brighten and we could see our surroundings again. Shorty after that, James noticed the subject thrashing in the litter. We maintained C-spine throughout the seizure and she came out of the seizure about three minutes later. That woke everyone up and got us ready to go. A group of four climbers approached and came down to help carry. We left shortly after 0600.

Kevin and Doug of RGCSAR arrived, responding to a 0100 request for additional assistance by Mark S. They had ridden a RGCSAR four-wheeler through the night to meet us at 0600. We received word that the FFL helicopter was due in the area in 30 minutes. I decided to wait at Crater Lake until we could find out if the helicopter would land there. After a 30-minute delay I got confirmation that they would not land there and we continued to Blue Lake. We met another group of climbers a little lower who helped carry. We had a dozen people to carry and switch-out at regular intervals and we made very good time with long hauls and fewer and shorter rests. We met the FFL crew and arrived at the helicopter approximately 0830. From there we walked down the road to Como Lake and got a ride with some 4x4ers. I gathered a package of gear that was the subject's and loaded in the Jeep. Per D.J., we left the gear at the car that was supposed to be Elisabeth's. We arrived at the command post around 1230, debriefed briefly and left about 1300.

At the end of the report, Andrew added some bullet points for the AAR. This is an edited version of the list, but here are a few worth pointing out in retrospect:

The AVSAR team had weak attendance mainly in the 4x4s. This crippled our gear supply. We do not take these folks for granted.

Altitude affected a high number of members. Only five members made it to the accident site and subject, although other factors, including weather, were at play. There was at least one member who had to return to the command post for AMS s/sx, and others who had to descend early for similar reasons.

The private climbers on the mountain came to help, and we are so glad. We know how hard that carry would have been without them. The meager ranks of AVSAR were supplemented by RGCSAR to produce a functioning team that fulfilled its duty to the subject. D.J. was beyond selfless to stay with the subject until she was handed over to FFL despite a lack of gear and getting drenched in the storms.

During the AAR, the rescuers involved expressed how grateful they were to Roy, the jeep driver who was able to shuttle personnel and gear up to a point where his Jeep broke down. The 4x4 members of the team worked in teams with each other and friends, so Roy would find ways to fix his jeep, but at great personal cost in time, parts, and money.

Everyone on scene had been fearful of lightning during the storm that occurred just after initial SAR responders reached Elisabeth. In the AAR, I communicated that while I was proud of everyone, I also reinforced the training all of us had received as wilderness EMTs, Wilderness First Responders, and Wilderness First Aid Certified techs: when lightning moves in proximity to a large group of personnel, everyone should spread apart fifty feet or more; that way if a strike does hit nearby, it only electrocutes one or two people, not the entire group. If a strike occurs with everyone spread out, survivors can begin rescue breathing and CPR on the one or two victims instead of everyone being victims and no one left to provide treatment. Those individuals who were on scene with Elisabeth as the storm passed over were risking their lives for her; Elisabeth and those rescuers are blessed that that was not their last evening on earth.

At the AAR, everyone expressed that after the storm had rolled out, it was just the beginning of a long, difficult night for Elisabeth. She had endured a dangerous electrical storm that could have left her and several rescuers dead, she had suffered several seizures throughout the night while lying down in a litter with dislocated shoulder pain so intense it was causing nausea. For several hours Elisabeth was very angry with the universe and let her rescuers know this. When the techs who were on scene recounted Elisabeth getting pretty ornery in the middle of the night, I chuckled. Who could blame her? Who could blame the SAR personnel and other volunteers for being equally cranky about the situation? There was no one to blame. All that could be done was simply cope with the damp, cold, uncomfortable, long night.

Like many past AARs, the team discussed the frustrating protocol conundrum of using prescription-level pain killing medications in wilderness settings. Because SAR teams are all volunteer, the team may contain several EMTs, nurses, M.D.s, etc., but because they are off-duty, smaller rural teams like AVSAR don't have the resources, medical direction, or support of on-duty EMTs. In most small, rural, mountainous counties, until a patient is evacuated to an ambulance (either land or air) with an on-duty paramedic, she cannot expect to be treated for pain. This shocked Elisabeth, whose father is an M.D., as it shocks nearly everyone when they learn of this fact.

We also discussed the unfortunate reality of Flight For Life not landing at backcountry LZs at night. The risk to the aircraft and the aircrew is just too high. The team said that because of several rescues that culminated in a first-light evacuation of a patient via FFL, having to provide overnight care for patients in extremely challenging conditions (or any conditions that exist), had to be the standard and expected.

The meeting concluded with several people validating the Wilderness First Responder training and skills that had become the norm for many members of the AVSAR team. Everyone also expressed a great deal of gratitude for the support and action of bystanders.

Several months later at the annual AVSAR awards ceremony held in November 2010, the team's awards committee awarded the AVSAR techs who responded to rescue Elisabeth Perry with Life-Saving Awards (for their actions during the mission). As the team's director at the time (I was known as a "hard driver"), I overruled those techs receiving our team's prestigious Courage Awards because I did not want to reinforce that taking such extreme personal risk is standard operating procedure, expected, or rewarded.

I hope that my teammates will forgive me. My intent was only to make them as hardcore, survivable SAR techs as I could, and often this meant implementing "tough love" methods and reinforcements. In retrospect, I point out to those SAR technicians (and similar SAR techs everywhere) the information in the following paragraph regarding the level of recognition they truly deserve.

On July 22, 2015, Specialist First Class Dwayne J. Enderle was awarded the prestigious Soldier's Medal for his courage and action in the rescue of Elisabeth Perry. From Wikipedia, "The distinguishing criteria for the award of the Soldier's Medal as per Army Regulation 600-8-22, para 3-13 states that 'The performance must have involved personal hazard or danger and the voluntary risk of life under conditions not involving conflict with an armed enemy. Awards will not be made solely on the basis of having saved a life.' It is the highest honor a soldier can receive for an act of valor in a non-combat situation, held to be equal to or greater than the level which would have justified an award of the Distinguished Flying Cross had the act occurred in combat."

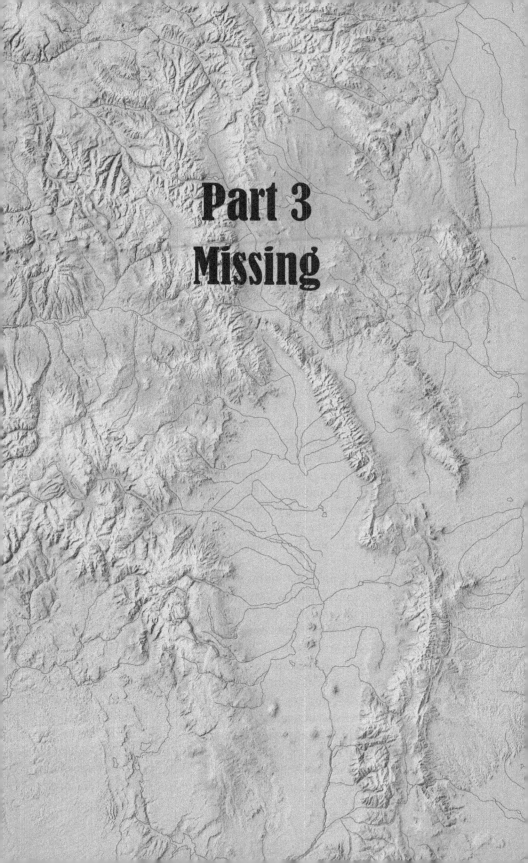

Part 3
Missing

The Skull
Near The Great Sand Dunes, September 11, 2008

"When you get to the top of the mountain, keep climbing."
—Zen Proverb

On Wednesday, September 10, 2008, a young woman was taking a walk on private land in the piñon pine forests southeast of The Oasis Restaurant and Convenience Store near the entrance to Great Sand Dunes National Park. In the middle of the piñon forest, after a flanking side jaunt into the woods, the woman's dog emerged with a peculiar bone in his mouth. It's not unusual for dogs that live in areas such as this to fetch any number of skulls such as fox, badger, or coyote skulls, but as the dog dropped this skull, the young woman knew this was the unmistakable skull of a human being.

Although the spot where the dog dropped the skull was hundreds of yards from the nearest road, investigators and deputies quickly located the source of the skull—a shallow grave containing the decomposed remains of a person. Still present in the grave was the majority of the person's ribcage and vertebrae, but the pelvis and extremities had been dragged away from the grave and dispersed by scavengers. Investigators and deputies did a coarse line search through the area surrounding the grave and found many pieces of the body's skeleton, but still missing was a very vital piece of the puzzle, the pelvis.

The afternoon of September tenth, as the sheriff and his deputies were in the middle of their initial shallow grave investigation, my caller ID showed an incoming call from Carol, the office manager of the Alamosa Sheriff's Office. Because SAR emergency calls came through the Colorado State Patrol dispatch center, I assumed Carol's call was a SAR administrative question.

I was surprised when this wasn't the case; instead, Carol passed along that the sheriff and the sheriff's office lead investigator, Sergeant Harry Alejo, were requesting that me and two three other top SAR personnel, preferably trackers, report to the sheriff's office the next morning. When I asked what it concerned, Carol said it was sensitive, and she was not allowed to say, but we should all show up expecting a search and rescue mission that would last all day. She also asked me not share with anyone what was occurring (except those on the mission). Without specifics and the "sensitive" nature of the request, I was highly curious. "Did the sheriff or sergeant indicate what sort of equipment I should bring?"

"The sheriff and Sergeant Alejo said to show up with your usual 72-hour SAR pack, ready to lead a small team of personnel in a wilderness setting. The sheriff said don't forget your GPS."

"That's a good copy, 0900 hours tomorrow, wearing our 72-hour packs including GPS units."

"Check-in with Sergeant Alejo in the morning."

"Affirmative. Check-in with Alejo."

Carol and I chit-chatted briefly about the SAR team's last mission recovering Dr. David Boyd, and as I hung up the call, my mind was already brainstorming what the possible reasons were for such a request. Why so secretive?

I thought about the more extreme things SAR personnel are called on to do, such as track lost children, or sometimes they help with the tracking of criminals who don't want to be found. Maybe if the group of us were the reserve deputies and trackers, but our group also contained victim's advocates. Victim's advocates, like reserve deputies, made up a separate department within the sheriff's office. Their jobs consisted of meeting with victims of crimes to provide support. Why would a team of old retired cops, victim's advocates, and SAR trackers be needed?

Maybe it would be a "babysitting" mission in which us SAR techs were functionally mountain guides for specialists who needed help negotiating the technical mountainous terrain. I thought about one of the most outlying, extreme cases I'd heard about in SAR.

In 1997, Craig Button, an air force A-10 pilot in an act of suicide, flew his aircraft into the side of a mountain approximately fifteen miles southwest of Vail, Colorado. The crash site, above treeline on high-angle, technical terrain, required that the Alpine Rescue Team techs contracted as the crash investigators' technical mountaineering guides keep their work secretive. The classified nature of the investigation for the warplane crash included accounting for the ordinance it carried. Eventually, the military disclosed to the public that more than one large bomb the warplane was carrying was unaccounted for and remained missing. In that incident's case, a SAR acquaintance was on the Alpine Rescue Team and one of the techs contracted for the crash site investigation and recovery. That mission took several weeks to complete.

What would require secrecy but only one day out in the field? Why reserve deputies and victim's advocates?

I arrived in the Alamosa sheriff's office parking lot a few minutes early, said hello to Cameron Roberts, Steve Morrison, and George Rapoza, the three other AVSAR team members I had invited to "the party." I also introduced myself to an older male reserve deputy and two young female victim's advocates. Sergeant Alejo and Kevin Rogers emerged from the building and introduced themselves and the situation. Sergeant Harry Alejo was the lead investigator on a case, and Kevin Rogers was an assistant Alamosa county coroner. Sergeant Alejo rallied the small group, "I called you all together because I need your help in investigating a shallow grave on private property out near the dunes. The reason why I've asked you is that the usual investigators and deputies have gone through the scene once, and they've gathered major evidence, but I need a more sensitive group to go in and comb through the scene again. You're all a sensitive group of people—medics and trackers, an old cop, and advocates for victims. Kevin's also going to help us document the evidence we find on scene with GPS."

Sergeant Alejo summarized what had occurred the day before—the dog emerging from the pines carrying a human skull. He then began to break down the plan. We were going to head out to the scene in two vehicles—both were newer model SUVs, blacked-out tinted windows, Kevin's having regular license plates, Sergeant Alejo's "GVT" plates hinting at the classified nature of the Secret Service-like convoy speeding down the highways. I asked, "Do you want us to bring our 72-hour packs?"

"Yes. Well, at least your medical equipment. The forest we'll be searching is relatively dense, and people are bound to get stabbed by branches and roll ankles on the baby heads."

"Sounds good. We'll bring our packs." I secretly wondered if any of the deputies had issues the day before, but I refrained from asking.

Sergeant Alejo, "Any of you have firearms in your possession or available?"

The reserve deputy and I both raised our hands. I was happy that none of my SAR techs raised their hands as it indicated to me that they were demonstrating our team's ethos of the victim's needs always being the priority.

In 99 percent of our standard "run-of-the-mill" SAR operations, firearms are not only unnecessary but are a liability. Our team promoted a culture of making every ounce we carried count. Any saved energy could be spent on evacuating the subject. Even a small handgun is extremely heavy for backpacking standards, and sometimes that one small additional medical item instead of the gun is the thing that means the difference between life and death.

The sheriff and undersheriff had completed a background check on me during my SAR application process, as well as for a concealed carry permit. In that process it came up that I had received small arms training while I was enlisted in the air force, including a law enforcement academy. The undersheriff tried to recruit me as a full-time deputy; I graciously declined. The sheriff, undersheriff, and Sergeant Alejo would have known had I been asked to help track a fugitive or be at-risk visiting a crime scene that I was properly trained to use a firearm. On this day I thought a possible mission scenario might include a situation in which a firearm was appropriate, and its weight wouldn't cost someone their life. Sergeant Alejo took a far more pragmatic way of explaining why he asked. "It's just the three of us who will be armed out at an isolated potential crime scene. Keep that in mind if we run into anything or anyone near the scene."

Sergeant Alejo explained that the initial investigators had already recovered most of the larger pieces of the body. What we were doing was a much finer search of the immediate area around the grave, and then a much larger sweep of the overall area. We were to collect and catalog all potentially related evidence as well as GPS map the locations of the evidence.

We transferred our gear into the back of the unmarked sheriff's SUV and the coroner's SUV, and in the shaded air-conditioned vehicles we cruised out to the site. Similar to other SAR missions, we were headed into the region of the Blanca Mountain Group—the Blanca Massif. Mount Blanca, known as Sisnaajini to the Navajo, is the nation's eastern cardinal boundary, one of the nation's holiest sites—hallowed ground. Were we investigating the secret burial of a Navajo elder who had died of natural causes and then been lovingly transported and buried on the holy mountain's feet? When we were near the location, we stopped off at the residence of the woman who had originally found the skull (with the help of her four-legged companion).

We stopped the vehicles along a small, private two-track dirt road, the closest we could get to the site before walking, but we were still several hundred yards away. I shouldered my pack and turned on my GPS. It quickly acquired satellites, the southern sky being easily visible and it only being a light overcast day, and we all started our walk through the woods.

As we walked through the environment, I remembered our mission was to become extremely attuned to evidence, so I began focusing on my senses. I thought about all the generations of human beings who had walked this same place for the thousands of years preceding that afternoon. I envied our Paleolithic ancestors and how incredibly sensitive they must have been to their environment. To miss a rabbit would be to miss a meal. Without speaking, everyone slowly sauntered through the pines following Sergeant Alejo. As we walked, I listened to the quiet footsteps of all my companions. I felt like the modern embodiment of an ancestral patrol on a holy mountain. The pines had the hint of fall in their scent. It was the smell of rich earth, moisture, the humidity in the air on an overcast day, delicious decomposition.

Within a few minutes, we were circled up around the shallow grave. The previous day, law enforcement and the coroner removed the body, but the shallow grave had obviously been visited by both scavengers and investigators recently. Normally one associates death going into the ground, not emerging from it and spreading all over the area.

Sergeant Alejo described what he and others found in the grave. One very important anatomical key that had not been recovered was the pelvis. We knew finding the pelvis would be very helpful in identifying the body.

From the grave, we all walked approximately thirty yards south through the trees. Here we found a fence line. Sergeant Alejo asked that I direct the line. This meant that I would keep the line of searchers aligned and moving together through the search area. I began by having everyone line up along the fence in a straight line. We didn't spread out too far as we wanted our probability of detection of small things, such as teeth, to be extremely high. When we lifted our arms in T's, there was only a couple feet between our fingertips. I explained that my plan was to slowly progress the line through the woods, like old school revolutionary war troops, and after a couple steps, everyone would carefully search the ground around them, in their minds targeting objects as small as teeth and earrings.

Once we moved up to the grave, we would continue past it for another fifty yards. Upon reaching the imaginary northern boundary of the search area, we'd walk the line westerly and then turn around and sweep southerly, combing the section of woods just south of the grave. We'd continue this process until we had swept fifty yards to the west. Then we'd return to the first sweep's location and sweep east until we had covered the fifty yards east of the grave. Using this grid-search method, we'd cover the hundred square yards surrounding the grave.

After giving the command to begin walking north, we all began combing the grass and piñon pine forest floor. The forest was just sparse enough that when I looked down the line of personnel, they were mostly visible, but not always. We SAR personnel were wearing our standard bright orange emergency clothing, thus far easier to see in the brush. Like a well-drilled boot camp unit, the line remained fairly straight as the search progressed. Not too long into the sweep, someone yelled, "I've got something!" I commanded the line to stop.

With everyone stopped, I ran to the searcher who had discovered evidence. Behind the line, the coroner, Kevin, and Sergeant Alego watched the process. When the line stopped and I approached potential evidence with the GPS, the coroner would make the initial call upon whether it was likely animal or human remains, and then as the investigator bagged and cataloged the item, I recorded its latitude-longitude coordinates, then I returned to my spot and continued the line.

The stopping of the line and cataloging of evidence continued monotonously for several hours. I kept reminding everyone that we were in no rush, in fact we wanted to be as relaxed and mindful as possible. Live in the moment, I encouraged, letting our eyes grid search as many of those square inches as we could. This was our one opportunity to potentially discover evidence that could reveal who was buried here and why. I kept encouraging all of us to look for things as small as rings, earrings, or cigarette butts. I thought of all the ancestral hunters who had done the same thing for millenniums hunting rabbits. As if reinforcing my feeling connected to the past, one of the searchers discovered a perfectly intact arrowhead. It was a small black obsidian point, likely used by a more "recent" Apache hunter (rather than more ancient, larger Folsom-era points). I felt a great deal of connection to history and the arrowhead reminded me we were on the slopes of the Navajo's Sisnaajini, sacred ground.

We cataloged everything from small bones (likely metacarpals or metatarsals) to an obviously human scapula (shoulder blade). We recovered a semi-intact heal quite a distance from the grave (this evidence was found at the boundary of our grid searching). As I had suggested everyone train their mind to look for teeth, we found two teeth. In addition to this important evidence, we also found many items that may or may not have had something to do with the scene. In the list of cataloged items in my notes, I listed items as seemingly unrelated as a beer can and a CO_2 cartridge. I figured the CO_2 cartridge was similar to a modern version of the arrowhead artifact, most likely lost in the practice or actual act of hunting bunnies with a pellet gun. We were searching through time as well as space.

After our final easterly sweep about 3:00 p.m., we all slowly walked back to the vehicles, a few hundred yards downhill from our search area. I stopped at the gravesite as we passed, closed my eyes, and said a short prayer asking that whomever's soul had been laid here to rest was at peace. I also asked that whomever had laid this body in its final resting spot also was at peace. I wondered if what we were carefully, ritually, respectfully documenting and accounting for was simply the off-record burial of a loved one and not the result of murder.

I stood with my eyes still closed listening to the breeze flow through the millions of pine needles around me. I could hear the far away cawing of crows. I listened to the sound of my peers' footsteps retreating out of the woods. I was at peace, and it felt as if the Great Spirit was at peace also.

In gratitude for our support, Sergeant Alejo took us out to The Oasis

Restaurant for lunch, just outside Sand Dunes National Park. We sat reviewing the additional evidence we had gathered, and we were disappointed that we were unable to recover the body's pelvis. Without it, it would be virtually impossible to know if the body belonged to a man or a woman. We talked about all the possible scenarios that could have led to the scene that we had processed. It was obvious animals had strewn body parts all over the woods, but what led to the body being there in the first place was still a mystery.

On Monday, September 29, 2008, nineteen days after the skull was originally dropped by a dog on the ground in front of its owner, the *Valley Courier* printed an article by Eric Mullens titled *Body found in shallow grave*. From the article, "After 19 days of a close-to-the-vest investigation, Alamosa County Sheriff Dave Stong announced Monday that his office is investigating the discovery of the human remains in a shallow grave in the vicinity of the Great Sand Dunes. Stong did not say the sheriff's office is investigating the discovery as a homicide yet, but said evidence located at the discovery site and the remains have been sent to the Colorado Bureau of Investigation and the El Paso County Medical Examiner's Office respectively." In an article titled *Mayhem in the Valley*, which references several unsolved mysteries in the San Luis Valley, printed on October 2, 2008, Eric ended the article quoting Sheriff Stong, "'As for the terrestrial mysteries of the Valley,' Stong said, 'now is the time for those who know something to come forward and tell their stories. Some people have carried secrets with them for years, decades, and now is the time for the truth to come out.'"

To this day, this case remains unsolved.

Mark Stice
Crestone Peak Region, September 17, 2013

"As for me, I am tormented with an everlasting itch for things remote. I love to sail forbidden seas, and land on barbarous coasts."
—Herman Melville, *Moby Dick*

I saw the movie *Stand by Me* when I was about the same age as the movie's protagonists—twelve. The movie is a screen adaptation of Stephen King's short story "The Body," and King brilliantly tells the story through the eyes of a group of twelve-year-olds who are in search of finding the remains of one of their peers. They've heard credible information that a train killed one of their classmates, so they profile what their peer was likely doing, where he would have been, and they set out on a journey walking the tracks. As a twelve-year-old at the time, the idea of searching for a body was frightening, but even then, I recall identifying with the fictitious characters—what about the boy's family? His family would be heartbroken, but they would want closure. Curiosity motivated the characters, but compassion also drove them.

As an adult, I ended up responsible for leading nonfiction searches for bodies; it should be no surprise that even as an adult, I have been motivated to serve because of the same reasons of the characters in *Stand By Me*, namely a curiosity and compassion.

In a book by Dr. Robert Sapolsky titled *Monkey Luv*, the Stanford professor examines why human beings put so much energy into recovering the dead.

> The desire for tangible proof of the death of someone we know or love is a natural human impulse. But often that desire extends well beyond a purely rational need for certainty. In circumstances where there is not the remotest chance that someone is still alive, even where the dead died centuries ago, we still expend great energy, have lawsuits and diplomatic standoffs, even risk and lose lives, all to retrieve the dead.

Later in the book, Sapolsky continues,

> I suspect that another reason for wanting the body back has much to do with the irrational energy that we put into denial. Beginning with our first

toddler encounter with a dead robin in the backyard and our parents' uncomfortable "It's only sleeping," or with Grandpa going to the hospital and
simply not coming back, our Western model of death is one of euphemism
and denial, complete with our tiptoeing and whispering around the dead
as if they really are just napping. As first demonstrated in the landmark
work of Elisabeth Kübler-Ross, people in our society tend to react to
tragedy—death, the news of terminal illness—with a fairly stereotyped
sequence of stages, the first being denial (most typically followed by anger,
bargaining, despair, and, if one is lucky, acceptance). To eventually reach
that state of grace of acceptance, the denial must be passed—and thus
the tendency of so many of us to consider it almost a bracing necessity,
taking the bull of denial by the horns, to ask that the coffin be opened, to
look upon the loved one's face. And you need the body for that. Some of
the time, we want the body back not so much to be convinced that they
died, but more to learn how the person died. This can be a vast source of
solace—"It was a painless death, he never knew what was happening." This
can be the ghastly world of forensics, where sequence is everything—"She
was already dead by the time X was done." Sometimes, the solace of "how"
comes from learning something about the deceased by the nature of his or
her death, the heroic act, the sacrifice that affirmed a group's values. In *A
River Runs Through It*, Norman MacLean wrote of the youthful murder of
his hell-raising brother. He had been beaten to death by thugs unknown,
and the autopsy revealed that the small bones in his hands were broken.
And thus, "like many Scottish ministers before him, [MacLean's father]
had to derive what comfort he could from the faith that his son had died
fighting." Similarly, many people were relieved to discover that passengers
on the hijacked plane that crashed in Pennsylvania on 9/11 had apparently
put up a valiant struggle.

On the evening of Sunday, September 22, 2013, I logged onto my email
and social media and discovered several messages and links to articles about
a missing hiker in the Sangre de Cristos.

On the 14ers.com website, I read the following request,

NEED YOUR HELP—Missing hiker in the Crestones
Sun Sep 22, 2013, 5:08 pm
We currently have a 37 YOM solo hiker that took a 5 day trip into the
South Colony basin to climb some or all of the 14,000-foot peaks in that
area last Tuesday 9/17/13. His vehicle was located at the lower gate on the
south colony road today. It is a 1995 White Suburban. Our missing party's

name is "Mark." We have limited information about him except for the following—We believe he is wearing cargo pants, he doesn't wear glasses, no beard, is 6'2" and weighs apx. 220 and may have a rope. We understand he has a tent but do not know the color. We do not know what peaks he was going to climb but understand he has climbed 13 of the 14,000-foot peaks this year.

At this time SAR personnel are on the mountain and additional SAR units will be assisting tomorrow. If anyone believes they might have seen this person on one of the peaks or at a campsite in the South Colony or Cottonwood basins, we are asking you to call. Please call:

Paul "Woody" Woodward
State Coordinator—Colorado Search and Rescue Board
303-393-7297
Last edited by Alpine Rescue Team on Mon Sep 23, 2013, 7:40 am, edited 1 time in total.

I had resigned from active service with AVSAR in 2011, but I was still in contact with many active SAR members, so I contacted a few in leadership and learned that the subject, Mark Stice, had a wife and two little girls. In just the last year and a half, he had ascended thirteen of the fifty-four fourteen thousand foot peaks in Colorado.

I looked up Mark's Facebook profile and saw the banner picture of his two little girls. I scrolled his wall and saw his last posted picture of his brother and him at the summit of Longs Peak. In a foreshadowing, there were also pictures from the previous spring, taken in the Sangre de Cristos. Mark posted them in May, from what appears to be near the summit of Crestone Needle. There was a picture looking north toward Humboldt Peak and south toward the Blanca group.

I sat back and thought about Mark's little girls. Mark had several strong reasons to fight to live if put in a situation in which fighting were necessary. Although he had climbed many peaks, it was in a relative short amount of time, and he had considerably increased his risk by traveling solo in the backcountry. He was capable of getting himself deep into the wilderness, beyond the capability of many peak-bagging weekend hikers, thus far away from a confirmed last known point (his car) and less likely to be found. If Mark were patient and calculating, the traits of many mature hikers, he could have chosen routes throughout the mountain group that were very isolated and rarely traveled.

I have taught all my friends, loved ones, and students to never go backpacking into the wilderness alone, especially without leaving a very clear itinerary and map of locations of objectives, routes, and times. One must then follow that schedule and route as closely as possible, for straying from it and getting injured could mean disaster. I suggest to people they read Aron Ralston's *Between a Rock and a Hard Place*, to experience a pretty extreme narrative that reinforces the additional risks of going solo and no one knowing your plans.

I occasionally break this rule. I do it very rarely, like the times I've free-soloed the standard Third Flatiron route in Boulder or gone backpacking in the wilderness for nine days without an itinerary. The chances of something happening are very slim; however, if something does happen, it would be catastrophic. When I do this, I am honest about the potential consequences. If possible, I leave an itinerary, I take few or no unnecessary risks, and I chose low-risk objectives (such as fly-fishing treeline lakes). When I have gone "off grid" into a mountain group for many days solo without an itinerary to seek solitude and deep communion with nature, I have been very cautious and take less risk than if I were with a partner or group. I hope to do this until I die, or ideally even be doing this when I die. If I were on a solo backpacking trip and died like James Udall, the sixty-one-year-old brother of former Colorado Senator Mark Udall, I'd be happy and content.

When I return from these periods of communion, I am that much more grateful and mindful of my human connections upon returning. Tragically, Mark never returned from one of his communions with nature; or another way I look at it was that Mark's journey into the Sangre de Cristo wilderness was his *ultimate* communion with nature and the universe.

I immediately identified with Mark's profile, and I was curious and compassionate. Mark had hiked a number of fourteen thousand foot peaks, he was a male in his late thirties, and he traveled solo in mountainous wilderness. On a personal vacation, he had chosen the Crestone Mountain Group as his vacation playground. Who would blame him? The Crestone Mountain Group is one of the finest playgrounds an alpinist can imagine.

In early September of 2005, similar to the time of the year Mark entered the Sangre de Cristo wilderness, I had some vacation time so I traveled to the town of Westcliffe. Mark had driven his Suburban to the upper 4x4 parking lot, a long, steep 4x4 two-track, similar to the 4x4 roads on the other side of the Sangres. I had parked my two-wheel drive Toyota pickup in the lower parking lot out on the Wet Valley flats, and starting at 7:00 p.m., I hiked up the 4x4 two-track that leads up to South Colony Lake and the surrounding peaks. I hiked the majority of the six-mile-long 4x4 road that night in the dark. After sleeping a few hours in a comfortable bivouac, I set up a base camp a mile past the upper parking lot, just below South Colony Lake. From there, I spent four days enjoying solo hikes throughout the area, including ascents of Crestone Needle and Humboldt Peak. I attempted Crestone Peak's northwest couloir, but it spooked me. I left the area after that trip without having seen the world from atop Crestone Peak. I returned a couple weeks later with Mike Laxague, a mountain-loving American-Basque friend, and ascended Crestone Peak using its southern "red couloir" route.

I thought about Mark, a husband and father of two little girls. He wouldn't have ever meant to make a mistake, ever abandon anyone, he wouldn't have knowingly taken too many risks; yet, he walked into the wilderness and vanished.

I wondered what routes Mark had traveled. Did he attempt the same circuit that I had, the one in which, just a few hundred vertical feet from the summit, I turned around? I was so close to the summit of Crestone in the northwest couloir I could have thrown a pebble to it, but to get there would have been a few steps across steep, hard water-ice and unprepared, I knew those steps could cast me into eternity.

I had turned around. Had Mark?

I wondered where Mark's remains were. In SAR, to help in the planning of search operations, planners speak in terms of Probability of Areas (POAs). I thought of all the spots in the mountain group with high POAs: There were the wrong couloirs off Crestone Needle's standard route; there was the ridge between Crestone Needle and Crestone Peak; there was Crestone Peak's northwest couloir, and there was the ridge connecting Bear's Playground with the Kit Carson group. All of these extremely remote locations have high POAs of being locations where Mark's remains could be.

Custer County Search and Rescue (CCSAR) responds to all SAR incidents that occur on the eastern slope of the Crestone Mountain Group, including Crestone Needle, Crestone Peak, and Humboldt Peak. Within the team's jurisdiction are some of the most magnificent alpine mountaineering peaks in the Lower Forty-eight.

Nearly all people accessing Crestone Peak and Crestone Needle approach from the east, out of Westcliffe. The Wet Mountain Valley, especially compared to the San Luis Valley, is lush and green. Upslope weather patterns along the Front Range precipitate moisture that falls in the Wet Mountain Valley. On many upslope weather days, clouds will "pour" over the San Luis Valley's eastern passes, and as the clouds descend into the valley they evaporate. It can be a bluebird sunny day in the dry air basin of the SLV while the eastern slope is under a blanket of stratus clouds creeping in from the south. From Highway 17, the Sangres are often silhouetted and backlit by the strobe effect of thunderstorms over the Wet Valley.

In my experience, three groups of people are very sensitive to the weather—pilots, sailors, and mountaineers, because the weather is a major factor in their survival. Those venturing into the Sangres during Colorado's monsoon thunderstorms should be prepared for extreme weather. Above treeline, thunderstorms are thunder-blizzards.

The week that Mark Stice had been camped in the Crestone region the weather had been overcast in the San Luis Valley, including a rare day of rain on the Sunday I heard of Mark's disappearance. Higher up in elevation, I imagined that a wet, wind-blown snow accumulated quickly on everything. What could have been a warm alpine paradise when Mark first entered the wilderness could have turned into a far less forgiving, winter-like environment with the passing of a weather front. I visited weather websites and looked at records for the days Mark had gone missing.

The websites confirmed that the weather had begun relatively good on the 17th, when Mark embarked into the Sangre de Cristo wilderness. The following days, the weather stayed relatively predictable for that time of the year—foggy mornings, partly cloudy warm late mornings and early afternoons, and potential rainstorms and/or thunderstorms later in the afternoon and early evening. Above treeline, the rain showers would have been sleet and grapple.

Then on the 21st, the barometric pressure plummeted and over the next couple days a storm system moved in that dropped several inches of snow on the entire Sangre de Cristo mountain range.

As I sat and stared at the Facebook picture of Mark's little girls, the picture of him and his brother standing at the top of the home stretch of Longs Peak, my heart ached. Somewhere in a deeply intuitive part of my soul I knew Mark's spirit had already passed. His communion with nature, for him, was complete; but as I thought of his loved ones, especially his wife and his daughters, my heart filled with sadness and compassion. I thought of Lygon Stevens' family and their desire to have final closure.

I hoped that the Custer County SAR folks, as well as any assisting SAR personnel stayed safe. Winter conditions in the Sangres set a stage for extremely dangerous conditions. A few years prior, I had contacted a contemporary SAR leader named Bob Pruiksma, then the captain of the CCSAR team, and I had asked him for advice while I led the recovery of Lygon Stevens. Bob passed along guidance in the form of conveying the experience he recently had losing a subject during a winter rescue on Humboldt Peak.

Bob explained the extra dangers that the rescuers had taken to respond to the subject, David Worthington, who had fallen while descending a circuit route that he had not ascended. After spending a night out in subzero windchill conditions, David was barely conscious, murmuring his 14ers.com moniker, "Talus Monkey."

It was sad listening to the toll that losing David Worthington took on the rescuers, the climbing community, his friends and family, and it reinforced a lesson I had learned on several occasions related to SAR missions: be extra careful when on a route that doesn't descend the same route that one ascended.

A group of teacher friends and I were hiking Mount Holy Cross on the weekend of September 24, 2005. We had agreed to meet at the trailhead of Mount Holy Cross Saturday morning and hike the peak. I hadn't been able to leave Denver until late in the evening, which put me at the trailhead outside of Minturn in the middle of the night. Rather than going from tent to tent looking for my friends, I had thrown out my sleeping bag on top of my Toyota truck's flat pickup camper.

At first light Saturday morning, I awoke as a couple walked passed me. They asked for directions to the trailhead. I said I wasn't sure, but pointed in the direction I thought it to be. The parking lot was under construction at the time, so there were no signs.

Had I known at the time that this was going to make me one of the last people on earth to speak to Michelle Vanek while she was alive, I would have been more mindful of the conversation. As the day and weeks panned out following, Michelle Vanek would become one of the most searched for missing persons in Colorado's SAR history.

The author on Mount Holy Cross the day Michelle Vanek vanished (the author was one of the last people to speak with Michelle). Author photo.

I left the same trailhead an hour later with several of my friends, and we all successfully summited Mount Holy Cross around noon. About the same time we were summiting, Michelle Vanek's partner saw her for the last time, just a few hundred feet from where we were celebrating a successful ascent of the holy mountain.

Michelle's disappearance and the scenarios explaining it reinforce that hikers and mountaineers should take extra caution when they are on circuits (routes that don't turn around and follow the same trail back).

I wondered if Mark Stice, like myself, had intended on turning his summits of Crestone Peak and Crestone Needle into a circuit, rather than a more traditional method that used the same route for ascent and descent. In the classic guidebook by Gerry Roach, *Colorado's Fourteeners*, he describes the Crestone Peak to Crestone Needle combination traverse. Roach rates this route as a Grade II, Class 4 "*Classic.*" He describes its crux as, "Traverse around the southernmost gendarme on a ledge and climb another knobby slab leading up to the ridge crest (Class 3). This is an exposed place and the crux pitch is above you. The Class 4 crux pitch is airy and beautiful. Climb 100 feet of steep, knobby rock directly on the ridge crest."

Gerry Roach, an acquaintance of my mountaineering mentor, Lindon Wood, is a world-class legendary mountaineer. Outside of his guidebooks to Colorado's fourteeners and high thirteeners, Gerry is also known for his mountaineering exploits in the Himalayas as well as other big mountains. When I successfully summited Mount Rainier in Washington, having narrowly escaped falling into a crevasse above the Ingraham Flats, Gerry texted me and congratulated me on my summit as well as my survival. I use his guidebooks and I trust their information completely, however, over time I've learned that I am not at Gerry's level of professional mountaineering skills.

My class system follows the usual criteria: class three means using your hands often, such as in steep talus fields; class four requires four point climbing and falls are potentially catastrophic (however, ropes are rarely implemented); fifth class is roped, technical climbing. Over time, I've learned that if Gerry rates a climb as a class four, for me this often equates to class five. What Roach feels comfortable free soloing and classifying as an "airy" class four move, I want to have a roped belay.

I was still learning about the subjective nature of rating systems on that day in 2005 when I walked up the 4x4 road bound for South Colony Lake. I had a well-worn copy of Roach's guidebook, and I had a plan to summit two of Colorado's gnarliest fourteeners in one circuit by traversing the ridge between them, just as Gerry suggested moving from Peak to Needle.

Probably similar to Mark, I had wanted to spend my precious personal vacation days enjoying some of the state's prime mountaineering grounds. Late summer and early autumn can be perfect for mountaineering. Looking through Mark's publicly available Facebook page, I could see from his pictures he had recently discovered the Sangre de Cristos, but upon his discovery he became somewhat obsessed.

The previous May Mark had climbed Humboldt Peak and taken pictures from a perspective near the summit of Crestone Needle. I imagine Mark would have pondered choices that would help him summit the peaks he had yet to claim including the Needle, Crestone Peak, and even a possible traverse of Bear's Playground over to No Name, Kat Carson, Kit Carson, and Challenger Point.

On my solo trip into the South Colony Basin, I spent my first day relaxing, journaling, reading, writing about a recent trip to Mount Rainier, and generally acclimatizing. In early June I had traveled with a couple friends to Washington state to climb Mount Rainier. One of my teammates popped through a snow bridge over a crevasse and nearly dragged the second and me into a crevasse. I was still thinking about the incident and pondering why I loved mountaineering.

In my small mountaineering journal that I took along on trips, I was filling up the pages following my notes from Rainier with inspirational quotes about risk-taking and the outdoors. One of John Muir's had especially called out to me, and so I had transcribed it into my journal. It was from Muir's *The Mountains of California* writings. In this case, chapter five, in which he's comparing the risks of mountain living to others.

> To the timid traveler, fresh from the sedimentary levels of the lowlands, these highways, however picturesque and grand, seem terribly forbidding—cold, dead, gloomy gashes in the bones of the mountains, and of all Nature's ways the ones to be most cautiously avoided. Yet they are full of the finest and most telling examples of Nature's love; and though hard to travel, none are safer. For they lead through regions that lie far above the ordinary haunts of the devil, and of the pestilence that walks in darkness. True, there are innumerable places where the careless step will be the last step; and a rock falling from the cliffs may crush without warning like lightning from the sky; but what then? Accidents in the mountains are less common than in the lowlands, and these mountain mansions are decent, delightful, even divine, places to die in, compared with the doleful chambers of civilization. Few places in this world are more dangerous than home. Fear not, therefore, to try the mountain-passes. They will kill care, save you from deadly apathy, set you free, and call forth every faculty into vigorous, enthusiastic

action. Even the sick should try these so-called dangerous passes, because for every unfortunate they kill, they cure a thousand.

After a day of acclimatizing, I was ready to go out and explore the mountainous playground. My plan was to get up just before sunrise, ascend the saddle just west of Humboldt Peak and then traverse the ridge west to Bear's Playground. From there I would traverse the ledges to the base of Crestone Peak's northwest couloir, ascend the chute to the summits of the peak, and then follow Roach's traverse to the Needle. From there I would descend the traditional route back to South Colony Lake.

An unexpected addition to my plan was that I had befriended another solo backpacker and peak bagger, a young engineer from Littleton named Nick. He asked if he could join my attempted circuit of the Crestones. Neither one of us had brought technical climbing gear, not even helmets, so I invited him to join me, but I reminded him we were two soloists in each other's presence, and if at any time either one of us wanted to turn around, there would be no hard feelings about separating. Nick agreed.

Nick and I awoke before sunrise, hitting the trail around 5:00 a.m. Mostly to aid in staying warm, we moved quickly and ascended to the saddle between Humboldt and Bears Playground around sunrise. By 9:00 a.m., Nick and I had traversed from Bears Playground across the ledges into the base of the northwest couloir. Although it was September and dry relative to the rest of the year, the couloir's air was still cool and damp, descending off the snow and water-ice still clinging above.

Once every few minutes a golf ball to softball sized rock came bouncing out the base of the couloir. I cursed myself for not having brought my helmet. Hopefully, I could climb far off to one side of the route, out of the path of the majority of the rocks trickling from above.

Nick and I carefully picked our way up the steep class four couloir until the rock fall lessened. However, as the rock fall stopped, the rock we were climbing on went from dry to covered in water. Our shoes quickly became wet and slippery—this was not good under such steep technical conditions.

Just a few hundred feet shy of the summit, the couloir split into a "Y" and to continue our ascent Nick and I would have to cross from one side of the Y to the other. Unfortunately, there was a thick slab of water-ice that ran the length of the upper part of the couloir, and we only had our approach shoes. Neither of us had crampons or an ice axe.

Precariously perched on a small table-top sized wet rock slab, we took turns chipping away the first of a couple footsteps into the snowfield. As I reached farther out over the steep icy slope, I knew that if either Nick or I were to slip off our footholds, we'd plummet hundreds of feet down an icy chute, tumbling to a stop on steep rocky ledges below the couloir. I stopped chipping the footstep and turned to my new hiking buddy, now feeling a bit foolish and responsible for our precarious position. "Nick, I'm stopping and turning around here. I don't feel safe crossing here or anywhere else nearby. If we had a bit of rope for a belay, sure. But we don't. I'm down climbing. You think we can down-climb this? I was climbing up, not taking into account having to turn around this close."

"Neither was I. I really don't want to have to give up."

"Nor do I, but the conditions just aren't right for what equipment we've got. The mountain will be here forever. We can come back and snag 'em another time. I just don't want to cross this luge chute without crampons or a belay."

"Yeah. It's just hard."

For a young, driven, type A engineer, I was impressed by Nick's reason and detachment. How many other young men would have continued to chip away footsteps into the ice? How many would have gotten away with crossing and not slipping? How many would have slipped?

I wondered about Mark Stice. Where had his metaphorical, or maybe literal, foot slipped? Where did Mark's final ultimate communion with nature occur?

On the way down Nick and I hiked over to the peak with no name, the easternmost high point on the ridge that runs back toward Kat Carson, Kit Carson, and Challenger Point. We looked for an easy passage to Kat Carson

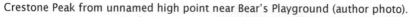

Crestone Peak from unnamed high point near Bear's Playground (author photo).

Crestone Needle from a saddle south of Brokenhand Peak (author photo).

and all we found were impassable cliff bands from our perspective. In Roach's guidebook, he describes the route as exposed class three moves. This is where Nick and I again turned around. I wonder, did Mark try and continue traversing the ridge toward Kit Carson?

Nick and I returned to the saddle between Bear's Playground and Humboldt Peak with enough time and cooperative weather to hike up Humboldt Peak. From the saddle to the summit and back wasn't too much more than an hour. The next day Nick hiked out and I hiked up Crestone Needle via its standard Brokenhand Pass southeast route.

I returned to the same group just a couple weeks later and successfully summited Crestone Peak via its south-facing Red Couloir. My friend Mike and I, standing on top of Crestone, took a long look across the ridge from Crestone to the Needle and pondered all the possibilities. None of them seemed enticing to us. We had found our limits and quickly descended the Red Couloir to our camp.

Where had Mark Stice found his limit?

The areas of highest probability for Mark's location are those places along the routes of travel that would bring Mark to the summits of the peaks. What remains of his body are likely along the Peak to Needle traverse, the northwest couloir being a higher than usual probability. Another high POA would be the ridge between Bear's Playground and Kit Carson.

How does a 220-pound man vanish in the wilderness? The scenario that seems very plausible to me is one in which Mark was on an isolated route bagging as many summits in the mountain group as he could, and he fell on a north-facing slope and was immediately covered in a blanket of snow (explaining lack of evidence thus far, it is still covered by ice and snow). Some spots, such as Crestone's northwest couloir are safest and most often visited in the late spring. At that time of the year, the route is a long set of kick steps into styrofoam snow instead of a crap shoot of dodging rock fall. In September, the northwest couloir is a melted-out gun range with bullet-like projectiles whizzing by every few minutes. This is the time of the year that it can be possible to ascend the couloir rock climbing, although this is unlikely, as even in late summer the couloir contains pockets of snow and ice.

In my proposed scenario in which Mark fell and perished in such a location, the storm that moved in the weekend he was reported missing would have immediately begun the process of covering up evidence. Then storm after storm, layer after layer could have built up, potentially preserving evidence until it melts out years later.

In the last couple of winters, snowfields higher up and hidden in the north-facing pockets did not melt out. Mark's remains may be under a protective layer of ice, potentially for years, until a series of warmer summers melt out all the couloirs and pockets to levels similar as mid-September 2013. Of the few mountaineers who are capable of accessing the northwest couloir, all but a very, very small percentage would prefer to kick step it filled with snow than venture near it in late summer. Mark's final resting place may remain a mystery for a long time, if not forever.

***

When I contacted the regional sheriffs asking to speak with their SAR specialists about cases that could be used to teach the public about the mountain range's dangers, I was pleased to be contacted by Captain Cindy Howard. I first met Cindy in 2009 on a mutual aid mission. Both of our teams (Alamosa Volunteer SAR and Custer County SAR) were giving support to Saguache County SAR. In my field notes from that mission (I was in an operations manager role while Cindy was one of the Custer County SAR personnel who boarded the Blackhawk):

> On Saturday, October 3, 2009, at 2054 hours, Alamosa Volunteer Search and Rescue leadership was contacted by Saguache County SAR leadership requesting assistance. Earlier that day, between 1300–1400 hours, a 51 y.o. male fell while descending the standard route of Challenger Point and Kit Carson Peaks. The subject had dragged himself for approximately four hours before cell phone service became available. The subject called a friend who then called 911. The subject reported that when he fell he did not lose consciousness, but that he had "shattered his knee ... feel woozy ... lightheaded."

By the description of his location, Saguache SAR leadership estimated his position to be on the eastern slope of Challenger Point above Willow Lake. With low temperatures in the upper teens forecasted for elevations above treeline, at approximately 2000–2100 hours, Saguache SAR leadership deployed a two-man hasty team, "Hasty Team One," consisting of a high-angle SAR tech and a SAR EMT to locate the subject and stabilize his condition. Beginning at 2115 hours, AVSAR leadership requested a call-out of all members who were Flight For Life "Lift Ticket" certified or who had hiked the standard route of Challenger Point. All these members were requested to rally at the command post, the Baca Grande Firehouse, in Crestone at 0545 hours the next morning. The San Luis Valley American Red Cross was notified at approximately 2300 hours.

On Sunday, October 4, 2009, at 0600 hours, AVSAR, the Red Cross, and Saguache SAR personnel rallied at the command post and were briefed by Saguache SAR leadership regarding the situation. Hasty Team One had reached the subject approximately 0130–0200 hours, and they had medically stabilized the subject as well as treated him for hypothermia. The subject's location was verified to be approximately a quarter mile above the headwall cliffs above Willow Lake. At 0700 hours, a five-person team made up of AVSAR personnel, "Search Team Two," deployed from the command post to reach the subject and Hasty Team One via the standard Willow Lake trail. At 0800, one of the AVSAR techs on Search Team Two experienced a knee problem resulting from a mild hyper-extension, and he returned to the command post.

At approximately 1030 hours, a four-person team comprised of high-angle personnel from Custer County SAR arrived at the command post. At approximately 1100 hours, the Forest Service notified SAR leadership that five horses were available for subject evacuation from below Willow Lake, in case the subject could not be evacuated via helicopter. Also at 1100 hours, a military Blackhawk helicopter from Eagle, Colorado, arrived at the command post to support the insertion of additional SAR techs. At approximately 1110 hours, the four-person SAR team from Custer Country, designated "Search Team Four" boarded the helicopter and began flying to a landing zone (LZ) near the subject above Willow Lake.

At approximately 1200 hours, Search Team Two reached the location of the subject and Hasty Team One. All personnel on scene packaged the subject for evacuation. On scene, all SAR personnel worked together to transport the subject via litter to the LZ where the Blackhawk waited. At approximately 1230 hours, the Blackhawk returned to the command post LZ with all deployed personnel and the subject. The subject was

Picture of Cindy Howard (with the white helmet in front of the litter) departing and unloading a patient from a Blackhawk helicopter near Crestone, Colorado (author photo).

transferred to a Baca Grande Fire Department ambulance and personnel until Flight For Life's Lifeguard Four arrived at approximately 1300 hours from St. Mary Corwin, Pueblo. At approximately 1330 hours, the subject began transport to St. Mary Corwin's ER via Lifeguard Four. The subject is expected to fully recover.

Cindy had been one of the techs on the SAR Four team that day. She had flown near the scene, helped evacuate the patient back to the helicopter, and then boarded the helicopter to fly back to the command post and transfer custody of the patient to Flight For Life.

Interviewing Cindy for this book and listening to her summarize the team's initial response to "hastily" cover the ground that Mark Stice had potentially traveled, as well as to then listen to the team's disappointment and frustration transitioning from a potential rescue operation to a long-term recovery plan reminded me very much of my own experience leading the mission to recover Lygon Stevens' body. The stress of not having final closure and laying a loved one to rest is punishing. Going through Mark's case documentation, I thought of his wife, daughters, mother, and those most affected by his death.

On September 29, 2013, Custer County SAR released the following statement:

Officials in Custer and Saguache counties have suspended their search for a missing hiker in the Sangre de Cristo Mountains near Westcliffe, as of 1500 hours, Sunday, September 29, 2013.

The search began on September 22, when Mark Stice of Arvada was reported overdue by his wife, after failing to return from a camping and hiking trip that began September 17. He was due home not later than September 21.

Stice was known to have hiked thirteen of Colorado's 54 fourteen thousand foot peaks in the past 1½ years. He had previously hiked Humboldt Peak in May and Long's Peak in early September.

The search lasted eight days, with objective hazards including difficult terrain, significant snowfall, ice, encrusted rock, and falling rock and ice during the daily freeze-thaw cycle.

Stice's vehicle was found parked at the South Colony trailhead on September 22; his campsite was not located until the 24th. He did not sign any trail or summit registers and did not have a cell phone or emergency locator beacon. It is also believed that he would not have been adequately prepared for the rapidly changing weather conditions.

While Stice had summited Humboldt Peak earlier in the season, he was not known to have any local knowledge of the technical challenges that he might encounter on the more difficult peaks in the area. He was also reported to frequently descend off-route.

Stice left no itinerary with family, friends, co-workers and few other clues. Volunteer Search and Rescue teams from Saguache, Custer, El Paso, Fremont, Douglas, Vail Mountain Rescue, and Western State participated in the search. The Colorado Search and Rescue Board assisted in providing resources to the mission, including both a Lakota and a Blackhawk helicopter from the High-Altitude Army National Guard Aviation Training (HAATS) division from Gypsum, Colorado. Over 800 man hours were expended in the eight day search.

***

My primary technical mountaineering mentor, Lindon Wood, kept an enormous, elegant collection of mountaineering books that he donated to the Alpine Rescue Team's archives and museum. When I was still in high school, he helped start my own mountaineering literature collection, which quickly turned into my continuing fascination and collection of mountaineering and SAR related stories. In 2005, I was involved in a crevasse incident on Mt. Rainier in which a team of three of us nearly fell into a deep, deadly crevasse. I returned home very shaken and guilty with how close I had been to vanishing from many people's lives, people who loved me deeply and would be forever negatively affected by my passing. At that same time I added a new book to my mountaineering literature collection, one by a mountaineer named David Roberts. In *On the Ridge Between Life and Death: A Climbing Life Reexamined*, he details his accomplishments as well as failures, failures that included watching friends and climbing partners die. The book's synopsis on Goodreads.com:

> By the time David Roberts turned twenty-two, he had been involved in three fatal mountain climbing accidents and had himself escaped death by the sheerest of luck. At age eighteen, Roberts witnessed the death of his first climbing partner in Boulder, Colorado. A few years later, he was the first on the scene of a fatal accident on Mount Washington, New Hampshire. Months afterward, while pioneering a new route in Alaska with the Harvard Mountaineering Club, Roberts watched as his climbing partner and friend fell wordlessly 4,000 feet to a glacier below. Despite these tragedies, Roberts insists that the greatest pleasures in his life have come in the mountains. Several of his challenging routes in Alaska have never been climbed again in the nearly forty years since those first ascents.
>
> Roberts continues to climb today, and like all climbers, he still grapples with the cost-benefit calculus of his sport. In a well-known essay that he wrote twenty-five years ago, "Moments of Doubt," Roberts insisted that the benefits of climbing were "worth it." More recently, however, he has gone back to interview relatives and friends of some of his deceased climbing partners. He discovered that even decades later, the wounds had failed to heal, the terrible losses were still acutely felt. And so in this book he comes to a different conclusion about climbing, one that is sure to stir controversy in mountaineering circles and among adventurers generally. Anyone who has ever wondered why mountaineers take the risks that they do will be moved and enlightened by *On the Ridge Between Life and Death*, as will anyone who appreciates vivid, dramatic storytelling and an unflinchingly honest self-examination of a lifetime spent pursuing a dangerous pastime.

I look back and examine my own life, my own mountaineering choices, near misses. Deep in my soul I know there is no greater time than that spent sauntering in wilderness; however, when wilderness can result in eternally leaving one's loved ones, I make my risk-taking choices carefully.

As I age I like to think of myself getting wiser, and I marvel at how relatively easy it is to die whether it be from mountaineering, car wrecks, or cancer. I am more and more deeply affected and see the long-term effects that any single person's passing has on those close to the person as well as on the interconnectedness of us all. I look back and think about having almost disappeared into that crevasse, and for me, "rubber-banding" behind my two teammates into eternity would have been a relatively quick demise. The long lasting effect my death would have had on my family, friends, students, community? This is why as I left Rainier National Park and called my mom to brag about having summited Mount Rainier after so much planning, training, obstacles, including nearly being lost into a crevasse, I began crying and apologized. I apologized for nearly robbing her of me.

Sebastian Junger, a journalist and author who has made a living studying courage, did an interview with *National Geographic* in which he speaks to the ideas of adventure, risk, courage, and heroism. In the interview Junger defines heroism as a brave act in the service of someone else.

I think back to all the human beings who have experienced emergencies in the mountains we refer to as the Sangre de Cristos. Before they were named for the Blood of Christ, they were a mountain range that ancient Native American trails crisscrossed. Cultures thousands of years old consider the region and mountains holy. Blanca Peak, known as Sisnaajini to the Navajo, is one of four sacred cardinal points to their nation's people. I close my eyes and see a vision of a Navajo brave, high up on a ridge, guarding the peak. Off to the north, I see Zebulon Pike looking down on the Great Sand Dunes. The Sangres have long been the setting preferred by some of the most extreme characters in the southwest.

I think of the heroes I've known who've taken huge risks in the service of others. I have known no finer characters on earth. I think of my friends Jess Caton and George Rapoza, both fathers, and I think of their faces as we were dropping to the earth in a broken helicopter. I think about Cindy and empathize with her challenge of succeeding in bringing closure to a case while balancing the safety of her team's personnel, and I remember how deeply frustrating it is to watch a family be tormented by an open case. I think about all the SAR heroes all over Colorado and the world who follow the creed, "So that others may live."

I think of the patients we've rescued. The moment we loaded Jim Cornwall onto the Flight For Life helicopter and he lifted off for the hospital will be one of the highest points of my life, albeit following such a desperate, dark night.

I think back to the bodies I've recovered, many of whom I've written about in this book. I think back to Lygon Stevens, David Boyd, Kristen Weiss, and Kevin Hayne. I think about their families, friends, loved ones.

I think back to when I was twelve and saw the movie *Stand by Me*. I think about a group of kids going out on a journey to look for a body.

I think about Mark Stice, still missing, and I think about his family and friends.

I think about those who, in the future, will be involved with and affected by SAR in the Sangre.

Conclusion

"We thrive on tales of the dead. Paradoxically, it's the lifeblood of our passion. We even subscribe to newsletters that recount the crashes of our fellow pilots in loving detail, and we pore over them obsessively. It would seem morbid to those who do not fly, but the stories embody our own invincibility. And in our meditations we find no augury of our own fate. On the contrary, the detailed technical analyses of fatal crashes bestow on us a completely illogical sense of mastery. We rehearse the drama to avoid taking part in it."
—Laurence Gonzales, *House of Pain*

In the publication *Appalachia*, December 15, 1995, on page 42 begins an article titled "Let 'Em Die: The Case Against Search and Rescue" by Robert Kruszyna. As one can guess from the article's title, it is an essay arguing for an extremist libertarian perspective toward organized, government-based search and rescue. It's extreme, but it represents the sincere philosophical sentiments of many citizens when it comes to SAR. From page 50 of the publication:

> We come to what, in a practical sense anyway, is the heart of the issue: Who pays? Search and rescue is an expensive business, even though most of the manpower is provided by volunteers. Helicopters cost something like $400 per hour, and other items—radios, snowcats, gas-powered winches, etc.—are not cheap, either. To give you an idea of the sums involved, in 1984, Denali National Park paid out more than $50,000, primarily for chartering search aircraft and rescue helicopters. This does not include any costs associated with park staff or equipment.

On page 53, Mr. Kruszyna argues:

> In our society we have decided somewhat arrogantly and self-righteously, it seems to me, that we should be our brother's keeper. And we have assigned government to the task. But the moral obligation of watching out for our brother ends at that point when he knowingly and willingly places

himself in the way of danger. Surely society feels no obligation to protect or rescue an Al Unser or a Reinhold Messner. We have a responsibility, perhaps, to point out the potential hazards to those who would climb in the mountains, but if, despite our warnings, they persist in exposing themselves to risks, that is solely their business, not society's.

We talk a great deal about freedom with accountability, but seldom do we do much about it. Thankfully we who climb mountains still have the freedom to pursue our somewhat demented sport, but what kind of accountability do we have if we expect the government (or anyone else) to bail us out when we make mistakes? Therefore I offer the least expensive, the least complicated, the least regimented, and the most moral solution to the problem of what to do about people in trouble in the mountains: DO NOTHING! Abandon all contingency plans. Disband all mountain rescue groups. At every trailhead, erect a sign bearing the inscription Dante found over the gate of hell: "Abandon all hope, ye who enter here." For, if it is immoral for the climber to exercise his freedom at the expense of placing a burden on others, it is equally immoral for a society to seduce him into exactly that position by promising him rescue, no matter what.

When I taught the Adams State University course, Introduction to Search and Rescue, I finished the course with a review of why I felt government SAR teams were vital to the public's trust and to ease the suffering of many whose circumstances were completely outside of their control (such as a plane crash), the opposite of Mr. Kruszyna's argument (although I can appreciate certain philosophical points his article makes about small elements of the public becoming enabled by wilderness SAR organizations).

At the end of my SAR course, I challenged university students to answer the question for themselves: what is the value of SAR? I also assessed and celebrated the knowledge and skills they gained over the semester. I especially reinforced the lessons that I felt would directly contribute to my students' future survivability operating in wilderness environments as SAR volunteers (or recreating personally). In that same spirit, I offer this conclusion.

Many of the lessons within this book's narratives require no explicit mentioning or definitive analysis; however, there are a few consistent lessons worth noting. I've arranged the following points in order from minor methods to increase survivability to broader concepts that delve into values regarding risk-taking and heroism.

In 2010, I was interviewed by the *Denver Post* regarding "Are you ready to hike Colorado," and when asked about wilderness survival information that could help raise the survivability of everyday hikers, I explained that everyone should understand and carry the list of the "mountaineer's ten essentials." The following ten essentials (listed below using the systems approach) will significantly add to anyone's survivability if carried and caught in a wilderness survival situation:

1. Navigation
2. Sun protection
3. Insulation (when possible, acquire bright colors as potential attraction tactic use)
4. Illumination
5. First-aid
6. Fire
7. Multi-tool/knife
8. Nutrition
9. Hydration
10. Emergency shelter

When my family and friends go hiking with me, they know that in addition to the basic ten essentials, I expect them to be genuinely prepared to render aid to others (carry extra gear they can "donate"). In the military I learned the mantra, "Hope for the best but prepare for the worst." The last time I led a group of friends up Longs Peak, each of us had the gear to not only get ourselves up the peak but also help others. The decision was validated when we passed three college boys in shorts and t-shirts on the Narrows—the ledges near the summit. The boys laughed at us for carrying such big packs, and they were obviously proud to be so ultralight. I was not impressed that they did not even have water bottles. Just a couple weeks later, a young male student from CSU was caught in the Trough in an unexpected early season blizzard and died. The ultralight, ultrafast culture that is transforming mountaineering, such as recent record-breaking ascents of classic alpine routes by the legendary Uli Steck and similar athletes, are amazing and worthy of idolizing, but if choosing to engage in such extremely high-risk styles, I would read and reread the chapter about Dr. David Boyd.

Mark Scott-Nash uses the David Boyd incident as a case study in the book, *Colorado 14er Disasters* (in the chapter about solos). In my opinion, David Boyd exhibits a phenomenally in-shape, driven, super-smart athlete (he had just completed the Leadville Ultramarathon successfully), who tragically died on Little Bear Peak because of a convergence of multiple factors such as trading weight on his back (better preparation for storms) for an ultra lightweight, ultrafast style. David chose to go solo, and he was at the end of a day summiting three major fourteeners, a storm was moving in (or had hit), David could have had an injury and been under additional duress, ultimately the fatal mistake being trying to descend a technical cliffed-out couloir instead of the nontechnical descent route.

The thing that stuck with me as I recovered David's body was that I was recovering someone who could have been a good friend. I kept thinking, if this mountain can do this to this man, it can take any of us, from the inexperienced and foolish to the experienced and brilliant.

While recovering David, I kept looking up the couloir from which he had fallen. It was all but obvious that during his descent he had mistaken one chute for another. This mistake has happened to me on more than one mountain, luckily not during my descent of Mount Rainier in 2005. After summiting, a blizzard moved in and in the low visibility our team found ourselves in a junction in the wands; it appeared we were at a "Y" and now we had to choose to go right or left. As I had led on the way up, I kept turning around to check on my teammates, and I had turned around and remembered the route visually backwards. On the way down, I asked that my partners trust my memory, and we chose the correct wands to the left (we had an initial disagreement). We realized as we descended, had we followed the other set of wands to the right, we would have been walking into a highly crevassed area that was no longer being used.

As a child backpacking with my father, he would saunter along and about every fifteen minutes, especially at decision points, he would stop us and make me turn around and memorize what the route looked like backward. As a child this behavior became a pattern without realizing the excellent reasoning behind it. The way down, even if it is the same route as the way up, is visually and experientially a different route. It is easy to go the wrong way if the trail forks on the way down, especially if it's dark, raining, and one is under duress from an injury. Above treeline, it's easy to mistake one couloir for another.

Another small mountaineering survival method my father and my Alpine Rescue Team mentor taught me was to get to know and "profile" the mountaineers around you. On many occasions, I have been called on to help others on the mountain, and I have asked for the help of bystanders while acting as a SAR field-team lead. Sometimes keeping track of the people around you can help in retrospect, even after you've left the mountain.

The morning of September 24, 2005, I was asleep on top of my Toyota pickup's flat camper top on the edge of the Mount Holy Cross trailhead parking lot. I was awakened by a young, athletic-looking couple asking for directions to the trailhead. Even half-asleep I began my mental list of hikers who I expected to see on the mountain that day. A short time later I genuinely awoke and joined a group of teachers that I worked with on a hike of Mount Holy Cross.

Throughout and at the end of the day I thought about the couple we had never passed, and I wondered how they had started before me, but I had never passed them. At the trailhead I remembered and assumed that they had hiked the peak in a circuit rather than the same route up and down (as my group did). Maybe they had detoured off the trail while we passed by?

The next day, one of my hiking buddies called and told me to go through all my videos and pictures from our hike. "Look for a woman, a young mother named Michelle Vanek, who went missing yesterday."

After combing through all my media at length, I also meditated and combed through all my memories of the day, and as I thought about everyone I had met and spent time learning about and knowing, I was positive that the only interaction I had with Michelle was when she and her hiking partner woke me up and asked for directions.

***

When one puts himself or herself at risk as a SAR tech, they should remember that rescuing an injured subject is *not* the number one priority of rescuers. As a first responder, the *safety of rescuers is the number one priority*. There is no other priority until reasonable safety for responders can be assured. If one chooses to take additional risks in the wilderness such as traveling solo, traveling in winter, being caught exposed during unexpected storms, one chooses to face potentially long, painful consequences with *less* support from SAR. If I am an EMT, and I respond to a car that has crashed into a fire hydrant and electric light pole, and I see that a civilian rescuer has been electrocuted trying to extricate the driver, it makes no sense at all for me or any other rescuer to go into that situation until the electricity has been turned off.

It is very rarely advantageous to keep moving or "shortcut" out of the wilderness; it is advantageous to stay put, or under certain circumstances to backtrack the route one used to ingress. Put most simply, if you get lost, *stop* moving. Set up a shelter and conserve energy until rescuers can locate you and aid in your wilderness egress. Parents and teachers should teach children to stay put, set up a shelter, and methods of attracting searchers' attention (from air and ground searches). For children and adults, I emphasize attraction tactics: for a child, hanging something brightly colored over their shelter; for adults, sets of three are a universal emergency signal. Build fires in a set of three, in a triangle, and from a plane this is a universal distress signal. Blow your whistle three times and pause. Wait and listen for a response. Then repeat. The rule of three indicating an emergency signal is the same with firearm reports—three signifies an emergency.

Although the media, Hollywood, and even some stories in this book would lead one to believe that helicopter air support is routine in wilderness rescue, it is not. Especially compared to flat, low-elevation wildernesses in places such as Minnesota where planes can safely operate at functional levels to aid in searches for individuals, in Colorado planes are of *no* use in high altitude mountain SAR searches for individuals. By the time the aircraft keeps a safe enough distance from the terrain, especially taking into consideration mountain turbulence, the proximity to possible subjects is too distant to be of any help. Generally, fixed wing aircraft are used in SAR to search for other aircraft crashes. Aircraft crashes leave big enough signatures that Civil Air Patrol pilots can spot them. Once in a while, if the weather is cooperative and the need is high, Flight For Life will aid in searches for children. This is extremely rare; it is not routine.

The actual use of helicopters, especially military aircraft, is rare. The use of air ambulances is extremely hazardous, especially in mountainous environments, and danger limits its use to extreme emergency cases—those in which the risk to the air crew's life is worth the potential benefit of saving a patient's life. Calling in a helicopter for a noncritical injury puts people in undue risk. Using a helicopter and putting its crew at risk for someone who could die without immediate critical medical care is appropriate.

Even when it is appropriate, one should recognize that rescuers cannot utilize helicopters in anything but ideal weather (daytime, no wind, long range visibility), and then the helicopter is not always immediately available (they're in the middle of an interstate call when the SAR call comes in). Too often the general public's fantasy of a helicopter rescue is just that—a fantasy. Adult, professional mountaineers are prepared for self-rescue.

Regarding battery-operated equipment such as cell phones, radios, satellite-based navigation and communication devices, these are all tools that are extremely helpful when they function; all too often something annihilates their use. In the Sangres, because of the steep and deep nature of most of the mountainous valleys relative to the valleys, there's minimal spots that line up with radio repeaters or cell towers (no communication), and satellite-based devices will often stop working or function inconsistently (especially in pockets where ridges block the southern sky). Be prepared to operate and self-rescue without battery operated support.

If one engages in risky behavior, one might be disappointed but shouldn't be surprised to become a victim of the potential consequences. Mountaineering is risky no matter one's level of intelligence, skill, experience, and denial. If one engages in backcountry skiing long enough, one will be caught in an avalanche. One hopes for the best, but prepares for the worst. I ask my fellow mountaineers, "Do you have a will? Is it clear with your loved ones exactly what they should do in the case of your demise? What if they can't find your body? Does your post mortem plan take into account your body missing? Your family won't be able to collect life insurance and could end up destitute if your body isn't found."

If one's body vanishes, many insurance companies will not pay out policies until many years have passed. Take into consideration what would happen in the worst-case scenario. When I left for hazardous duty in the Middle East, I wrote a "death letter" meant to be delivered to my parents in the case of my death. Most of us were only eighteen and nineteen, and yet we were taught the basic courtesy of taking into consideration those we might leave behind (hope for the best, but plan for the worst).

Any mountaineer engaging in high-risk activities should take into consideration those they leave behind. Mountaineers who do not take others into consideration seem, from my perspective, immature or egocentric, and by definition are demonstrating they are not mature enough to be participating in high-risk endeavors.

Is it possible to quantify comparably high-risk activities? This is difficult as I am neither a statistician nor could I ever account for so many variables and ways to interpret and criticize the use of quantifiable statistics; however, for the sake of pointing out that mountaineering is a relatively dangerous activity in a class of other dangerous activities, here are recent statistics regarding the number of fatalities per 100,000 people who participate in the activity (usually in a given year, but the soldier fatality rates are for the entire war). I have kept this list personally for years to remind me of the odds. I prefer the odds to be in my favor. Below are activities I have listed in order of least to most deadly:

- **6/100,000 Colorado fourteener hikers die per year.** In an average year there are approximately ten deaths of Colorado 14er hikers (http://www.100summits.com/articles/colorado-mountaineering-deaths/2013), and divided by the average number of people who climb Colorado 14ers per year 150,000 (http://www.14ers.org/blog/how-many-people-climb-the-14ers-anyway/), 10/150,000
- **11/100,000 cops die on duty per year.** (http://fee.org/freeman/detail/by-the-numbers-how-dangerous-is-it-to-be-a-cop)
- **57/100,000 rock climbers die per year.**_(http://www.besthealth degrees.com/health-risks/)
- **104/100,000 "Deadliest Catch" fishermen die per year.** (http://www.bls.gov/iif/oshwc/cfar0020.pdf)

- **392/100,000 Iraq War veterans died.** (http://repository.upenn.edu/cgi/viewcontent.cgi?article=1000&context=psc_working_papers)
- **2,179/100,000 Vietnam War veterans died.**_(http://repository.upenn.edu/cgi/viewcontent.cgi?article=1000&context=psc_working_papers)
- **4,053/100,000 Sherpas on Mt. Everest die.** (http://www.outside online.com/1922431/everest-deaths-how-many-sherpas-have-been-killed)
- **8,696/100,000 mountaineers die (who travel through avalanche terrain, crevasse fields, in close proxmity to seracs)** http://www.nzma.org.nz/__data/assets/pdf_file/0010/17947/Vol-118-No-1208-28-January-2005.pdf), pg. 80.

These statistics hint at the dangers of mountaineering, especially depending upon the specific type of mountain climbing in which one engages. Seeing how the survival statistics of war are similar to technical mountaineering, it makes me think of my mentor reinforcing, "There are no old, bold mountaineers."

This reminds me of another soldier anecdote. There are three stages to a combat soldier: the first is the rookie stage with the soldier straight out of training. The rookie is usually young, feels immortal, is eager for action, "Send me into combat! I'm ready! I'll come back a hero, don't worry." The second stage is the soldier who has seen a few tours. This soldier isn't immortal. This soldier has lost a few friends in combat, and he knows, "I do this long enough, and I can easily die, and I need to be ready to die." The third stage is the old veteran soldier who has embraced the inevitable, "I do this long enough, and this *is* the way I will die."

In the world of technical climbing, free soloing is a completely different endeavor than free climbing; choosing to go into the wilderness solo is analogous to choosing to free solo. Most folks would be very well advised to simply not go into the wilderness solo, but just as there are the occasional soloists such as Dean Potter and Alex Honnold and backcountry rangers who spend months at a time solo in the wilderness, there are the occasional outliers who choose to raise the stakes of their risk-taking by going alone.

One of my favorite solo trips is a parallel trip to Mark Stice's in the Crestone Mountain Group. Over a decade ago, for a week in September, I made South Colony Lake my base, and enjoyed the changing aspen colors at my own pace from my preferred elevations. If one goes solo, leave as detailed an itinerary as possible with a person who will launch the search if you fail to return. If you improvise and leave the routes of travel you indicated in your itinerary, accept that your chances of being found are slim to none.

SAR leadership and those involved with the media should be wary of using the media in regard to unvetted volunteers showing up. Even though SAR teams in Colorado are made up of "all volunteers," this does not mean that anyone, at any time, can show up at a SAR mission command post and be expected to be included in the operations. Paradoxically, this choice could distract SAR leadership at a time when they least need distractions.

SAR teams, especially those that cover Colorado's most technical and dangerous terrain, train regularly (in AVSAR's case this is monthly) so that the members can gain skills, build relationships, and become a trusting, cohesive team. As a leader for AVSAR, I too often saw new applicants join the team and then be surprised when none of us were impressed by anything they wrote down on their applications. That was a good start, and the paperwork and background checks indicated what we could hope to expect from a potential team member, but it is simply too easy for well-meaning folks to exaggerate their skills or flat out lie. When one is in the middle of trying to save a subject's life (or recover their body) and she is standing on a ledge that's only a couple of feet wide, working with a team of fellow high-angle technicians—knowing that any small mistake or lack of skills could result in a thousand-foot fall to one's death—this is *not* the time to be "building rapport" with teammates. Missions requiring winter-time response in extreme temperatures in extreme avalanche conditions fall well into this category of responders needing to be a very cohesive team that has spent significant time training together. Extreme avalanche conditions in Colorado's backcountry can be as dangerous as wandering around crevasses with seracs hanging over one's head.

I always encouraged my university students to read *Deep Survival* by Laurence Gonzales in addition to the required textbook, *Fundamentals of Search and Rescue*. These texts give insights about survival methods that apply to wilderness survival situations.

I would end the semester with a quote from the *Deep Survival* Prologue,

It's easy to imagine that wilderness survival would involve equipment, training, and experience. It turns out that, at the moment of truth, those might be good things to have but they aren't decisive. Those of us who go into the wilderness to seek our thrills in contact with the forces of nature soon learn, in fact, that experience, training, and modern equipment can betray you. The maddening thing for someone with a Western scientific turn of mind is that it's not what's in your pack that separates the quick from the dead. It's not even what's in your mind. Corny as it sounds, it's what's in your heart.

In the Introduction of this book, I shared four reasons for writing this book. I wanted to honor the heroic men and women of SAR; I wanted to honor SAR subjects and their families; I wanted to educate mountaineers and the public about the realities of isolated, rural, small county mountain SAR; I wanted to educate people about wilderness survival.

I hope that I stayed true to my intentions, and I hope in the future less blood is spilled in the Sangre de Cristos.

Search and Rescue 72-hour Field Pack List

- **Navigation:**
  Map
  Compass
  GPS unit

- **Sun protection:**
  Sunglasses
  Sunscreen
  Lip balm w/ sunblock
  Sun hat

- **Insulation (avoid cotton—think layers):**
  Fleece or wool sweater
  Water resistant shell (top & bottom)
  Sock hat (wool or fleece)
  Gloves
  Extra shirt
  Extra bottoms
  Extra socks
  Footwear, sturdy, adequate for climate and environment
  Waterproof extra clothes bag (treated nylon, garbage bag)

- **Illumination:**
  Headlamp
  Extra bulb or headlamp

- **Basic first-aid:**
  60 cc suction syringe
  Exam gloves
  Face mask (cpr / ppvs)
  Roller gauze
  SAM splint
  Trauma gloves

Trauma pads, large
Trauma pads, small (maxi pads)
Trauma shears
OTC drugs as needed

- **Fire:**
Lighter or matches
Flint (back-up fire source)

- **Tools:**
Cell phone
Leatherman multi-tool
Whistle
Watch
Mirror (signaling)
Pen / pencil
Mission log (small notebook)
Extra aa batteries (headlamp, GPS)
Parachute cord 10 ft lengths: 10+
Lg ziplock bags: 5+ (trash, evidence)
Fluorescent flagging tape
Monocular / small binoculars
Disposable camera / digital camera w/removable memory card
Sewing kit (small)

- **Nutrition** (no cook items, 72 hours worth of food):
Energy bars, gel packets, gorp, cheese, bagels, etc.

- **Hydration:**
Liter bottles (2 min)
H_2O treatment or water filter

- **Emergency shelter:**
Bivy sack or large nylon poncho
Sleeping bag

- **Miscellaneous:**
Toilet paper
Pack (large—2000 cubic inches+)
Helmet
SAR identification

Optional additional equipment or seasonal equipment:

- **Optional extra personal gear:**
  Extra water
  Foam pad
  Stove/pot

- **Seasonal (winter):**
  Gaiters
  Mittens
  Balaclava
  Goggles
  Down jacket
  Long underwear (2 sets total)
  Crampons
  Stove/pot
  Snowshoes
  Ski poles
  Avalanche probe
  Avalanche beacon
  Ice axe
  Snow shovel

Glossary and Acronyms

A-10: A military attack jet designed for close-combat support (tank killing).

AAR: After Action Review

ALP: Adventure Leadership and Programming

AMS: Acute Mountain Sickness

Anchor: In mountaineering a point that connects a climber to the mountain. Anchors are often rocks with webbing tied around them, active or passive camming devices put into cracks, or pitons that are hammered into cracks.

ANG: Air National Guard

ASAP: Adams State Adventure Program

ASU: Adams State University

ATV: All Terrain Vehicle

AVSAR: Alamosa Volunteer Search and Rescue

Belay: Refers to either the verb or the noun. In the verb's case this is the act of one climber letting out or taking in rope to keep another climber protected in case the climber falls, the belayer can catch the climber. In the noun's case, a belay is the anchored spot from which a climber belays.

Bivouac (bivy): A temporary camp without tents or cover, used especially by soldiers and mountaineers.

BLM: Bureau of Land Management

Boilerplate: A term used by mountaineers to describe large domes/low-angle hard rock faces.

Bushwack: A term mountaineers use to indicate going off trail.

C-130: A large cargo plane used by the military.

C-collar: A neck splint put on a patient to stabilize possible neck injuries.

C-spine: The cervical (neck) part of the spine.

CAIC: Colorado Avalanche Information Center

Cache: A collection of provisions/equipment that has been hidden in a secret location to secure for later use.

Cairn: An identifiable pile of rocks that mark a place or trail.

Carabiner: A metal spring-hinged link used as a connector in technical climbing systems and to hold freely moving ropes.

CCSAR: Custer County Search and Rescue

COSAR: Colorado Search and Rescue (an organization made up by all the state's SAR teams)

Couloir: A steep mountainside gorge that is often an avalanche path in the winter.

CP: Command Post

CPR: Cardiopulmonary Resuscitation

Crampons: Sharp metal points attached to a mountaineers boots that allow more secure contact with snow and ice.

CSP: Colorado State Patrol

CSPD: Colorado Springs Police Department

CWO: Chief Warrant Officer (a title and rank for army helicopter pilots)

DP: Decision Point

ER: Emergency Room

ETA: Estimated Time of Arrival

Exposure: In mountaineering this term refers to being exposed to risk by a long fall or from weather.

FEMA: Federal Emergency Management Agency

FFL: Flight for Life

FOB: Foreign Objects Debris (usually used in conjunction with an aircraft landing zone)

GIS: Geographical Information Systems

GPS: Global Positioning System

HAATS: High-Altitude Army National Guard Aviation Training

Hypothermia: A condition in which the body's temperature is too low.

IC: Incident Commander

Ice axe: A tool carried by mountaineers that looks like an axe. The tool is used to aid climbers in staying secure in steep ice and snow terrain.

ICP: Intracranial Pressure

ICU: Intensive Care Unit

IV: Intravenous

Jaws 1, 2, 3, 4: Four major obstacles encountered by 4x4s on the Lake Como Trail.

KED Splint: An upper body splint useful for stabilizing the spine.

Kilonewton: A measurement of force equal to about 100 kilograms, the average weight for a man, hanging on a rope (two kilonewtons equals the force that approximately two men hanging on a rope exert on the rope).

LEO: Law Enforcement Officer

Litter: A stretcher used for carrying an injured subject.

LKP: Last Known Point

LZ: Landing Zone

Massif: A mountaineering term for a group of mountains (i.e. the Blanca Massif refers to the group of mountains near Mount Blanca including Little Bear Peak, Ellingwood Point, and Mount Lindsey.

MRA: Mountain Rescue Association

NOAA: National Oceanic Atmospheric Administration

NODS: Night Optic Devices

OR: Operating Room

Piton: A large metal nail-like spike that can be hammered into rock cracks and connected to as an anchor.

PJ: Air Force Pararescue Jumper

POA: Probability of Area

POD: Probability of Detection

POS: Probability of Success

Prusik knot: A hitch that can be used to ascend a rope.

Rappel: To descend high-angle terrain using ropes and technical equipment.

SAM Splint: A multi-use splint developed by military special forces used by SAR medical personnel in expeditionary settings.

SAR: Search and Rescue

SARDOC: Search and Rescue Dogs of Colorado

SAROP: Search and Rescue Operations

Scree: Loose rock on steep slopes up to the size of soccer balls. Rock bigger than a soccer ball is referred to as talus.

Self-arrest: If a climber falls on snow or ice, this is the act of stopping the fall.

Sign Cutting: Another term for tracking usually applied at the beginning of a search when the last known point of the subject is searched carefully for sign of direction of travel.

SKED Litter: An expeditionary-style litter that is not the usual metal "basket" but instead a large, rollable piece of hard plastic that can be carried in a backpack and used to wrap around and transport patients.

SLV: San Luis Valley

SOP: Standard Operating Procedure

SPOT Device: A GPS satellite-based electronic tracking device.

Talus: Rock fields on slopes or on flat terrain including rocks bigger than the size of soccer balls.

Topographic Map: A map that shows three dimensions using contour lines.

Treeline: The elevation at which trees cease growing. Treeline is different depending upon where one is. In Colorado, the average treeline is at 11,000 feet. In Washington state it is 4,500 feet. In Nepal it is 14,000 feet.

USAF: United States Air Force

USAR: Urban Search and Rescue

VC: Visitor Center

WEMT: Wilderness Emergency Medical Technician

WFR: Wilderness First Responder

Windchill: The effect that wind has of making air feel colder than it actually is.

YOM: Year Old Male (as in 37 YOM subject)

Bibliography

Cooper, Donald C. *Fundamentals of Search and Rescue*. Jones and Bartlett Publishers. Sudbury, MA. 2005.

Cummins, Joseph. *The Greatest Search & Rescue Stories Ever Told*. Lyon Press. Guilford, CT. 2002.

Gonzales, Laurence. *Deep Survival: Who Lives, Who Dies, and Why*. W.W. Norton & Co. New York, NY. 2003.

Gonzales, Laurence. *House of Pain*. University of Arkansas Press. Fayetteville, AR. 2013.

Hill, Kenneth. *Managing the Lost Person Incident*. National Association for Search and Rescue. Chantilly, VA. 1997.

Mountaineering 6th Edition. The Mountaineers, Seattle, WA. 1997.

Potterfield, Peter. *Over the Top: Humorous Mountaineering Tales*. The Mountaineers. Seattle WA. 2002.

Roach, Gerry. *Colorado's Fourteeners, 2nd Edition*. Fulcrum Publishing. Golden, CO. 1999.

Roberts, David. *On the Ridge Between Life and Death: A Climbing Life Reexamined*. Simon & Schuster. New York, NY. 2005.

Sapolsky, Robert M. *Monkeyluv: And Other Essays on Our Lives as Animals*. 2005.

Scott-Nash, Mark. *Colorado 14er Disasters: Victims of the Game*. Johnson Books. Boulder, CO. 2009.

Syrotuck, William. *Analysis of Lost Person Behavior*. Barkleigh Productions, Inc. Mechanicsburg, PA. 2000.

Syrotuck, William. *An Introduction to Land Search Probabilities and Calculations*. Barkleigh Productions, Inc. Mechanicsburg, PA. 2000.

Newspapers and Magazines
The Alamosa Valley Courier, Alamosa, Colorado
Appalachia, Boston, Massachusetts
The Crestone Eagle, Crestone, Colorado

Kevin Wright grew up near Evergreen, Colorado, and has been technical mountaineering since he was twelve. Near deadly experiences in Nepal in 1995 and on Mt. Rainier in 2005, both requiring self-rescues, catalyzed a personal desire in Kevin to volunteer to serve others in their times of need in the mountains. From 2008–2011, the Alamosa Volunteer Search And Rescue (AVSAR) team elected Kevin as president. During this time, he served as an adjunct instructor for Adams State University teaching a course he designed, Introduction to Search and Rescue. In 2011, after a Chinook helicopter "hard landing," Kevin resigned from active duty SAR service. In the past, Kevin has been licensed as a Wilderness First Responder (WFR), a nationally registered EMT, and he has served as a National Park Service Ranger Teacher. Kevin has received life-saving awards from multiple organizations, however, Kevin admits that his favorite "awards" are the phone calls and letters he receives from former SAR subjects and their family members. Kevin works as a high school English teacher in Monte Vista, Colorado. He appreciates time with his wife and dogs sauntering along the Rio Grande or in the wilderness throughout the Sangre de Cristos.